최신 ③ 10회분

토익 급상승
Part 5&6

실전문제집 + 해설집

저자 니오어학원장 임동찬

토익 인텐시브과정으로 유명한 니오어학원을 운영하고 있습니다. 지난 2000년 초반부터 지금까지 토익강의와 30여 권의 토익 교재를 집필한 우리나라 토익계의 산증인입니다. 독자와의 직접적인 소통을 중시하는 니오강사는 카카오톡(neoteacher)과 페이스북 (https://www.facebook.com/neotoeicteacher/)을 통해 독자들의 토익 고민을 실시간으로 해결해주고 있습니다.

최신 토익 급상승 ❸
Part 5&6 10회분[실전문제집 + 해설집]

저 자 임동찬
발행인 고본화
발 행 반석출판사
2019년 7월 20일 초판 1쇄 인쇄
2019년 7월 25일 초판 1쇄 발행
홈페이지 www.bansok.co.kr
이메일 bansok@bansok.co.kr
블로그 blog.naver.com/bansokbooks

07547 서울시 강서구 양천로 583. B동 1007호
(서울시 강서구 염창동 240-21번지 우림블루나인 비즈니스센터 B동 1007호)
대표전화 02) 2093-3399 **팩 스** 02) 2093-3393
출 판 부 02) 2093-3395 **영업부** 02) 2093-3396
등록번호 제315-2008-000033호

Copyright ⓒ 임동찬

ISBN 978-89-7172-895-6 (13740)

최신 ③ 10회분

토익 급상승
Part 5&6

실전문제집 + 해설집

반석출판사
Bansok

저자는 지난 20여 년 동안 토익시험을 치르면서 실제 경험의 중요성을 느껴왔습니다. 많은 학생들이 이런 경험적인 요소를 무시한 채 막연히 토익을 공부하지만 이는 효율적이지 않습니다. 처음에는 저 역시 토익에 문외한이었지만, 많은 경험을 쌓으면서 토익 전문가가 되었습니다.

저자는 학생들이 가능한 한 많은 문제를 풀어보면서 실전감각을 익히는 게 점수 획득에 유리하다는 확신을 가지고 있습니다. 본 교재에 실린 문제들은 실제 토익시험에 출제된 기출문제를 변형해서 만들었기 때문에 시중의 어떤 실전문제집보다 수준이 높습니다. 특히 저자는 여러 차례 실전문제집을 발간해왔습니다. 이런 경험을 토대로 만든 본 교재의 파트 5, 6 문제들로 공부를 한다면 단기간에 고득점 획득이 가능할 거라고 확신합니다.

이 책의 특징은 다음과 같습니다.

- 최신의 신토익 출제 경향과 난이도를 반영했습니다.
- 토익 파트 5, 6 실전문제 10회분(460문제)이 실려 있습니다.
- 저자의 카톡과 페이스북을 통해 토익문제 고민을 실시간 해결해드립니다.
  카톡 neoteacher 페이스북 https://www.facebook.com/neotoeicteacher/

끝으로 가족이라는 이름으로 희생만을 강요하는 건 아닌지, 항상 미안함이 앞서는 아내와 아들에게 감사와 사랑의 마음을 전하면서 이 글을 마칩니다.

저자 임동찬

목차

이 책의 특징 및 활용 방법

1. 신토익 출세가 예상되는 파트 5,6 10회분(460제) 제공!

2. 전체 문제에 대한 해석과 꼼꼼한 해설 제공

3. 저자의 카톡과 페이스북을 통해 토익문제 고민을 실시간 해결

TALK 카톡 neoteacher 페이스북 https://www.facebook.com/neotoeicteacher/

『최신 토익 급상승 ❸ 파트 5&6 10회분』은 그동안의 기출문제들을 분석하고 앞으로 출제가 예상되는 문제들을 모아서 파트 5, 6 문제 10회분을 제공합니다. 또한 전체 문제에 대한 해석과 꼼꼼한 해설을 제공합니다. 많은 문제를 접하는 것과 동시에 이 책이 제공하는 해설을 꼼꼼하게 리뷰하는 것이 토익 파트 5, 6 점수를 빠르게 올리는 지름길임을 잊지 마세요. 또한 문제를 풀다 막히는 부분이 있으면 위의 카톡이나 페이스북을 통해 실시간으로 질문하세요! 니오토익이 실시간 해결해 드립니다.

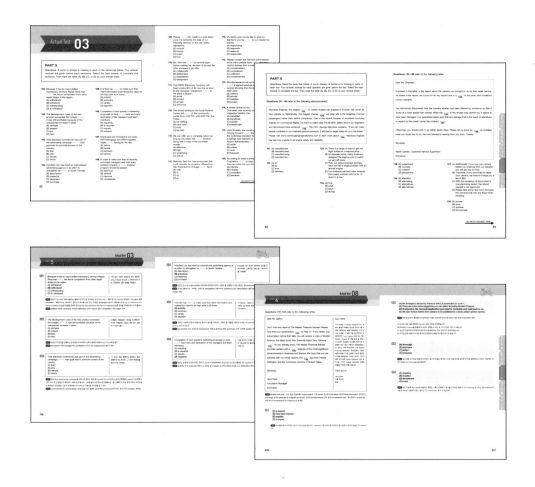

6

최신 ③ 10회분

토익 급상승
Part 5&6

Actual Test 01~10

PART 5

Directions: A word or phrase is missing in each of the sentences below. Four answer choices are given below each sentence. Select the best answer to complete the sentence. Then mark the letter (A), (B), (C), or (D) on your answer sheet.

101. Ms. Hwang's ------- sponsor for the survey program has ensured its continued funding.
(A) enthuse
(B) enthusiastic
(C) enthusiastically
(D) enthusiasm

102. Upon successful completion, ------- will receive a printable Certificate of Completion for their records.
(A) participants
(B) participation
(C) participant
(D) participating

103. Because our company is highly safety-conscious, each employee is thoroughly ------- to follow our safety manual.
(A) trained
(B) train
(C) trainer
(D) trains

104. At Panawi, we ------- safety and reliability in manufacturing products of the highest quality so that consumers can enjoy them with peace of mind.
(A) deliberate
(B) emphasize
(C) impact
(D) analyze

105. ------- you find the manual to be unclear, note that there are customer support centers throughout the country where an expert can help you.
(A) Whether
(B) So that
(C) Until
(D) If

106. Although the keynote speech has been verified for March 8 at 6:30 P.M., the rest of the conference schedule has not yet been -------.
(A) equalled
(B) announced
(C) reminded
(D) informed

107. Most candidates are ------- being reviewed for the annual staff excellence award.
(A) new
(B) now
(C) after
(D) once

108. Brisbane-based David Delivery Service will repay all business-related travel costs ------- three weeks of their submission.
(A) within
(B) between
(C) into
(D) when

109. ------- chooses to work in our head office must have five years of experience in a related field.
(A) Another
(B) Anyone
(C) Somebody
(D) Whoever

110. In order to continue their operation, manufacturers must satisfy the standards set ------- by regulatory agencies.
(A) along
(B) away
(C) forth
(D) in front

111. Software intended for use in the diagnosis of an abnormal physical state should meet the definition of a medical device and must ------- comply with the requirements of the Medical Devices Regulations.
(A) how
(B) often
(C) sometimes
(D) therefore

112. Even though most of the computer programmers work by themselves, weekly staff meetings will give an opportunity for them to cooperate with -------.
(A) one another
(B) the same
(C) much
(D) this

113. Celine Park ------- insisted that purchasing stationery items from another supplier could reduce operating expenses at Marc Industries.
(A) rights
(B) rightful
(C) rightly
(D) right

114. Service animals must follow all ------- laws pertaining to vaccinations as well as any registration requirements.
(A) local
(B) locally
(C) localize
(D) locals

115. Workshops at the Central Convention Center will be ------- to ten people to allow for interactive discussions and Q&A sessions.
(A) remained
(B) ended
(C) limited
(D) asserted

116. Corrie Kim, founder of Power Athletic Clinic, recently received an ------- for her research in the field of sports medicine.
(A) interpretation
(B) ability
(C) apology
(D) award

117. Mr. Heo accepted the position of assistant financial analyst at his company, ------- he was also offered a higher position by a big bank.
(A) even though
(B) likewise
(C) whether
(D) due to

118. By consistently providing customers with high quality products and services, Omitt Corporation is able to win back clients that it had ------- lost to bigger competitors.
(A) previously
(B) behind
(C) formally
(D) ahead

GO ON TO THE NEXT PAGE ➤

119. Existing members of the committee should introduce ------- to new people and briefly describe their involvement with the organization.
(A) their
(B) themselves
(C) they
(D) their own

120. Madacas Packaging ------- employees who are highly motivated to work at our manufacturing facility located in Scotia.
(A) are sought
(B) seeking
(C) have been sought
(D) is seeking

121. If you are under the age of 18 at the time of application, you will also need to show ------- of your enrolment in the East Boston school system.
(A) proof
(B) process
(C) basis
(D) analysis

122. The personnel manager had ------- forgotten that she had an appointment with the new employees until her assistant reminded her.
(A) completed
(B) complete
(C) completion
(D) completely

123. As an assistant manager, Mr. Roy's main role is to facilitate cooperation ------- Syscho Corporation's numerous directors.
(A) onto
(B) among
(C) above
(D) inside

124. Mr. Johns suggested that I drive a company car while ------- is being repaired.
(A) mine
(B) I
(C) my
(D) myself

125. Even employees who ------- were rather sceptical about the PEP training, afterwards appear to have accomplished improvements they did not think of as realistic.
(A) annually
(B) inadvertently
(C) initially
(D) successively

126. Sales ------- has dropped dramatically despite efforts to boost recognition by increasing the marketing budget.
(A) action
(B) response
(C) appreciation
(D) revenue

127. Dr. Morgan has been involved in a car accident this morning and will be ------- to attend the seminar today.
(A) impossible
(B) doubtful
(C) remote
(D) unable

128. Even though many of our employees have lived in foreign countries, ------- few of them are fluent in another language.
(A) once
(B) hardly
(C) far
(D) very

129. The site manager told the new worker that ------- certain kinds of construction equipment needs several years of experience.
(A) operated
(B) operate
(C) operating
(D) operates

130. The general manager finished his weekly report ------- schedule because his earlier presentation had been cancelled.
(A) on account of
(B) aside from
(C) ahead of
(D) far from

PART 6

Directions: Read the texts that follow. A word, phrase, or sentence is missing in parts of each text. Four answer choices for each question are given below the text. Select the best answer to complete the text. Then mark the letter (A), (B), (C), or (D) on your answer sheet.

Questions 131-134 refer to the following e-mail.

From: Robertnatale@cellrite.net

To: Customer Service Department (Mckinney Electronics)

Subject: Ordered Items

Date: May 17

Dear Customer Service Department:

Thank you for shipping the items earlier than I had expected. -------. However, I would just
131.
like to inform you that the Samsung DVD player I received is not the Blu-Ray DVD player that I

ordered. I ordered the Samsung Blu-Ray DVD player BDC 8200, but the model no. of the DVD

player I received is BDC7500. ------- they have ------- identical features, such as built-in WIFI
132. **133.**
and media sharing, I still prefer the BDC8200 since I can record 250GB of HD videos with it.

Please let me know when you can ship the correct model so that I can also make plans to ship

the DVD player I received. I am hoping that you can ship the unit within 48 hours, which is

earlier than your ------- shipping schedule. Thank you in advance.
134.

131. (A) Unfortunately, the shipping charge
cost more than we had anticipated.
(B) But the receipt I requested wasn't
included.
(C) Please confirm receipt of payment for
these items.
(D) Everything was in good condition.

132. (A) Although
(B) Therefore
(C) Whether
(D) Moreover

133. (A) frequently
(B) intentionally
(C) previously
(D) nearly

134. (A) regular
(B) regularly
(C) regularity
(D) regularness

GO ON TO THE NEXT PAGE

Questions 135-138 refer to the following e-mail.

From: Jack Clark

To: Summer Martin

Subject: RE: Phone Order

Date: March 8 15:20:35

Dear Mr. Martin,

Regarding your email today, I have no problem ------- the toy cars with the transformers, so
135.
please go ahead and process my order. I may have forgotten to mention this to your staff

member, but please make sure that in the seven sets of toy cars there is ------- one red model.
136.
Blue and green would also be nice, but they are not as ------- as the red one.
137.

I would prefer that those items be sent to my office at this address: Prime Holdings Co., 45
James St., New Heights, NJ. My telephone number is (201) 836-9127. My secretary, Elena
Kirstein, will receive them if I am not in the office.

-------. That will give us some time to prepare them for a children's party that same day.
138.

---

135. (A) repairing
(B) redeeming
(C) replacing
(D) recharging

136. (A) at least
(B) instead of
(C) by means of
(D) so that

137. (A) importance
(B) important
(C) importantly
(D) imported

138. (A) As a customer, I'm always satisfied
with the quality of your product.
(B) Thank you for delivering items earlier
than expected.
(C) Because of the rather tight schedule,
it would be best if you could deliver
them on or before 1:00 P.M. on March
14.
(D) I received an e-mail with discount
coupons that can be used next time.

Questions 139-142 refer to the following memo.

TO: All Employees

FROM: Managing Director Elena Kirstein

This is to ------- you that after 30 years of dedicated service to Rakestraw Industries, CEO and
     139.
President Smith Barren will step down. He and his wife will be moving ------- to their summer
                    140.
residence in Florida, and we all wish them well. -------. Thanks to his persistence on this project,
                    141.
our company is now a global leader in selling baking equipment. -------, sales of the XR-800
                      142.
have tripled over the last two years. We are very grateful for his dedication and commitment.
We will certainly miss him.

---

139. (A) inform
    (B) access
    (C) announce
    (D) describe

140. (A) approximately
    (B) permanently
    (C) moderately
    (D) consecutively

141. (A) In fact, we asked Mr. Barren to put off
his retirement for two years.
    (B) Throughout his presidency, Mr.
Barren was in charge of the
development of the XR- 800 system.
    (C) CEO told company shareholders
that he believed the new product line
would be very profitable.
    (D) Mr. Barren's outstanding contribution
to Rakestraw Industries over the
past 30 years will be highlighted in
speeches at his retirement dinner
next month.

142. (A) In addition
    (B) For example
    (C) In short
    (D) By comparison

GO ON TO THE NEXT PAGE

Questions 143-146 refer to the following letter.

To Whom It May Concern:

Davis Lewis & Partners placed an order with your company for the book entitled Yoga for Health by Theresa Woolsley on November 27 (invoice number 394-DI).

-------. I have spoken with several customer service representatives by telephone ------- this
143.   **144.**
matter, and they ------- me that the Shipping Department sent the books on December 1.
                  145.

I am sure that your company faithfully filled the order, but I would appreciate a replacement shipment as soon as possible so we can have the books in stock for the holiday season.

If this is not -------, then I will expect a full refund. I have enclosed a copy of the invoice for your
                  146.
reference. Thank you in advance for your assistance in this matter.

Sincerely,

Philip Moore
Inventory Control Manager

143. (A) Unfortunately, due to high demand,
the item is out of stock until
December 13.
(B) Although our record shows that
payment was made, we have still not
received the books.
(C) Because we received the defective
item yesterday, I'd like to return it.
(D) The shipment is scheduled to be
delivered in 2 weeks, but it's too late.

144. (A) regard
(B) regards
(C) regarded
(D) regarding

145. (A) assured
(B) appointed
(C) designated
(D) directed

146. (A) fortunate
(B) feasible
(C) urgent
(D) ultimate

Actual Test 02

PART 5

Directions: A word or phrase is missing in each of the sentences below. Four answer choices are given below each sentence. Select the best answer to complete the sentence. Then mark the letter (A), (B), (C), or (D) on your answer sheet.

101. Portland Airlines adopted the policy that it will no longer ------- whales and dolphins for aquariums and water parks.
(A) transported
(B) transport
(C) transporting
(D) transports

102. If the order is not dispatched ------- three business days, you will be contacted to offer partial shipment or full refund.
(A) in
(B) about
(C) into
(D) until
(A) in

103. The construction of gymnasium at the new State Middle School was ------- completed when we took a tour of the building Wednesday morning.
(A) nearest
(B) nearer
(C) neared
(D) nearly

104. In an ------- to reduce the amount of photocopier paper we use, please use recycled paper whenever possible.
(A) acceptance
(B) output
(C) account
(D) effort

105. After 10 years of ------- the company as a business executive, Mr. Pitt decided to quit his job.
(A) donating
(B) instructing
(C) competing
(D) leading

106. To sum up, ------- cranes and forklifts are great ways of transporting heavy goods, but cranes are capable of lifting heavier goods.
(A) this
(B) after
(C) both
(D) once

107. As a manager, ------- is important for Nicolas Janet to be able to delegate duties to subordinates rather than attempt to complete everything herself.
(A) it
(B) she
(C) there
(D) he

GO ON TO THE NEXT PAGE

15

108. Wide. R. Electronics is so ------- in the reliability of its domestic appliances that it offers a free two-year warranty on its new models.
(A) confident
(B) confidence
(C) confidential
(D) confidently

109. Please tell us about your recent experience with Brux Apparel Company ------- our web site so that we can improve our quality.
(A) on
(B) in
(C) up
(D) of

110. All researchers at Jansen pharmaceuticals must wear ------- goggles as a safety measure whenever in the workplace.
(A) protected
(B) protective
(C) protects
(D) protection

111. As soon as everyone in our tour group arrived, they were ------- served a delicious dinner in the main dining hall on the ground floor.
(A) prompting
(B) prompts
(C) promptly
(D) prompted

112. The release of Ms. Showna's building permit for her condominium was delayed because one of the documents required was filed -------.
(A) equally
(B) approximately
(C) importantly
(D) incorrectly

113. Business owners can rent booths to promote their products at the event, allowing them to get wider ------- to thousands of potential customers.
(A) exposure
(B) expose
(C) exposing
(D) exposed

114. Perth has flourished over the years and has ------- been named as one of the best places to live in Australia.
(A) frequenting
(B) frequently
(C) frequents
(D) frequent

115. We appreciate you taking time to let us know how ------- your stay was at Sunrise Edge Villa.
(A) considerable
(B) available
(C) additional
(D) enjoyable

116. It has been more than two years since the ------- episode of Find Wolly Season 2 aired on Tooniversal Network.
(A) lasts
(B) lastly
(C) last
(D) lasted

117. Construction is ------- 89 percent complete and the opening ceremony is scheduled for March 2nd.
(A) too
(B) quite
(C) now
(D) far

118. Studies have shown that the media is rarely ------- of the scientific findings they report.
(A) criticize
(B) critic
(C) critically
(D) critical

119. After ------- a client survey, Daniel's Restaurant decided to add more international options to its lunch menu.
(A) conducts
(B) conducted
(C) conduct
(D) conducting

120. Because the company's printer on the 4th floor has been repaired, Mr. Jackey's document can be printed without -------.
(A) refund
(B) favor
(C) delay
(D) action

121. H&D Department Store hired 12 cashiers ------- at all its branches during the busy winter season.
(A) assists
(B) have assisted
(C) to assist
(D) assisted

122. Ms. Magon will have to go to the Blitch office in July, so Mr. Ester will act as General Manager ------- her absence.
(A) among
(B) because
(C) during
(D) while

123. Visitors to the capital will be able to take advantage of a unique international package for tourists ------- in September 2017.
(A) start
(B) starting
(C) will start
(D) started

124. ------ after becoming the marketing manager of Commax Business Lenter, Jimmy Cotter expanded the market share by 20 percent.
(A) Soon
(B) Often
(C) Far
(D) Ever

125. The decision of the publishing company as to the number of books to be reprinted will be based on ------- many copies have been sold in the first quarter.
(A) very
(B) how
(C) as
(D) so

126. For seven consecutive months, the National Restaurant Association has given its highest ------- in food service to Lakeview Cafe.
(A) rating
(B) personnel
(C) demonstration
(D) reliance

127. Although the firm saw a 13 percent drop in revenue last year, specialists continue to express ------- in the future of Toshio Platinum.
(A) sympathy
(B) confidence
(C) challenge
(D) gratitude

128. Whole Multi Cultural Community depends on generous funding from local donors for ------- its teaching programs.
(A) maintaining
(B) maintain
(C) maintains
(D) maintenance

129. TF12 television station, ------- features the music of new recording artists, is expected to hold a fall concert event.
(A) which
(B) where
(C) what
(D) that

130. The agreement's terms are very ------- and state that all work must be completed by July 14th.
(A) straightforward
(B) negligible
(C) accomplished
(D) immediate

GO ON TO THE NEXT PAGE

PART 6

Directions: Read the texts that follow. A word, phrase, or sentence is missing in parts of each text. Four answer choices for each question are given below the text. Select the best answer to complete the text. Then mark the letter (A), (B), (C), or (D) on your answer sheet.

Questions 131-134 refer to the following memorandum.

DATE: March 3

TO: Petrisha Deaze

FROM: Steven Hernandaze

SUBJECT: Earned Vacation Credits

This year, I ------- in a number of advertising projects that did not allow me to use up my
131.
vacation credits. I had hoped to use the two weeks this month, but delays in the Cleanse Herbal

Tea project have made that impossible. -------. If we hope to finish this project by the end of the
132.
year, I will have to work on it continuously.

I am ------- of the company's policy that vacations should be taken between January 1 and
133.
December 21 each year. -------, because of my unusual workload this year, I am requesting
134.
permission to carry over the remaining two weeks of my vacation time this year into the next

year.

I would appreciate your favorable consideration for my request. I look forward to receiving your

answer.

131. (A) have been involved
(B) have involved
(C) will be involved
(D) involved

132. (A) I'm wondering what the vacation policy is.
(B) Could someone else help me with the project?
(C) Is it possible to put off the project?
(D) We are now running three weeks behind schedule.

133. (A) proposed
(B) known
(C) aware
(D) confident

134. (A) However
(B) Additionally
(C) Thus
(D) Otherwise

Questions 135-138 refer to the following e-mail.

To: Adam Eastbourne <adam@mmedia.com>

From: Rosalin Hopes <hope@mmedia.com>

C.C: Richard Wagner <rich@mmedia.com>

Subject: Tardiness

Attach: Februarysummary.doc

Date: March 10

This is to call your attention to the excessive tardiness you ------- last month. ------- our
135.   136.
records, there were five instances when you came in beyond the normal start of office hours.

Because you have accumulated more than 60 minutes of tardiness, your monthly pay for

March will reflect a deduction ------- to the time in question. -------. Otherwise, we will have no
137.   138.
alternative but to put you on suspension should the same thing happen again in the future.

We look forward to seeing an improvement in your record soon.

---

135. (A) to incur
(B) incurring
(C) incurred
(D) incur

136. (A) Regarding
(B) In spite of
(C) Based on
(D) Owing to

137. (A) equivalent
(B) official
(C) intended
(D) outstanding

138. (A) This action of a monthly salary cut
was also notified to your direct
supervisor.
(B) If there are any problems that make
it difficult for you to be here on or
before 9 A.M., please discuss those
issues with your manager.
(C) If this happens repeatedly, there will
be a cut in salary for six months.
(D) New regulations about tardiness have
been implemented since last year.

GO ON TO THE NEXT PAGE

Questions 139-142 refer to the following information.

New Policy at the Palo Alto Public Library

-------. However, due to a significant increase in the number of overdue books, cardholders
139.
from outside the Palo Alto area will now have to pay an annual membership fee in order to use

the library. -------, the lending of books outside the library will no longer be allowed for non-Palo
140.
Alto area residents. This new policy will go into ------- on May 3.
141.

To obtain a non-resident library card, simply fill out the required form and pay the $ 40 annual

fee at the library's front desk. Your card ------- within three business days.
142.

Although we regret to introduce this policy, we feel it is a necessary measure that must be taken

to protect our library's valuable resources.

---

139. (A) The Palo Alto Public Library is conveniently located near both the bus stop and the subway station.
(B) Information on using the library is available on the website or at the front desk.
(C) The Palo Alto Public Library was founded by the mayor Peter Adams 30 years ago.
(D) Since its opening in 1995, the Palo Alto Public Library has always allowed the lending of books for free to residents of neighboring communities.

140. (A) Specifically
(B) Instead
(C) In addition
(D) As a result

141. (A) creation
(B) effect
(C) practice
(D) composition

142. (A) is issued
(B) has issued
(C) will issue
(D) will be issued

Questions 143-146 refer to the following letter.

Dear Wells,

-------. Over the past few years, we have organized fun runs, which ------- enthusiastic
143. **144.**
responses from kindhearted people like you. As you know, our organization is ------- to raising
145.
awareness of the disease, educating the public about its signs and symptoms, and raising
money for more effective detection and treatment methods.

I hope you will join us on October 30 at Midtown Park for this year's fun run. If you can't be
there but would like to contribute, please make your check ------- to the American Diabetes
146.
Society and mail it to our office address. If you want to register for the race or pledge online,
please go to www.diabetes.org.

Thank you for your support.

Sincerely,

Matthew Saltmarsh
President, ADA

ACTUAL TEST 01 ACTUAL TEST 02 ACTUAL TEST 03 ACTUAL TEST 04 ACTUAL TEST 05

143. (A) I am writing to express my gratitude
   for helping us finish the event
   successfully.
   (B) According to the expert, the number
   of diabetes patients is increasing
   dramatically.
   (C) Diabetes can be prevented by eating
   healthily and exercising regularly.
   (D) I am writing to invite you to participate
   in person or through a cash pledge
   to help raise money for children with
   diabetes.

144. (A) draw
   (B) draws
   (C) have drawn
   (D) drew

145. (A) expressed
   (B) scheduled
   (C) designed
   (D) committed

146. (A) pay
   (B) to pay
   (C) payable
   (D) payment

PART 5

Directions: A word or phrase is missing in each of the sentences below. Four answer choices are given below each sentence. Select the best answer to complete the sentence. Then mark the letter (A), (B), (C), or (D) on your answer sheet.

101. Because it has so many skilled mechanics, Jimmy's Repair Shop has ------- the fierce competition from other repair shops in the region.
(A) withstands
(B) withstood
(C) withstanding
(D) to withstand

102. The development costs of the new product exceeded the budget, ------- it was still profitable because of the unexpected increase in sales.
(A) perhaps
(B) instead
(C) but
(D) next

103. That television commercial was part of the advertising campaign ------- main goal was to promote tourism of the country.
(A) that
(B) who
(C) whose
(D) which

104. Holyfield Ltd. has hired an international advertising agency in an effort to strengthen its ------- in South Canada.
(A) description
(B) presence
(C) treatment
(D) purchase

105. It is their top ------- to make sure that client information and transaction reports are kept safe at all times.
(A) priority
(B) summary
(C) variety
(D) segment

106. Completion of next quarter's marketing proposals on time ------- hard work and dedication of the managers and team members.
(A) requiring
(B) is required
(C) require
(D) requires

107. Employees are reminded to put away their belongings and office supplies neatly ------- leaving for the day.
(A) before
(B) beside
(C) between
(D) behind

108. In order to make sure that all recently promoted managers deal with every problem properly, a ------- training program should be passed.
(A) spacious
(B) various
(C) rigorous
(D) considerate

109. Please ------- Ms. Caitlin's e-mail dated June 2 to schedule the date of our following seminar on the new safety regulations.
(A) consult
(B) inquire
(C) invest
(D) look

110. Ms. Gao has ------- for several days before making her decision to accept the other company's job offer.
(A) collaborate
(B) deliberated
(C) established
(D) designated

111. The KMDH Electronic Company will begin production of its new line as soon as the necessary equipment ------- at the plant in Busan.
(A) arrive
(B) arrived
(C) arrives
(D) will arrive

112. Free blood testing by the local Physical Center will ------- in the community center from 3:30 P.M. until 6:00 P.M. this Friday.
(A) be holding
(B) have held
(C) hold
(D) be held

113. We can offer you a complete refund as long as you return the ------- product along with a copy of the purchase receipt.
(A) defective
(B) high
(C) underlying
(D) untrue

114. Malcolm Tech Inc. has announced that it will relocate its company offices from San Francisco to Chicago ------- April.
(A) with
(B) in
(C) on
(D) at

115. My family and I would like to give our thanks to you for ------- to our request so quickly.
(A) responding
(B) responds
(C) respond
(D) responded

116. Please contact the network administrator since many people have ------- that they cannot access their e-mail accounts.
(A) compensated
(B) complained
(C) collected
(D) complimented

117. Reimbursements will not be processed ------- a signed expense form and valid receipt showing that the amount has been paid.
(A) without
(B) across
(C) besides
(D) except

118. A review article on the ------- aspects of Chia seed was recently published in the magazine Healthy Life.
(A) benefited
(B) beneficial
(C) benefit
(D) beneficially

119. Unfortunately, the construction is not moving forward ------- the proposal for the footbridge between the two terminal buildings was rejected by the Portland Airport Administration.
(A) while
(B) unless
(C) until
(D) because

120. According to today's press release, Bio Cosmetics ------- to open a plant in Toronto within the next three years.
(A) intends
(B) initiates
(C) considers
(D) previews

GO ON TO THE NEXT PAGE

121. ------ an elementary school and then a women's health club, the red brick building will be completely renovated before opening as Victory High School.
(A) Directly
(B) Before
(C) Formerly
(D) Since

122. ------ of a central apartment building where fire broke out on Thursday night have been allowed to return to their units.
(A) Resided
(B) Resides
(C) Residing
(D) Residents

123. The White Pages lists addresses and telephone numbers of business establishments in the city, including ------ outside the city limits.
(A) their
(B) that
(C) them
(D) those

124. Please ------ the maintenance crew that repairs of the equipment must be done no later than next Monday.
(A) confirm
(B) inform
(C) neglect
(D) refer

125. As soon as all passengers board the ferry, they must show their tickets ------ keep their ticket stubs as proof of payment.
(A) so
(B) as
(C) and
(D) both

126. If Ms. Elliot had not filled in the new agreement completely, the landlord of the property ------ back to the old agreement.
(A) have reverted
(B) will revert
(C) would have reverted
(D) being revert

127. The advertising team worked ------ over the weekend to complete the project by the deadline.
(A) hardly
(B) heavily
(C) diligently
(D) repeatedly

128. The Institute of Arts and Sciences ------ $ 35,000 to the Public Broadcasting corporation this quarter.
(A) is donated
(B) was donated
(C) has donated
(D) has been donated

129. Mr. Richards was ------ to start his managerial research because he had not yet received enough funding for it.
(A) hesitantly
(B) hesitant
(C) hesitated
(D) hesitation

130. Phil McKnight's ability to increase revenue through team coaching and training is well known ------ the business world.
(A) throughout
(B) regarding
(C) aboard
(D) toward

PART 6

Directions: Read the texts that follow. A word, phrase, or sentence is missing in parts of each text. Four answer choices for each question are given below the text. Select the best answer to complete the text. Then mark the letter (A), (B), (C), or (D) on your answer sheet.

Questions 131-134 refer to the following advertisement.

CERN Medical Service has begun to ------- our new services and longer opening hours to help
131.
better serve our customers. We have added 5 new locations ------- the city, where our patients
132.
can access our full range of services. -------. However, we have added more laboratory space
133.
to handle patient blood analysis from our new locations. All locations will now be ------- from
134.
7 A.M. until 10 P.M. Monday to Friday, and Saturday and Sundays from 11 A.M. to 3 P.M. For
more information on all our services, along with the addresses to the new locations, please visit
us on the web at www.medical-service.com.

131. (A) find out
(B) roll out
(C) agree with
(D) meet with

132. (A) among
(B) onto
(C) off
(D) across

133. (A) CERN Medical Service has been
continually trying to provide better
service.
(B) Our main building is still on Orface
Road.
(C) These new locations are conveniently
located.
(D) Our patients will be more satisfied
with this service.

134. (A) progress
(B) open
(C) potential
(D) limited

GO ON TO THE NEXT PAGE

Questions 135-138 refer to the following article.

Hostile Takeover Brings Judicial Review

California (27 November) - Since Sam Cleaning ------- Waste Removal Service last week in a
                                              135.
hostile takeover, Washington lawmakers have been ------- watching the court case developing
                                                     136.
against Sam Cleaning and the U.S. government. If the takeover is allowed to go on, -------. The
                                                               137.
government is concerned that the lack of competition could ------- a 30% increase in bills for
                                                            138.
hospital waste within the next 5 years.

---

135. (A) generated
     (B) informed
     (C) acquired
     (D) merged

136. (A) closed
     (B) close
     (C) closing
     (D) closely

137. (A) Sam Cleaning will be the best
         medical waste disposal company in
         the region.
     (B) Jobs and salaries of Waste Removal
         Service's employees will remain
         same.
     (C) The processing procedure of a
         takeover will start immediately.
     (D) Sam Cleaning will be the only
         company left in the market of medical
         waste disposal on the southwest
         coast.

138. (A) lead to
     (B) retrieve
     (C) grant
     (D) comment on

Questions 139-142 refer to the following letter.

Alabama Ski and Sports Club

Dear Mr. Radnor,

This is to ------- receipt of your membership check for $65 last July 20 and to welcome you to
            139.
ASSC. -------. We are also allocating 5% of your membership fee to our designated beneficiary,
        140.
the Boys and Girls Club of Alabama.

In a recent meeting with our travel agency partners, however, we ------- that they can no longer
                                                                    141.
afford to extend the 30% discount to our members. Instead, they are willing to grant a 25%
discount to anyone who presents their ASSC card.

Other than this slight change, all other membership benefits still hold. Rest assured that we
are ------- trying to develop partnerships with other service providers for the benefit of our
     142.
members.

Again, thanks for joining ASSC and we look forward to seeing you at our events.

Sincerely,

Jim Cassidy

---

139. (A) review
(B) submit
(C) acknowledge
(D) publish

140. (A) Our annual membership fee increased nearly 10 percent this year.
(B) If your friend decides to join the ASSC, you will be eligible for additional membership benefits.
(C) As a new member, you are entitled to all the privileges we mentioned in our notice.
(D) ASSC has added new equipment and upgraded the facility.

141. (A) tells
(B) are telling
(C) were told
(D) told

142. (A) continuously
(B) continuous
(C) continuity
(D) continue

GO ON TO THE NEXT PAGE

Questions 143-146 refer to the following e-mail.

To: Colin Falconer <colin@aol.com>

From: David Faber <davidfaber33@buckhead.com>

Date: Sept. 8

Subject: Your inquiry

Dear Mr. Falconer,

Thank you for your inquiry about our ongoing promotion. Based on the details you have provided, we are pleased to recommend a package ------- of three family-sized pizzas, five
143.
plates of pasta, and three servings of Chicken Marsala with bottomless servings of our popular iced tea. The total bill would ------- cost you $200, but with our ongoing promotion, that will go
144.
down to $160 after the 20% discount.

Your preferred date of September 15 falls on a Friday, which is a busy day for Buckhead Diner. More so, you plan to come in at 7 P.M. which is the peak time of our operations. -------. Please
145.
call us two hours before your arrival so that we can ------- the seats for your party of seven. We
146.
look forward to seeing you and your friends at Buckhead Diner.

Sincerely yours,

David Faber

General Manager

Buckhead Diner

143. (A) consisting
(B) consist
(C) consisted
(D) to consist

144. (A) recently
(B) fairly
(C) openly
(D) normally

145. (A) The usual peak time for Buckhead Diner is between 6 P.M.-9 P.M.
(B) In peak times, our restaurant may be very busy.
(C) Therefore, we request that you confirm your reservation on the same day.
(D) Buckhead Diner is the most popular restaurant in the area.

146. (A) keep up with
(B) take on
(C) deal with
(D) set aside

PART 5

Directions: A word or phrase is missing in each of the sentences below. Four answer choices are given below each sentence. Select the best answer to complete the sentence. Then mark the letter (A), (B), (C), or (D) on your answer sheet.

101. Suzan Fridley was offered the human resources director position last Thursday ------- has not yet accepted it.
(A) while
(B) unless
(C) but
(D) even if

102. ------- the lanes of St. Anthony Street should result in a 15 minutes decrease in commuting hours for traffic in and out of the city.
(A) Expanding
(B) Expansive
(C) Expand
(D) Expansion

103. The vehicle manufacturer ------- that the filter be changed every year or 25,000 miles.
(A) recognizes
(B) remembers
(C) registers
(D) recommends

104. The latest spring collection designed by Charles Elster is available for a ------- time only.
(A) limited
(B) limit
(C) limiting
(D) limits

105. All new employees preparing their first report are encouraged to help ------- by writing together.
(A) whichever
(B) each
(C) either
(D) one another

106. In the first quarter of 2017, Norwich Kitchenware Company reported a 30 percent increase ------- profits despite the fact that domestic sales declined.
(A) off
(B) in
(C) up
(D) at

107. All clients in the waiting room are ------- to use an outlet to charge their laptop computer batteries or any other electronic device they may have with them.
(A) pending
(B) expectant
(C) customary
(D) welcome

GO ON TO THE NEXT PAGE

108. This free web site is of use to those ------- familiar with the Korean and Chinese language.
(A) less
(B) little
(C) fewer
(D) none

109. Downpours over the last two weeks ------- the city government from reinforcing patrolling along riverbanks.
(A) will prevent
(B) has prevented
(C) prevented
(D) have prevented

110. It is ------- for people to raise concerns about the way we are extracting certain kinds of natural resources.
(A) reasoning
(B) reasonable
(C) reasoned
(D) reasonably

111. The latest developments in navigation systems allow drivers to know where there is congestion ------- in advance.
(A) nor
(B) well
(C) ever
(D) now

112. Sommet Mattresses provides its customers ------- only the best quality at incredibly low prices.
(A) over
(B) onto
(C) with
(D) for

113. The exact date of completion for Anne's software installation has yet to be announced, but it will be ------- between September 20 and October 10.
(A) current
(B) tomorrow
(C) sometime
(D) there

114. With over 15 years experience in the field, we are capable of ------- roads, houses, and bridges.
(A) designs
(B) design
(C) designed
(D) designing

115. Richard was selected for the lead patent attorney position because his educational background was very -------.
(A) knowledgeable
(B) impressive
(C) qualified
(D) pleased

116. After you complete the ------- permit applications, please detach the pages from the booklet and bring them to the Public Service Center.
(A) relevantly
(B) relevance
(C) relevancies
(D) relevant

117. It is imperative you do not attempt to ------- items that are too heavy for you, whether you are on your own or with someone else.
(A) draw
(B) select
(C) lift
(D) damage

118. The most ------- way to get motivated to exercise is to make it a part of your everyday routine.
(A) practically
(B) practice
(C) practicing
(D) practical

119. In Canada, new teacher's salaries differ ------- according to which province they are teaching in.
(A) great
(B) greatest
(C) greater
(D) greatly

120. You can change the departure date of your flight without any extra charge, ------- seats are available.
(A) will assume
(B) assume
(C) assuming
(D) assumed

121. The Board Charter describes the ------- of the responsibilities between the Chairman and the Chief Executive Officer.
(A) division
(B) support
(C) statement
(D) enforcement

122. Complete the form below with the required information and we will send you a ------- that you have been successfully added to our system.
(A) notifies
(B) notify
(C) notification
(D) notifying

123. All new employees are on a probationary period when their performance is ------- monthly by managers.
(A) experimental
(B) built
(C) evaluated
(D) understood

124. Tickets are not ------- under any circumstances other than cancellation of the event.
(A) refunding
(B) refund
(C) refunds
(D) refundable

125. Mr. Lim asked ------- Ms. Hwang would be available to photograph the food for the party in July.
(A) although
(B) whether
(C) whenever
(D) either

126. It would be hard for ------- who has watched the movie to deny that Mr. Neo's performance is the best of his career.
(A) some
(B) you
(C) anyone
(D) those

127. All applicants for a two-wheeled vehicle license are asked to pass a driving test ------- by the National Police Agency.
(A) exchanged
(B) administered
(C) occupied
(D) exceeded

128. The committee members visited Mumbai last month to inspect the ------- site for the new airport.
(A) propose
(B) proposing
(C) proposer
(D) proposed

129. Of the ten members of the marketing team, Ms. Chi is the ------- about the new marketing strategy.
(A) most knowledgeable
(B) knowledgeable
(C) knowledge
(D) more knowledge

130. Jack and Associates provides a three-dimensional, ------- version of its full-scale interior designs.
(A) major
(B) fierce
(C) eager
(D) miniature

GO ON TO THE NEXT PAGE

PART 6

Directions: Read the texts that follow. A word, phrase, or sentence is missing in parts of each text. Four answer choices for each question are given below the text. Select the best answer to complete the text. Then mark the letter (A), (B), (C), or (D) on your answer sheet.

Questions 131-134 refer to the following announcement.

Mendoza Engines, the largest ------- of civilian aviation jet engines in Europe, will unveil its
          131.
new website on Wednesday. The biggest change ------- our older site is the targeting of actual
                                        132.
passengers rather than airline companies. Due to the recent number of accidents involving
engines on commercial flights, we want to make clear the 99.98% safety record our engineers
and technicians have achieved. -------. The CEO, George Mendoza, explains, "If we can make
                          133.
people confident in our business partner products, it will lead to larger sales for us in the future."

Please visit www.mendozaengineandturbine.com to learn more about ------- Mendoza Engines
                                                        134.
has become a leader in jet engine safety and reliability.

131. (A) manufacturer
(B) manufactured
(C) manufacturing
(D) manufacture

132. (A) at
(B) by
(C) from
(D) between

133. (A) There is a range of ways to get our flight tickets at a reduced price.
(B) An awarded artist, Kathy Anderson designed the engine cowl to match our aircraft body.
(C) Plus, our airline business partners have not had a single problem with an aircraft engine.
(D) Our business partners have renewed their yearly contract with us for 10 years in a row.

134. (A) how
(B) what
(C) each
(D) during

Questions 135-138 refer to the following letter.

Dear Ms. Sheridan,

Enclosed in this letter is the report about the camera you brought to us for free repair service. As stated in the report, we could not do any repairs due to a ------- of the terms and conditions
135.
of your warranty.

Our technician discovered that the camera shutter had been altered by someone so that it works at a lower speed than normal. When the ------- to the shutter was carried out, it seems to
136.
have been damaged. Our guarantee clearly says that any damage that is the result of alterations or repairs by the owner cannot be covered. -------.
137.

Otherwise, you should pick it up within seven days. Please let us know as ------- as possible
138.
what you would like to do. We look forward to hearing from you soon. Thanks.

Sincerely,

Sarah Lipinski, Customer Service Supervisor
Enclosure

---

135. (A) experiment
(B) courtesy
(C) violation
(D) perspective

136. (A) alteration
(B) alternating
(C) alternatives
(D) alternatively

137. (A) Additionally, if you buy one camera battery by ordering from our website, you will get one for free.
(B) Therefore, if you would like to repair your camera, we have to charge you a fee of $85.
(C) With the exception of the product's manufacturing defect, the refund request is not approved.
(D) Please take extra care not to immerse the camera body into any liquid when cleaning.

138. (A) sooner
(B) soon
(C) soonest
(D) the soonest

GO ON TO THE NEXT PAGE

Questions 139-142 refer to the following e-mail.

To: swhite@doverengineering.com

From: sschaefer@doverengineering.com

Subject: Approval of the Order

Attachment: Materials required for training

Dear Mr. Sandra,

I have ordered ------- of the materials that you require for the training sessions for summer
139.
interns. I have attached a copy of the purchase order I made.

However, our regular supplier has informed us that they ------- produce the folders with the
140.
client's logo on them. After I contacted several companies, I found that Conoco Marketing
produces the folders with the logo. -------.
141.

Please confirm at your earliest convenience the purchase of the folders. Once you authorize this
transaction, I will order the items -------.
142.

Also, I have been informed that we will have all items no later than June 10.

Sincerely,

Steve Schaefer

139. (A) every
(B) these
(C) anyone
(D) most

140. (A) no longer
(B) any more
(C) no later than
(D) not only

141. (A) The logo has been created by our
in-house designer and received many
compliments for its originality.
(B) Their folders are a bit more expensive
than the previous folders, but I think
the Conoco Marketing folder is better.
(C) Our folders are made of the highest
quality and we guarantee that you will
be satisfied with it.
(D) Since its foundation, our company
has never changed its logo, so this is
a good opportunity to do so.

142. (A) immediately
(B) impartially
(C) meticulously
(D) positively

Questions 143-146 refer to the following e-mail.

To: jsparshott@unam.com

From: sbean@ewdf.com

Subject: Response to the Inquiry

Dear Ms. Sparshott,

I appreciate the inquiry you made recently. As the host of the European World Dance Festival, European World Arts Center welcomes members of the news media, ------- freelance writers **143.** on commission, to come to report on special events held in our facilities since both Spanish and international media have a high ------- in the event, passes for journalists will be given on **144.** a first-come, first-served basis, except for some passes secured in advance. -------. The form **145.** is available through our website. All credentials attached must be written on official company letterhead. Successful applicants will receive an email notification, and their passes will be sent to them ------- mail. **146.**

Sincerely,

Star Bean

Public Relations Office, EWDF

---

143. (A) included
(B) was including
(C) to include
(D) including

144. (A) interest
(B) emphasis
(C) fragile
(D) impact

145. (A) To successfully host this festival, admission into the arena is restricted to the dancers and their family members.
(B) The Spanish media has a reputation for its impartial reporting and the full confidence of the public.
(C) Applicants who want to have a journalist pass must submit their request in writing to the dance festival committee.
(D) Secured passes are for disabled people, pregnant women, and the elderly.

146. (A) by
(B) during
(C) from
(D) across

PART 5

Directions: A word or phrase is missing in each of the sentences below. Four answer choices are given below each sentence. Select the best answer to complete the sentence. Then mark the letter (A), (B), (C), or (D) on your answer sheet.

101. Heavy machinery engineers at ------- check the fluid levels of the forklifts and bulldozers.
(A) regularize
(B) regular
(C) regularly
(D) regular

102. Thanks to technological innovation online, the future of mass media is less ------- than ever.
(A) predictable
(B) predicting
(C) predicts
(D) predict

103. Savings banks ------- the country are expected to recover from the recent economic downturn in two months.
(A) behind
(B) despite
(C) across
(D) among

104. Please be reminded that checks ------- at the National Australia Bank no later than 5 P.M. on weekdays will be credited to an account the next morning.
(A) deposited
(B) amounted
(C) borrowed
(D) coined

105. The Zenga Beauty ------- introduced new cosmetics products for the teenage market that include colorful eye and lip products.
(A) recently
(B) rather
(C) very
(D) still

106. The delivery fee listed on our website is an ------- and varies depending on the weight of items.
(A) estimate
(B) attempt
(C) objective
(D) omission

107. Tus Airways is happy to provide all the necessary services to ensure that passengers ------- special needs enjoy a comfortable flight in a perfect safety.
(A) over
(B) with
(C) of
(D) from

108. Requests from clients for ------- our office hours are positively being considered by executives.
(A) submitting
(B) offering
(C) reaching
(D) extending

109. Though Nature Organic introduced a new line of luxurious bed clothing made of organic cotton, its revenue has ------- the same.
(A) remained
(B) determine
(C) announced
(D) resulted

110. A guest speaker advised participants that rewarding outstanding performance is good way to increase employee -------.
(A) productively
(B) produce
(C) productivity
(D) to produce

111. Ms. Hwang's excellent managerial skills resulted in her being ------- as the general manager of the Taipan group of hotels.
(A) designated
(B) appealed
(C) processed
(D) conducted

112. After adopting a new marketing strategy, Woolworths made big profits this year, ------- surpassing last year's gains.
(A) easy
(B) easily
(C) easing
(D) ease

113. After thoughtful consideration, United Electronics ------- accepted Myer Construction's bid to renovate its Sydney plant.
(A) finally
(B) hardly
(C) previously
(D) seldom

114. ------- manager responds to the customer's inquiries just depends on the area the customer lives in.
(A) Each
(B) Which
(C) Something
(D) Either

115. Should your payment details be incorrect, the delivery will be postponed ------- the correct information is received from you.
(A) within
(B) from
(C) around
(D) until

116. Every stay at the Comfort Hotel ------- a free buffet-style breakfast each morning.
(A) inclusive
(B) including
(C) to include
(D) includes
(D) includes

117. To purchase a weekly ------- monthly pass, you will need to register on the website and pay by credit card.
(A) or
(B) out
(C) after
(D) still

118. Jin Airlines ------- a nonstop flight between Seoul and Osaka later this week.
(A) being announced
(B) announcing
(C) will announce
(D) announced

119. If you would like expedited shipping please contact us ------- you have placed your order at info@aco.com
(A) so that
(B) in fact
(C) as soon as
(D) meanwhile

120. Prior to booking any appointments, it will be ------- to send medical information related to the problem along with any imaging reports.
(A) necessarily
(B) necessities
(C) necessitating
(D) necessary

GO ON TO THE NEXT PAGE

121. Red Printing is a firm that ------- in printing business cards and resumes, using the latest laser technology.
(A) specializes
(B) special
(C) specialization
(D) specially

122. Compensation paid to workers must ------- with all applicable wage laws, including those related to minimum wages, overtime hours and legally mandated benefits.
(A) achieve
(B) authorize
(C) comply
(D) regulate

123. After ------- review the terms and conditions of the contract, please sign in the appropriate space below.
(A) yours
(B) yourself
(C) your
(D) you

124. One of the general complaints from apartment residents is that the volume of unwanted mail which they receive has become too -------.
(A) overwhelm
(B) overwhelmed
(C) overwhelming
(D) overwhelmingly

125. This letter is to ------- you that your subscription to Chronicle Science magazine ends with next month's issue.
(A) inform
(B) recommend
(C) persuade
(D) invite

126. Anyone ------- in receiving a box of food and care items has to get a voucher in advance by calling Neo Partners at (808) 569-2785.
(A) interest
(B) interested
(C) to interest
(D) interesting

127. The Surrey Delicatessen is very famous in the West Beach area for its quality of service and reasonable ------- on its delicious selection of baked sandwiches.
(A) priced
(B) price
(C) to price
(D) prices

128. BNK Financial Group will ------- its financial support so we must look for another major investor for the development project.
(A) detach
(B) withdraw
(C) correspond
(D) write

129. Due to our advanced technologies, we have increased the number of customers by ------- 15 percent.
(A) approximately
(B) approximate
(C) approximated
(D) approximating

130. Miterran State Library is not in charge of items left ------- in the reading room.
(A) unattended
(B) discounted
(C) ineligible
(D) nonrefundable

PART 6

Directions: Read the texts that follow. A word, phrase, or sentence is missing in parts of each text. Four answer choices for each question are given below the text. Select the best answer to complete the text. Then mark the letter (A), (B), (C), or (D) on your answer sheet.

Questions 131-134 refer to the following announcement.

Beginning next month, the Manchester Science and Technology Center will ------- its latest
131.
exhibition on the history of lighting. Beginning Saturday, June 1st, come and learn how humans
first learned to harness flame for ------- use, and later refined it in the form of candles, whale oil
132.
lanterns and gas fired street lights. As we approach the modern age, you will see how electricity
transformed night to day with the ------- of the incandescent light bulb. The Manchester
133.
Science and Technology Center address is 4587 Park View Drive, across the street from the
court house. -------. To learn more, call 543-2341-6582.
134.

131. (A) undo
(B) redeem
(C) recall
(D) unveil

132. (A) ourselves
(B) our own
(C) ours
(D) we

133. (A) arrive
(B) to arrive
(C) arrival
(D) arriving

134. (A) You can watch a video about how a
steam train was developed.
(B) This exhibition will be permanent and
will be updated every so often.
(C) Whale oil sale is prohibited by animal
protection law.
(D) We have to continue our efforts to
reduce the amount of electricity used.

GO ON TO THE NEXT PAGE ▶

Questions 135-138 refer to the following information.

Sandy's mountain Equipment

We make sure our products are of the ------- quality and tested in the outdoor environment
                                           135.
before making them available to our customers. Your satisfaction is our number one goal. -------
                                                                                            136.
you feel that any of our merchandise does not meet your exact needs, please feel free to return
it. -------.
    137.

Simply place your item to be returned in the package we included with your shipment, and we
will ------- the shipping expense. We guarantee to process your return immediately on arrival
       138.
and will have your replacement item sent back out on the same day.

135. (A) highly
    (B) high
    (C) highest
    (D) higher

136. (A) Should
    (B) Would
    (C) Had
    (D) Could

137. (A) We also supply our products to
       professional climbers.
    (B) You can personally see our product
       at our showroom.
    (C) We will gladly offer you an exchange
       or a complete refund.
    (D) Delivery takes normally 2 business
       days from the purchase.

138. (A) use
    (B) cover
    (C) persist
    (D) tend

MILO-Kurata Credit Services

Mr. Maria Shurn

84b Trilling Road

Calgarly, AB

Dear Mr. Shurn,

After ------- two years of negotiations, MILO Asset Management and Kurata Holdings have
139.
finally merged to become MILO-Kurata Credit Services. Two successful financial product
companies have now become the industry leader in the finance sector. We promise to continue
honoring our previous commitments to you, a ------- customer. However, we are also pleased to
140.
be able to offer you a range of new and exciting financial products to ------- your portfolio and
141.
lower your risk exposure. -------. Please look over the brochure we've included with this letter
142.
regarding our products. If you have any questions, a friendly and knowledgeable associate will
be only too pleased to help at any of our branches. We look forward to serving you better.

Sincerely,

Graham Carter

Asset Advisor

---

139. (A) following
(B) more than
(C) very
(D) much more

140. (A) first
(B) referred
(C) temporary
(D) valued

141. (A) broaden
(B) extend
(C) excel
(D) forecast

142. (A) After we used this service for 3 months, we decided to cancel our contract.
(B) Beginning September 17, these services will become available to all our customers.
(C) We are an awarded financial advisor and we are confident that our service will exceed your expectation.
(D) Making a huge profit through investing needs experts'insight from many year's experience.

GO ON TO THE NEXT PAGE

Questions 143-146 refer to the following e-mail.

To: Kolnas@stanfordcom.net

From: customerservice@zonacomcenter.com

Date: March 30

Subject: Invoice # 346750

Dear Ms. Kolnas,

As I mentioned in our conversation over the phone, we finished ------- your laptop on March 15,

143.

and we shipped it to you through Fedex on March 16. ------- you have notified us that you have

144.

not yet received the laptop, our only assumption is that it was lost in transit. Right after receiving

your letter, we informed the shipping agency about the loss, and one of its representatives is

now trying to locate the shipment. We expect a report from them within two days. -------. If it

145.

cannot be found within seven days, you will be refunded for the exact amount you paid for the

laptop by Fedex. We apologize for the inconvenience you -------, and look forward to doing

146.

business with you again in the future.

Sincerely,

Quincy Bishop

Customer Service, Zona Computer Center

---

143. (A) to repair
(B) repairs
(C) repairing
(D) repair

144. (A) Since
(B) While
(C) Though
(D) Due to

145. (A) After talking with one of the delivery staff, we concluded that your shipment has successfully arrived.
(B) The manufacturer informed us that the item will be included in our next regular shipment.
(C) If the Fedex representative can find your laptop, it will be delivered to you right away.
(D) The items left in baggage claim area will be kept in our lost & found office for 90 days.

146. (A) will be experienced
(B) are experienced
(C) have experienced
(D) will have experienced

PART 5

Directions: A word or phrase is missing in each of the sentences below. Four answer choices are given below each sentence. Select the best answer to complete the sentence. Then mark the letter (A), (B), (C), or (D) on your answer sheet.

ACTUAL TEST 06 ACTUAL TEST 07 ACTUAL TEST 08 ACTUAL TEST 09 ACTUAL TEST 10

101. ------- the goods have been delivered at the delivery address, the risk concerning the products is the purchaser's responsibility.
(A) In addition to
(B) Even so
(C) As soon as
(D) Other than

102. ------- four months, the management committee of Gold West Corporation checks if their policies are moving toward the right direction.
(A) Every
(B) Only
(C) During
(D) About

103. All employees who were hired last month must submit their first report to Mr. Stich's office ------- 5:30 P.M. on Friday.
(A) by
(B) within
(C) onto
(D) until

104. The Melbourne City Council will take its citizens' preferences into ------- when choosing a location for the new community center.
(A) construction
(B) participation
(C) account
(D) registration

105. The delegation ------- at ten in the morning tomorrow, so please go to the airport to meet them.
(A) arrived
(B) will be arrived
(C) is arriving
(D) have arrived

106. Since adopting non-toxic paint last year, Bridge Home Improvement Service has ------- doubled its profit margin.
(A) after
(B) until
(C) almost
(D) during

107. Only those who have the ------- to travel abroad for business are considered for the position of the overseas sales division head.
(A) commission
(B) flexibility
(C) relative
(D) destination

108. By the time this item is launched in the market, Big Chase Supplies ------- a new advertisement.
(A) is published
(B) will be published
(C) will have published
(D) had published

GO ON TO THE NEXT PAGE

43

109. Make sure to avoid covering the item's bar code when ------- new price stickers to books on sale.
(A) applies
(B) applying
(C) apply
(D) applied

110. The new tax policy is intended ------- local growth and development, but its effects may not be seen for a couple of years.
(A) facilitating
(B) to facilitate
(C) facilitate
(D) to be facilitated

111. Mr. Chan will announce the idea ------- has come up with to market our soap line.
(A) him
(B) his
(C) he
(D) himself

112. ------- is willing to apply for the sales manager position must submit their resume and previous employer's references.
(A) Another
(B) Someone
(C) Whoever
(D) Anyone

113. ------- working for the department store, Mr. Han had to handle about 20 complaints from customers per week.
(A) While
(B) During
(C) Meanwhile
(D) For

114. Ms. Oh will be transferred to the marketing department, in ------- she will take charge of web advertising.
(A) which
(B) what
(C) where
(D) that

115. Residents of Festival Tower and employees at Lakeview Manufacturing Company worked ------- to lessen water pollution in the area.
(A) collaboratively
(B) collaborative
(C) collaborating
(D) collaboration

116. The president of Hussy company commissioned Corrie Vernard to create a ------- designed company logo.
(A) profession
(B) professional
(C) professionals
(D) professionally

117. I-plan, a new mobile phone application, can help you organize your calendar schedule -------.
(A) yours
(B) you
(C) yourself
(D) your own

118. Our Engine Clean machine has been manufactured in Australia and delivers ------- results on your car engine parts.
(A) exceptional
(B) exceptions
(C) exceptionally
(D) exception

119. In honor of ------- achievements, Mr. Hwang was given the lifetime achievement award.
(A) perceptive
(B) noteworthy
(C) interested
(D) satisfied

120. The document attached in the file contains essential information about your newly ------- car insurance policy.
(A) issued
(B) expected
(C) expressed
(D) influenced

121. Since its founding fifteen years ago, Jamie's Kitchen ------- customer satisfaction to be a top priority.
(A) consider
(B) has been considered
(C) has considered
(D) considered

122. Please help us provide better service to our customers by taking a few moments to ------- to this short and simple written questionnaire.
(A) announce
(B) respond
(C) fill
(D) sign

123. Paul Gouguin faced many difficulties in his life, but he used them as ------- for his art.
(A) inspiration
(B) constructions
(C) suspicions
(D) apprehensions

124. If your passport is set ------- soon and you have travel plans, it will be a good idea to renew it as soon as possible.
(A) to expire
(B) expired
(C) expiring
(D) will have expired

125. Most specialists ------- with the construction market predict that construction of buildings will decrease over the next two years.
(A) familiar
(B) usual
(C) normal
(D) recognizable

126. Four years ago, at the age of 32, Kike Alfredo ------- to Tokyo to work in the financial sector.
(A) moved
(B) has moved
(C) would move
(D) moves

127. On behalf of the management and staff at Mega Mart, we would like to thank all of our loyal customers for their ------- and support.
(A) item
(B) backup
(C) usage
(D) patronage

128. Over the years, we have been ranked not just -------, but repeatedly by the Arizona Business Journal as the best Law Firm throughout North Carolina.
(A) still
(B) about
(C) so
(D) once

129. ------- among the reasons Victoria is a favored city to live in are the city's strong educational system, growing economy, and temperate climate.
(A) Proper
(B) Adept
(C) Similar
(D) Chief

130. Vancouver police are implementing a new model to train officers and are hoping to ------- the results of their research with other Canadian law-enforcement agencies.
(A) share
(B) split
(C) suggest
(D) taste

GO ON TO THE NEXT PAGE

PART 6

Directions: Read the texts that follow. A word, phrase, or sentence is missing in parts of each text. Four answer choices for each question are given below the text. Select the best answer to complete the text. Then mark the letter (A), (B), (C), or (D) on your answer sheet.

Questions 131-134 refer to the following memo.

To: All Employees

From: Lance Alvarez, Manager of Facilities

Date: March 20

Subject: Access card

On April 15, our company will install card-access systems ------- to the gates of the two parking
                                                                 131.
areas. Parking Lot A, just behind the Golden View Building, and Parking Lot B, adjacent to the

Calipso Building. -------. Nevertheless, employees in the maintenance and security departments
                   132.
who will be reporting to work on that day should be aware that they cannot enter the parking lot

while the installation -------. On Friday, a memo will be sent out about ------- parking spaces for
                       133.   **134.**
staff members who will be at work on April 15.

---

131. (A) nearby
(B) nearly
(C) close
(D) proximity

132. (A) This newly installed system has been
revealed to have a serious defect and
will be replaced.
(B) The security workers will inspect this
system on a monthly basis to find any
error.
(C) This new system will help increase
customer satisfaction by helping
them access our building more easily.
(D) As the installation will be completed
in a single day, the installation
process will not affect most
Manufacturing workers.

133. (A) is taking place
(B) will be taken place
(C) was taking place
(D) will have taken place

134. (A) alternative
(B) alternate
(C) alternatively
(D) alternation

Questions 135-138 refer to the following e-mail.

To: All employees

From: Floyd Mitchum

Date: April 1

Subject: Next Week's Assignment

Thank you, everyone, for finishing all of your tasks for this week efficiently. I will go on rotating you weekly so that the tasks are ------- distributed to all of us, in addition to our regular work.
135.

On April 4, Ela will take charge of ordering coffee, tea and other supplies from Superior Taste Coffee Supplies. She will also ------- the kitchen cabinets when items we have ordered arrive.
136.
Excess supplies must be stored in the closet in our storage room. Mariposa ------- the filing
137.
cabinets on the third floor. -------. There is also a request from the payroll department to help
138.
them organize their files. It should take about two hours to finish this job each day.

If you have any questions, please contact me in my office.

Floyd Mitchum

135. (A) commensurately
(B) expansively
(C) fairly
(D) compatibly

136. (A) replenish
(B) deplete
(C) neglect
(D) comprise

137. (A) has organized
(B) will organize
(C) organized
(D) will be organized

138. (A) Please make sure to arrange all the files in alphabetical order by customer name.
(B) Please be aware that we installed new copiers at each end of the 3rd floor hall way.
(C) I am writing to announce that we successfully passed the state fire inspection.
(D) It's two days before our quarterly evaluation of staff performance.

GO ON TO THE NEXT PAGE

Questions 139-142 refer to the following review.

Dining Review Exclusive

The Sicilias ★★★☆

by Shelly Croughton

Edisonburg City (April 20) - Chef Alfonso Prodi, a famous culinary artist who is a native of Cannes, France, ------- a pleasant French restaurant called The Sicilias on the Edisonburg
139.
Coast yesterday. Residents of Edisonburg were excited to ------- the dishes at the only French
140.
restaurant in the city. -------. Fortunately, the superb food more than compensated for the long
141.
wait to get a table. I suggest that you stay for dessert. The really delicious chocolate cake prepared by Chef Alfonso Prodi is ------- the best in Edisonburg. The Sicilias is the newest
142.
addition to the city'great restaurant scene, and I really cannot wait to go back!

---

139. (A) is opening
(B) opening
(C) opened
(D) will have opened

140. (A) sample
(B) remain
(C) satisfy
(D) expedite

141. (A) To reserve a table, please call 555-0812 and spell your name.
(B) Chef Alfonso Prodi is also serving as a professor at Edisonburg university.
(C) Ratatouilles and Beef Bourguignon are the signature dishes of Sicilias.
(D) Last night, guests waiting for a table formed long lines down the sidewalk.

142. (A) by far
(B) far away
(C) nearby
(D) far too

Questions 143-146 refer to the following letter.

Hottest Fit Fitness

San Francisco'Best Fitness Club

33 New Montgomery Street, San Francisco, CA 94105

Mike Winslow

9087 Appletown Avenue

San Francisco, CA 94105

Membership Number 32456

Dear Ms. Winslow,

We would like to inform you that your membership at Hottest Fit Fitness is scheduled to be renewed on 1 April. ------- our records, you signed up for the Automatic Renewal Program.
143.
Previously, you ------- us to charge your yearly membership fee to your credit card, which
144.
starts with the numbers 1108. If you would rather use ------- credit card or pay using a different
145.
method, please inform us before March 25 so that we can update our records. Also, you can update your billing information in three ways. First, you can visit www.Hottestfittown.com, our secure website, click on My Information Modification, and choose the section about your credit card. Second, you can call our customer service department at 9162-0228. -------. If you don't
146.
take any further action, we will continue billing the current credit card that we have on file.

Sincerely yours,

Regina Miller

Director of Club Membership

143. (A) Accordingly
(B) In accordance
(C) According to
(D) Accordance

144. (A) asked
(B) suggested
(C) allocated
(D) compensated

145. (A) other
(B) another
(C) the others
(D) each other

146. (A) Lastly, we have completed updating our website, so you can find more detailed information than before.
(B) Finally, you can drop by any Hottest Fit Fitness branch and talk to a representative at the reception desk.
(C) Thirdly, for every person you refer who then uses our service, you'll receive a 20% discount.
(D) Once more, your next payment is due on April 1, after which your name will be removed from our list.

PART 5

Directions: A word or phrase is missing in each of the sentences below. Four answer choices are given below each sentence. Select the best answer to complete the sentence. Then mark the letter (A), (B), (C), or (D) on your answer sheet.

101. The company may ------- ticket sales to a maximum number per person and reserves the right to cancel any tickets purchased in excess of this number.
(A) connect
(B) restrict
(C) claim
(D) deny

102. Dining at Roma Station Park is always a ------- and genuinely authentic experience in Calgary.
(A) delightfulness
(B) delightfully
(C) delight
(D) delightful

103. Ms. Najad requested two color printers to be used only to ------- brochures for the upcoming product campaigns.
(A) printed
(B) prints
(C) printing
(D) print

104. Sales Director Manuel Park thinks that advertising ------- in print is no longer a strong method to attract potential customers.
(A) closely
(B) solely
(C) otherwise
(D) indeed

105. Ramos Ramirez is going to distribute an ------- to each committee member before next Saturday's meeting.
(A) appointment
(B) agenda
(C) appearance
(D) expense

106. Part of Ms. Koop's job as production supervisor is to oversee daily operations, ------- providing support to her team members.
(A) so
(B) but
(C) as well as
(D) whereas

107. ------- Nike's sales have increased so dramatically is proof that its chief sales manager, Hochang Lee, has done a great job.
(A) With
(B) That
(C) If
(D) For

108. The human resources director is now evaluating trainees' performance ------- more thoroughly than the previous months.
(A) even
(B) too
(C) very
(D) so

109. As per the Canadian Railway guidelines, the railway does occasionally close at very ------- notice due to unforeseeable circumstances.
(A) brief
(B) short
(C) high
(D) low

110. ------- are the manuscripts needed to be reviewed and summarized.
(A) Encloses
(B) Enclosing
(C) Enclosed
(D) Enclose

111. Selecting a house is a big decision and requires patience and a willingness to view ------- properties as possible.
(A) so much
(B) so many
(C) as many
(D) as much

112. We will cease using the information you provided for the project ------- after your request has been received.
(A) vaguely
(B) measurably
(C) promptly
(D) originally

113. If you have problems with starting your car, please refer to page 17 of the instruction manual ------- contacting a customer service representative.
(A) before
(B) even if
(C) during
(D) except

114. The inspectors ------- that the school buses are compliant with all state regulations.
(A) replace
(B) influence
(C) associate
(D) certify

115. One year after the merger, the executive team has been able to draw its initial conclusions and they are ------- positive.
(A) exceptional
(B) exceptionally
(C) exception
(D) except

116. If you discover any physical ------- in our products, we will replace them free of charge or refund you the full amount.
(A) inconveniences
(B) mistakes
(C) misfortunes
(D) defects

117. With little difference between the services offered by logistics companies, contracts are awarded to ------- company offers the lowest price.
(A) whichever
(B) any
(C) these
(D) each

118. Health care providers are required to keep a patient's health information confidential ------- consent to release the information is provided by the patient.
(A) as
(B) unless
(C) nor
(D) either

119. KYL Accounting exclusively provides payroll services for restaurants, as ------- are their primary clients in the Hamilton area.
(A) their own
(B) these
(C) there
(D) them

120. Within a short period of time, Lotus Metal Corporation has established a reputation as a ------- importer of quality stainless steel.
(A) fragile
(B) reliable
(C) memorable
(D) comfortable

GO ON TO THE NEXT PAGE

121. As a pharmacist, Dr. Duchamp's most ------- quality is the passion and commitment he shows to his patients.
(A) admiring
(B) admiration
(C) admirable
(D) admire

122. A real estate developer is in need of an ------- to design high-tech double-story houses at a low cost.
(A) architecturally
(B) architectural
(C) architect
(D) architecture

123. To use the machine safely, extension cords should be ------- only when necessary and only on a temporary basis.
(A) usage
(B) used
(C) using
(D) uses

124. Fedex ground shipping takes about 5 business days to deliver ------- express delivery takes only 2 days.
(A) despite
(B) whether
(C) until
(D) while

125. Available in a wide variety of sizes, our newly ------- line of luxury shoes are still made with the finest leather.
(A) updated
(B) updating
(C) update
(D) updates

126. Distributing a memo by email ------- paper versions may save several hours of labor, which over time could save the company a substantial amount of money.
(A) according to
(B) instead of
(C) throughout
(D) except

127. ------- for changes to MYK membership must be made online using the electronic forms available.
(A) Requests
(B) Requested
(C) To request
(D) Requesting

128. There were some attempts to grow bananas commercially in Honduras in the 1980s but these were only ------- successful.
(A) intriguingly
(B) regrettably
(C) marginally
(D) eloquently

129. With the aid of wireless remote devices, our service team guarantees that your vending machines always remain ------- stocked with the most popular selections.
(A) fully
(B) full
(C) fullest
(D) fuller

130. It is important to keep in mind that new operating systems are not always ------- with existing software needed for your printers.
(A) compatible
(B) alternative
(C) external
(D) formal

PART 6

Directions: Read the texts that follow. A word, phrase, or sentence is missing in parts of each text. Four answer choices for each question are given below the text. Select the best answer to complete the text. Then mark the letter (A), (B), (C), or (D) on your answer sheet.

Questions 131-134 refer to the following article.

Around Town

-------. Marcus Verbeek, the event organizer, said that this year's performances were ------- the
131.   **132.**
best event ever and wished to thank all the artists who joined in the celebration of the famous
island music. Many of the reggae bands that ------- this year were locals who have never been
                                              133.
to Jamaica. Of course, the big names in reggae, especially Stephen Marley, who came all the
way from Kingston, Jamaica, were the ones that attracted the largest audiences. It is ------- that
                                                                                      134.
over 300 performers and more than 20,000 fans attended the concerts across the city. The local
tourism bureau estimates that this week-long event brought more than $500,000 in tourism
money to the local economy.

131. (A) Coming Tuesday, Cansas City is
holding a grand reggae festival at its
city hall plaza.
(B) Reggae Fest wrapped up its 10th
annual extravaganza Sunday night to
a cheering crowd.
(C) Stephen Marley has been nominated
for the reggae artist of the year
award.
(D) This weekend, the Cansas Stadium
will be closed to do a spring-cleaning
for the coming reggae Fest.

132. (A) chosen
(B) among
(C) polite
(D) prior

133. (A) will participate
(B) participate
(C) participated
(D) participating

134. (A) estimates
(B) estimating
(C) estimated
(D) estimator

GO ON TO THE NEXT PAGE

Questions 135-138 refer to the following letter.

Michelle Zapatos

48 Main St

Boulder, Colorado

Dear Mr. Zapatos,

Thank you for 32 years of dedication to our company. We at Pueblo Imports want to celebrate your decades of excellence in employment by hosting a huge retirement party ------- you and all our departing workers. We hope that you will join us December 13th at the Miami Pueblo Country Club for a banquet dinner and speech from the President of Pueblo. You, ------- the other retiring employees, will be seated at the head table with the board of directors. Of course, your family is ------- to join this prestigious event as well. If you will be attending, please respond by filling in the attached card and leaving it with reception by November 15th at the latest. -------.
135. **136.** **137.** **138.**

Sincerely,

Gabriel Daniels

Human Resources Manager

Enclosure

135. (A) will honor
(B) to honor
(C) would honor
(D) to be honored

136. (A) owing to
(B) even if
(C) along with
(D) in case of

137. (A) customary
(B) welcome
(C) pending
(D) exclusive

138. (A) Our janitor will then direct you to your reserved seat before the show begins.
(B) Your appointment as a new president will be announced at the end of the banquet.
(C) Don't forget to mark down the number of guests you will be bringing.
(D) This banquet attendance will be limited to permanent employees only.

Questions 139-142 refer to the following e-mail.

To: Auckland Office Managers <management@aros.com.nz>

From: Robert Fabian, IT Department <rfabian@aros.com.nz>

Re: Server Update

Date: 20 October

Attachment: admin password update procedure.txt

As the internal memo sent to all managers explained last week, we are ------- to upgrade our
139.
company servers. This will occur at midnight on August 24th and should be completed by
Monday morning on August 26th.

All security protocols will be reset, which means you will need to enter a new password for your
admin accounts. Please follow the procedure as ------- in the attachment included here. -------.
140. **141.**

In additon, you must enter your new password within 24 hours of the servers going online. Do
not use the ------- password as you had. Commit your new password to memory and do not
142.
write it anywhere.

139. (A) about
(B) reluctant
(C) concerned
(D) insecure

140. (A) explain
(B) explained
(C) explaining
(D) be explained

141. (A) You have to attend the training
seminar before accessing our new
network system.
(B) Our company's network has the top
security and is always protected from
any DDOS attack.
(C) You will not be able to access the
network until a new password has
been entered.
(D) You can now log in to our website as
regular maintenance has just been
completed.

142. (A) both
(B) equal
(C) eager
(D) same

GO ON TO THE NEXT PAGE

Questions 143-146 refer to the following letter.

Dear Mr. Moore,

We thank you for choosing Oceanblue Pools as your custom outdoor swimming pool contractor. Our professional pool installers ------- in the business for over 25 years and installed more than
143.
1000 pools over that time. If the pool vinyl liner does become ripped or warped, make sure to contact our service department -------. We promise to come to your home and have the pool
144.
back in perfect ------- within 2 business days. We also provide a full range of pool maintenance
145.
services. -------. Please contact us if you have any additional questions regarding your pool.
146.

143. (A) will be
(B) being
(C) have been
(D) has been

144. (A) later
(B) perfectly
(C) immediately
(D) extremely

145. (A) schedule
(B) term
(C) appointment
(D) condition

146. (A) Our mowing and gardening service is highly recognized across this county.
(B) This includes preparing your pool for the cold season and to reopen it in the spring.
(C) Swimming is a good exercise especially for those who have heart problems.
(D) We only use environmentally friendly detergent for cleaning your house windows.

PART 5

Directions: A word or phrase is missing in each of the sentences below. Four answer choices are given below each sentence. Select the best answer to complete the sentence. Then mark the letter (A), (B), (C), or (D) on your answer sheet.

101. ------- are already complete for the display booths at tomorrow's Wellness Food Fair.
(A) Preparations
(B) Preparation
(C) To prepare
(D) Preparing

102. Nowadays, many consumers find credit cards ------- and safe when they purchase items in stores.
(A) convene
(B) convenience
(C) convention
(D) convenient

103. Because the last board meeting focused on planning issues, it ran ------- late and left little time for important corporate issues.
(A) quite
(B) ever
(C) enough
(D) more

104. The new machines are simply designed, so they are easy to operate and require ------- repairs.
(A) few
(B) little
(C) many
(D) any

105. This series of ------- of the heroes of Korea were originally written approximately four hundred years ago.
(A) charts
(B) models
(C) careers
(D) biographies

106. Before you submit the monthly report, make sure that you go over it with great -------.
(A) care
(B) caring
(C) careful
(D) carefully

107. Our friendly, experienced staff will be happy to respond to any questions you may have ------- our vehicles, parts and services.
(A) regards
(B) regarding
(C) regard
(D) regarded

108. Cecelia Ahern wrote ------- first book at just 21 and recently released her 11th novel: The Year I Met You.
(A) she
(B) hers
(C) herself
(D) her

GO ON TO THE NEXT PAGE

109. Mr. Danilo Dalle needs to submit a ------- review of the book he read last week.
(A) future
(B) many
(C) short
(D) convenient

110. It is our ------- that staff members should not take care of personal business while on duty.
(A) approval
(B) manual
(C) policy
(D) guide

111. The hotel also boasts a fine-dining restaurant on its premises and ------- scenery on the grounds of the hotel.
(A) momentary
(B) picturesque
(C) multiple
(D) appeared

112. The downtown Hiltons hotel includes an ------- open-air courtyard that provides an informal seating area for guests.
(A) assessed
(B) entertained
(C) anticipated
(D) enclosed

113. With regional offices all ------- Australia, NASB provides support to help small businesses succeed.
(A) along
(B) across
(C) away
(D) broad

114. Replacement keys for your house can be ordered directly from the manufacturer ------- you have the house's proof of ownership.
(A) as though
(B) in fact
(C) more than
(D) provided that

115. Not only is this a fantastic way to save energy, but you can also save almost $ 730 per year when you make the ------- improvements to your home.
(A) suggested
(B) suggest
(C) suggests
(D) suggesting

116. The Regional Director of Operations will be responsible for leading a high performing team of sales representatives who consistently ------- company expectations.
(A) hail
(B) exceed
(C) believe
(D) command

117. In addition to being a leading domestic producer, Muritos has been ------- successful in overseas markets.
(A) markedly
(B) permissibly
(C) intimately
(D) initially

118. Krachen College is pleased to offer two new professional development opportunities ------- educators in Moreton during the 2017 academic year.
(A) at
(B) for
(C) in
(D) as

119. The results included in this report are ------- applicable to British pension plans.
(A) directs
(B) directing
(C) direct
(D) directly

120. Due to a high ------- of submissions, please understand that we will only contact you if your work fits our current needs.
(A) volume
(B) location
(C) point
(D) size

121. An evaluation will be completed -------
after all requested information has been
received by Creed Union.
(A) only
(B) when
(C) most
(D) now

122. FORTUNE's new main office building,
with floor space ------- 28,000 square
meters, houses modern production
facilities, warehouses and offices.
(A) processing
(B) completing
(C) earning
(D) totaling

123. We are going to replace the silver
knobs with ------- ones to match the
bookshelves, and we ordered a wall
mount to hang the TV.
(A) darkness
(B) darkest
(C) darker
(D) darkly

124. ------- of Mr. Ahn's mail should be
forwarded to his assistant while he is out
of town for a business trip next week.
(A) Everyone
(B) Each
(C) All
(D) Such

125. ------- the country's largest shopping
complex was finished, Lexis
Construction had already planned to
build a larger one.
(A) Unless
(B) By the time
(C) Due to
(D) Whenever

126. A majority of the organization's members
are physicians with an expertise in a
------- area of the neurological sciences.
(A) provided
(B) confident
(C) granted
(D) particular

127. We actively seek to support innovative
technologies ------- decrease
dependence on fossil fuels.
(A) if
(B) that
(C) when
(D) will

128. Australian Toy Corporate is slowly
inching its way ------- more entertaining
games that boys and girls of all ages can
play together.
(A) beside
(B) toward
(C) along with
(D) onto

129. Failure to comply with the rules ------- in
this manual will cause the warranty to be
declared null and void.
(A) outlined
(B) outlining
(C) outlines
(D) outline

130. Meriton, which was formerly known as
Riverside, is a desirable community to
live in because of its ------- to downtown
Brisbane and natural environments.
(A) direction
(B) diligence
(C) proximity
(D) site

GO ON TO THE NEXT PAGE ▶

PART 6

Directions: Read the texts that follow. A word, phrase, or sentence is missing in parts of each text. Four answer choices for each question are given below the text. Select the best answer to complete the text. Then mark the letter (A), (B), (C), or (D) on your answer sheet.

Questions 131-134 refer to the following letter.

Dear Mr. Gallon,

Don't miss any issue of The Weekly Financial Adviser! Please note that your subscription ------- **131.** on May 31. If you renew your subscription before that date, you will receive a copy of Modern Finance, the latest book from financial expert Tony Parsons. -------. As you already know, **132.** The Weekly Financial Adviser provides readers with a ------- analysis of the most significant **133.** advancements in business and finance. We hope that you are satisfied with our timely reports, the ------- tips from Harbie Dellington and the humorous columns of Anayeli Tapia. **134.**

Sincerely,

Jane Ryan

Circulation Manager

Enclosure

---

131. (A) is expired
(B) have been expired
(C) expires
(D) to expire

132. (A) We arranged a lecture by Parsons which is scheduled for June 1.
(B) There are a few more magazines you can select including Modern Finance.
(C) Enclosed is the renewal application you need to complete and mail back to us.
(D) We also receive letters from readers to be published in a newly added opinion section.

133. (A) thorough
(B) absorbent
(C) skilled
(D) temporary

134. (A) investing
(B) invested
(C) investment
(D) invest

Questions 135-138 refer to the following fax.

Dear Mr. Yamamoto,

The Sukusima School and Office Supply thanks you for bringing this to our ------- . We -------
that we made a mistake. We mistakenly delivered to you a different product due to the hectic
schedule of our newly hired inventory clerk, who was just hired a couple of weeks ago.

We deeply apologize for the inconvenience. For our part, we are ------- to replace the
equipment sent to you mistakenly free of charge. The correct set of audio-visual equipment will
be delivered to you at your office tomorrow.

------- . We will try not to make the same mistake in the future.

Thank you!

Respectfully yours,

Keiko Yamada
General Manager

135. (A) attendee
(B) attentive
(C) attention
(D) attended

136. (A) acknowledge
(B) impress
(C) carry out
(D) reserve

137. (A) ready
(B) hesitant
(C) qualified
(D) deliberate

138. (A) However, either way, you have to pay
an additional $10.
(B) He is the only person who knows the
situation.
(C) Your constructive comments are
greatly appreciated
(D) We are looking forward to hearing
your opinion about this new
technology.

GO ON TO THE NEXT PAGE

Questions 139-142 refer to the following letter.

Dear Mr. Andrew Nagorski,

I ------- to you to bring to your attention the outstanding service I received from one of your
139.
employees at the Sacranton branch of your pet cleaning company.

-------. I warned the shampooer, a Mrs. Clare, that Haru (my pet's name) can be very difficult
140.
around new people. She just smiled and approached my dog ------- hesitation. After playing
141.
with him for a few minutes, he was completely relaxed and even let her clean his ears without a

fight.

I've never seen someone with more genuine affection for the animals and I will definitely

recommend ------- to all my dog owner friends.
142.

Sincerely,

Robert Natale

---

139. (A) will write
(B) am writing
(C) to write
(D) wrote

140. (A) Last week, I brought my pet dog over
for a shampoo and cut.
(B) That day, your employee was very
impolite and didn't pay any attention
to my pet.
(C) Some time ago, my pet was trained to
be a guide dog.
(D) The day before yesterday, I kept my
pet outside for a long period.

141. (A) except
(B) without
(C) unless
(D) instead

142. (A) him
(B) her
(C) you
(D) them

Questions 143-146 refer to the following memo.

To: All staff of Telegraph Publishing

From: David Faber

Date: May 2

I am glad to give you some news about the exciting developments at Telegraph Publishing. For 25 years, our firm has ------- excellent publications in the English language in several countries
        143.
in Asia.

To make Baliplus News more successful, Colin Falconer has been hired as Director for Circulation. We are delighted that he came to work with us, and Mr. Falconer has already outlined ambitious plans ------- the number of readers for this publication.
        144.

Also, our recent project, Babak Namazian, will begin production next month with Amos Badeah as the chief editor. Mr. Badeah was chosen from ------- hundreds of applicants for the position
        145.
because he has expertise stemming from his 12 years with another publication. Mr. Badeah and the new art director, Donald Walf, will lead Babak Namazian.

-------.
146.

---

143. (A) distributed
(B) disturbed
(C) disordered
(D) discarded

144. (A) increase
(B) was increasing
(C) to increase
(D) increases

145. (A) despite
(B) among
(C) about
(D) between

146. (A) The recruitment is processed now and the successful applicant will be announced by the end of this month.
(B) Walf was an account manager for 7 years before being appointed for this position.
(C) Babak Namazian will be the last publication of our company because we decided to discontinue the other magazines.
(D) We are certain that these new employees will be valuable assets to our company and make the magazine successful.

PART 5

Directions: A word or phrase is missing in each of the sentences below. Four answer choices are given below each sentence. Select the best answer to complete the sentence. Then mark the letter (A), (B), (C), or (D) on your answer sheet.

101. The warranty does not ------- any damage caused by accident, misuse, fire, flood, or improper installation.
(A) covered
(B) cover
(C) covering
(D) covers

102. Please be informed that utility bill payments ------- in person at the Cashier's Office will be processed immediately.
(A) making
(B) make
(C) made
(D) makes

103. The Seal Inc. agreed to make an ------- in US-based Ecoline Ltd, a provider of software for the hospitality sector.
(A) effectiveness
(B) investment
(C) alternative
(D) indication

104. States have the right ------- or ban the purchase and sale of alcohol on Sundays.
(A) restricted
(B) to restrict
(C) restricts
(D) restricting

105. To feed a growing population, agricultural land is ------- to expand globally in the next decade to match the increase in food demand.
(A) presented
(B) preferred
(C) projected
(D) proceeded

106. ------- the parking lot in front is being repaired, employees are advised to park their vehicles behind the main building.
(A) So
(B) In addition to
(C) While
(D) During

107. ------- Furious Autos salesman could offer a company credit application to customers purchasing one or more vehicles.
(A) Whichever
(B) Future
(C) Every
(D) When

108. Many private art galleries and museums recently opened in the Burbank district, which was ------- an industrial area.
(A) immediately
(B) formerly
(C) fully
(D) closely

109. Consumers are advised to do some preliminary research ------- making a purchase an air conditioner.
(A) from
(B) before
(C) for
(D) with

110. The Expo on November 11th offers auto designers from various countries an opportunity to meet ------- and view many concept cars in Chicago.
(A) as if
(B) inclusive
(C) one another
(D) otherwise

111. In the event that both candidates are ------- qualified for a job, other factors to determine merit should be considered, such as community service and any notable awards.
(A) equally
(B) lately
(C) punctually
(D) often

112. ------- Elliot Electronics' stock price has increased recently, the company's board of directors is worried about the slowdown in the high-end electronics industry.
(A) Despite
(B) Whenever
(C) So that
(D) Although

113. Mr. Watson reviewed the sales report from our Langley agency ------- and found five areas that need further marketing research.
(A) interestingly
(B) usefully
(C) significantly
(D) thoroughly

114. Mr. Davison is a reliable lawyer who will help our company when we consider ------- our corporate headquarters to a new facility.
(A) has relocated
(B) to relocate
(C) relocating
(D) relocation

115. A number of quality ------- are made before new products are released to our customers.
(A) checked
(B) checking
(C) checkable
(D) checks

116. Free delivery is available to customers who ------- a two-year maintenance contract for the product purchased.
(A) agree
(B) drive
(C) offer
(D) sign

117. We are interested in learning ------- you still have an interest or might be available to work full-time this year.
(A) either
(B) nearby
(C) whether
(D) regarding

118. ------- of the two accounting directors will be available on Thursday.
(A) Each other
(B) However
(C) Neither
(D) Anywhere

119. The vendors also must demonstrate that they have ------- to all equipment needed and that it is available within twenty-four hours.
(A) accessible
(B) access
(C) accesses
(D) accessed

GO ON TO THE NEXT PAGE

120. The most popular digital cameras on sale today contain ------- functions such as video capture and automatic focus.
(A) many
(B) every
(C) each
(D) a lot

121. Before installing a new toner cartridge for the laser printer, it is extremely important that it ------- thoroughly first.
(A) shaking
(B) be shaken
(C) to shake
(D) shaken

122. ------- one of the four packages we sent last night by courier has arrived at the destination yet.
(A) Never
(B) Not
(C) None
(D) No

123. In spite of the scarcity of dependable skilled technicians, the office will open in June and the project will proceed as -------.
(A) planning
(B) is planned
(C) planned
(D) plan

124. The new software program can ------- organizations to share information more quickly and efficiently.
(A) acquire
(B) enable
(C) overcome
(D) except

125. The CEO's speech is scheduled ------- 11:30 A.M, following morning press conferences as part of Media Day activities.
(A) for
(B) upon
(C) in
(D) between

126. Use of the new accounting system is strongly recommend as it works much ------- than present one although it might look very complicated.
(A) efficiently
(B) more efficient
(C) most efficiently
(D) more efficiently

127. The necessary documents should arrive by June 30 ------- prospective applicants to be considered for admission to our law school.
(A) in order for
(B) yet
(C) so that
(D) when

128. Clients of County Corporation have increased ------- since the public relations director started actively promoting the campaign.
(A) considering
(B) considered
(C) considerable
(D) considerably

129. Queensland Elementary School offers a variety of after-school programs ------- on the arts and physical development.
(A) will focus
(B) focus
(C) have focused
(D) focusing

130. Translink International Co. has used a global consulting group in an attempt to re-establish its ------- in Korea.
(A) provision
(B) summary
(C) presence
(D) description

PART 6

Directions: Read the texts that follow. A word, phrase, or sentence is missing in parts of each text. Four answer choices for each question are given below the text. Select the best answer to complete the text. Then mark the letter (A), (B), (C), or (D) on your answer sheet.

Questions 131-134 refer to the following information.

Congratulations ------- your purchase of an Ichikami Food Processor. Our products are made
   131.
tough and are dishwasher safe. Our famous lifetime warranty is our guarantee to ------- any unit
                                                                                132.
which does not meet the high standards we hold. -------. Please make sure not ------- the food
                                                  133.   **134.**
processor's outer shell in water. Only the removable plastic parts with the 'dishwasher safe' logo
on them should be allowed to get wet.

131. (A) of
   (B) on
   (C) in
   (D) to

132. (A) replace
   (B) design
   (C) produce
   (D) convert

133. (A) However, the warranty does not cover
       any damage to the electronics inside
       the machine.
   (B) Therefore, you are not eligible to get a
       full refund for these reasons.
   (C) Additionally, we will deliver your items
       to your new address as specified in
       your previous letter.
   (D) Similarly, please contact the
       manufacturer directly for the parts
       needed to be replaced.

134. (A) to immerse
   (B) immersed
   (C) immerse
   (D) immersion

GO ON TO THE NEXT PAGE

Questions 135-138 refer to the following memo.

From: Jim O'Rourke

To: Eastbourne's Lumber employees

Date: March 23

Subject: John Greenspan retirement

------- more than 40 years working at Eastbourne's Lumber, John Greenspan will be retiring at
  135.
the end of this week. As such, we will be holding a dinner in his honor on Friday, March 28th at

6 O'clock at the Berry Mix restaurant. We hope that you will be able to attend this special event

to show Greenspan how ------- we are of his decades of hard work. -------. I will ------- your
           136.   **137.**   **138.**
desk to get the money. We recommend a minimum contribution of 20 dollars.

Thank you,

Jim O'Rourke

Human Resources Manager

135. (A) After
(B) Within
(C) Over
(D) Since

136. (A) appreciate
(B) appreciated
(C) appreciative
(D) appreciation

137. (A) We will pay for this dinner with
collections from all of you this week.
(B) To commemorate our 20th
anniversary, we prepared gold
medals for employees with long
service.
(C) This event was delayed due to
unavoidable circumstances.
(D) Greenspan will be out of town that
day to lead a seminar at the 2017
Missouri Lumber Conference.

138. (A) continue on
(B) found out
(C) look for
(D) come by

Questions 139-142 refer to the following e-mail.

To: Company Employees

From: Nicholas Baldwin

Date: September 12

RE: Vacation Scheduling

Attachment: spreadsheet

This email is to ------- all employees that our winter holiday vacation period has decreased from
                    139.
10 days to 1 this year. We will ------- longer close our offices from December 23rd to January
                                 140.
2nd, but instead will offer Christmas day only. Employees are still welcome to use their personal

vacation time over this period. -------. Therefore, we have implemented a merit system to
                               141.
determine ------- gets the most popular days. Employees recognized for the most dedication
          142.
to their job will have priority for Christmas Eve and New Year'day vacation. Please fill in the

spreadsheet with your desired vacation times.

Thank you,

Nicholas Baldwin, Human Resources Director

---

139. (A) comment
(B) imply
(C) remind
(D) speak

140. (A) not
(B) no
(C) none
(D) never

141. (A) However, we cannot afford more than 5% of the workforce to be away from the office on any day.
(B) During this company vacation period, two of our security guards will be on duty alternately.
(C) Supervisors of each team will have a priority to choose their vacation date.
(D) We aim to boost our sales during the Christmas and New year peak season by 50%.

142. (A) who
(B) what
(C) where
(D) when

GO ON TO THE NEXT PAGE

Questions 143-146 refer to the following letter.

Dear Valued Holsten Mall Customer,

Because of loyal Holsten Mall shoppers like you, we are happy to announce the continuation of the reward program.

After we announced last year that membership into the program would be free, many people -------. By spending just 500 dollars in one visit to the mall, shoppers were given a gift certificate **143.** for 10 dollars which could be used at ------- retail outlet in the building (food court and movie **144.** theatre not included).

Also, every month the top 100 spenders were entered into a draw for a ------- to win a $1000 **145.** shopping gift certificate. This year, we hope to get even more customers into our reward program and are offering all new members a $5 gift certificate to be put toward any purchase of an item of $50 or more value.

-------. To learn more about what membership means for you, please visit www.Holstenmall. **146.** com.

143. (A) will join
(B) joined
(C) joins
(D) joining

144. (A) no
(B) many
(C) any
(D) few

145. (A) chance
(B) result
(C) matter
(D) event

146. (A) This reward program is a temporary event and only available to existing customers.
(B) It's one of the many ways Holsten says thank you to our fabulous customers.
(C) Your order has been processed and will arrive in 2 days.
(D) On January 3rd, the last day of our business, we are planning to celebrate our store's history.

PART 5

Directions: A word or phrase is missing in each of the sentences below. Four answer choices are given below each sentence. Select the best answer to complete the sentence. Then mark the letter (A), (B), (C), or (D) on your answer sheet.

101. All manufactured goods from this production facility have been thoroughly ------- for quality control.
(A) considered
(B) reached
(C) inspected
(D) planned

102. Once you ------- your travel plans, we will send you an itinerary related to your plans by e-mail.
(A) confirmed
(B) would confirm
(C) confirm
(D) will confirm

103. Riverdale Restaurant changes menu ------- seasonally depending on the availability of the fresh produce and seafood.
(A) options
(B) occasions
(C) results
(D) payments

104. While most of the car dealers met their quota this month, ------- exceeded it.
(A) few
(B) much
(C) either
(D) whose

105. At this time of the year, catering service companies are busy ------- year-end parties and annual banquets.
(A) preparing
(B) prepares
(C) preparation
(D) to prepare

106. Employees are notified that conference rooms 1 and 2 will be ------- next Tuesday while the air-conditioning system is being repaired.
(A) irreversible
(B) allowable
(C) improbable
(D) inaccessible

107. In December, Heritage museum will feature over 45 works by the ------- oil painter Alex Bryson.
(A) completed
(B) renowned
(C) founded
(D) estimated

108. Located at the heart of the Docklands, this airport is very popular due to its ------- to the financial centre of the City.
(A) achievement
(B) proximity
(C) competence
(D) exception

GO ON TO THE NEXT PAGE

109. Please make sure that the lid is screwed on ------- so the sauce does not leak.
(A) tightly
(B) strictly
(C) largely
(D) thinly

110. Employers need to provide portable fire extinguishers by law ------- employees can access them in case of emergency.
(A) in order to
(B) owing to
(C) if
(D) so that

111. Even though the new policies were initially controversial, ------- effectiveness in assisting Quantas Papers Service has not been.
(A) they
(B) them
(C) their
(D) theirs

112. Below are a few ------- ideas for how you can build relationships with customers and create brand loyalty.
(A) specific
(B) specify
(C) specifics
(D) specifies

113. If possible, you should apply online and upload electronic copies of documents ------- submitting paper applications.
(A) because of
(B) which
(C) instead of
(D) through

114. The South English cruise industry ------- significant growth in its capacity and in the number of passengers embarking from U.K. ports.
(A) experientially
(B) experiential
(C) experienced
(D) experience

115. Thanks to the new high-tech scanner ------- other devices, it has become quite convenient for consumers to take superior quality prints.
(A) and
(B) yet
(C) only
(D) either

116. There are several ------- in the airport terminal that sell a wide variety of typical Korean souvenirs.
(A) stored
(B) storing
(C) store
(D) stores

117. The current version of the Win-Latex pillow has been lightened, making it the lightest ------- on the market.
(A) any
(B) either
(C) that
(D) one

118. The Pearl Bay Times article reports that several hospitals in the region have begun preparing ------- the shortage by recruiting new nurses.
(A) for
(B) to
(C) of
(D) as

119. Due to unexpected health problems of one member of the Quintet, the ensemble's European tour will be postponed ------- further notice.
(A) onto
(B) until
(C) all
(D) with

120. If you don't have a computer, the school buildings are equipped with computer kiosks that you may use to complete the ------- form, before you begin your study.
(A) reimbursement
(B) training
(C) inventory
(D) enrollment

121. Whether you are ------- seeking a new position or are simply interested in learning about exciting new opportunities, the Manhattan Lycos Network is a valuable tool to move your career forward.
(A) activate
(B) active
(C) activity
(D) actively

122. Every shipment must be ------- to the attention of Andrew Morrei, the inventory manager.
(A) directed
(B) positioned
(C) included
(D) conditioned

123. Requests to book conference rooms should be submitted in writing to Dr. Pavalov ------- three business days in advance.
(A) by means of
(B) at least
(C) so that
(D) instead of

124. The conference will be cancelled due to inclement weather, but the preparation for it should continue ------- there will be full attendance.
(A) so
(B) which
(C) that
(D) as if

125. For tourists who want to visit Germany and Spain, New Dutch Express Ways ------- passengers with a bus service to and from Berlin and Madrid.
(A) commutes
(B) offers
(C) transports
(D) provides

126. Established in 2001, Richmond has become a ------- manufacturer of tennis balls, basketballs and soccer balls in Austria.
(A) moving
(B) talking
(C) serving
(D) leading

127. Last year, the company's total sales rose ------- even the most hopeful predictions of its new president.
(A) beyond
(B) except
(C) besides
(D) therefore

128. Emit Otter ------- the shoe designs by the time he meets with the president of Onits Footgear next week.
(A) completes
(B) completed
(C) is completing
(D) will have completed

129. Towers Innovations is seeking employees who have a cooperative spirit, strive to meet expectations, and have a ------- for serving clients.
(A) benefit
(B) passion
(C) career
(D) confirmation

130. All participants can stay at Central Hotel or Residence Suites, ------- is more comfortable.
(A) neither
(B) whichever
(C) everyone
(D) other

GO ON TO THE NEXT PAGE

PART 6

Directions: Read the texts that follow. A word, phrase, or sentence is missing in parts of each text. Four answer choices for each question are given below the text. Select the best answer to complete the text. Then mark the letter (A), (B), (C), or (D) on your answer sheet.

Questions 131-134 refer to the following letter.

Dear Ms. Theresa,

My stay at your hotel was truly amazing, as it ------- me comfort and relaxation due to the many
131.
services you offer.

Hayatt Zilala is truly one of the best hotels in the U.S. as far as offering world-class amenities to

the guests is concerned. ------- During my 3-night stay at your hotel, I was really aware of the
132.

expenses I ------- by using the hotel's services. I was genuinely shocked when I went to pay my
133.

bill. I checked in on July 21 and checked out on July 24. For 3 nights' accommodation, I was

charged not $ 675 but $ 750. This is much higher than expected, and I ------- there is a mistake
134.

with the bill. I hope you respond promptly to this letter and provide a refund for me.

Thank you very much.

Respectfully yours,

Jared Jones

---

131. (A) brought
(B) kept
(C) deposited
(D) consisted

132. (A) Additionally, I met several business
colleagues there.
(B) However, there is just one thing that
bothered me when I was there.
(C) Therefore, I would like to take the
opportunity to visit your hotel again.
(D) Nonetheless, this was the best trip
I've ever gone on.

133. (A) incurred
(B) incurring
(C) was incurred
(D) have been incurred

134. (A) consider
(B) describe
(C) expect
(D) assume

Attention to All Residents in the Edison Building

Please be informed that annual maintenance work on the building's heating system will be ------- on Friday, April 12 from 9:00 A.M. until 4:00 P.M. This routine maintenance will prevent
135.
problems from occurring during the winter. To make work -------, some equipment will be
136.
placed in the upper hallways and main lobby. We are sorry for the noise and disturbance this work will cause. If any serious problems are found during the maintenance work, proper -------
137.
will be taken and we will do our best to finish the additional work as quickly as possible. -------.
138.
You can also call 339-1672.

We appreciate your patience and understanding.

Rose Arkansas

Building Manager

135. (A) recognized
(B) waived
(C) conducted
(D) demonstrated

136. (A) easier
(B) more easier
(C) easily
(D) more easily
(A) easier

137. (A) subscriptions
(B) trouble
(C) transactions
(D) measures

138. (A) This work has been successfully completed and you can access anywhere in this building.
(B) Please move all your stuff to the employee lounge located on 3rd floor.
(C) For updates about this project, drop by the janitor's office next to the elevator.
(D) Please come up with ideas for making this transition more convenient for everyone.

Questions 139-142 refer to the following letter.

From: International Radio Network

Date: January 12

Subject: Membership

Mr. Hernandez,

Thank you for considering ------- our growing radio network. -------. Our goal is to join together

139.   **140.**

as many different voices as possible from different cultures and languages for the purpose

of expanding an understanding and tolerance of each other. All stations in the network have

access to the best professionally produced programming of their sister stations. These

programs can be custom tailored to your listeners'-------. Your membership fee will go into

141.

our legal fund which helps to keep all our stations on the air when they are threatened by

government cutbacks. We have included a document that details some of the other benefits

you ------- when you join the network.

142.

Thank you,

International Radio Network

---

139. (A) to join
(B) joining
(C) joins
(D) joined

140. (A) We are seeking some qualified
applicants to take the chief producer
position at our new location.
(B) We are focusing on covering the
irregularity of the Korean government
these days.
(C) We are preparing to deliver our next
issue to you and you will get it soon.
(D) We are looking to expand our global
reach by gathering partner stations.

141. (A) tastes
(B) absences
(C) alteration
(D) sense

142. (A) experienced
(B) experience
(C) to experience
(D) will experience

Questions 143-146 refer to the following e-mail.

To: Addington Stickler <astickler@ceprocookware.com>

From: Tira West <twest@ceprocookware.com>

Date: June 10

Subject: Brochure

Attachment: Revised draft

Dear Mr. Stickler,

Our marketing personnel are getting ready for the World Food and Cooking Exposition ------- in **143.** Vancouver from June 20 to June 23. As you already know, we will be displaying our ------- line **144.** of stainless steel cooking and dining utensils ------- your team designed. Attached to this e-mail **145.** is a recently revised draft copy of the cookware brochure that we plan to give out at our display booth. We have put in more images and reflected the changes in the brochure that you have asked for. -------. Therefore, please go through it and let me know if there is anything you want **146.** to change before Wednesday afternoon.

Thanks,

Tira West

143. A) holding
(B) is holding
(C) will be held
(D) to be held

144. (A) latest
(B) late
(C) last
(D) lately

145. (A) it
(B) who
(C) that
(D) what

146. (A) The printing division has informed us that they've finished printing our brochure.
(B) We tried the utensils you recommended, but they were not durable enough.
(C) We want to send the final version to our printing division by the end of this week.
(D) Without your help, we would have not taken those photographs.

최신 ③ 10회분

토익 급상승
Part 5&6

정답 및 해설

101

Ms. Hwang's ------- sponsor for the survey program has ensured its continued funding.
(A) enthuse
(B) enthusiastic
(C) enthusiastically
(D) enthusiasm

Hwang 씨의 설문조사 프로그램의 열정적인 후원자는 계속된 자금을 보장해왔다.

해설 빈칸은 소유격 뒤에 그리고 명사 앞에 어울리는 품사가 들어갈 자리이다. 명사 앞이라는 점을 고려할 때 형용사가 어울리는 자리이다. 정답은 (B) enthusiastic(열정적인)이다.

어휘 ensure ~을 보장하다, 반드시 ~하게 하다 sponsor 후원자 enthusiastic 열정적인 funding 자금

102

Upon successful completion, ------- will receive a printable Certificate of Completion for their records.
(A) participants
(B) participation
(C) participant
(D) participating

성공적으로 수료를 하자마자 참석자들은 그들의 기록을 위해 인쇄 가능한 수료증을 받을 것입니다.

해설 빈칸은 주어자리에 어울리는 단어가 들어갈 자리이다. 뒤에 동사가 will receive(받을 것이다)이므로, 이 동작에 대한 주체가 될 수 있는 사람명사가 정답이다. participant는 셀 수 있는 명사이므로 관사 없는 복수형태가 쓰여야 한다. 그래서 정답은 (A) participants(참가자들)이다.

어휘 printable 인쇄할만한 completion 완성, 완료 record 기록 participant 참석자 participation 참석

103

Because our company is highly safety-conscious, each employee is thoroughly ------- to follow our safety manual.
(A) trained
(B) train
(C) trainer
(D) trains

우리 회사는 안전을 매우 중시하기 때문에 각각의 직원들은 안전 매뉴얼을 준수하기 위하여 철저하게 훈련됩니다.

해설 빈칸은 부사 그리고 그 앞의 be동사 is 뒤에 어울리는 단어가 올 자리이다. 이 두 가지 모두를 충족시키는 선택지는 수동태의 구조인 trained(pp형태)이다. is throughly trained 철저히 훈련받다

어휘 highly 매우 safety conscious 안전을 중시하는 thoroughly 대단히, 완전히 follow 따르다, 준수하다 each 각각의

104

At Panawi, we ------- safety and reliability in manufacturing products of the highest quality so that consumers can enjoy them with peace of mind.
(A) deliberate
(B) emphasize
(C) impact
(D) analyze

Panawi에서 소비자들이 편안한 마음으로 제품을 사용할 수 있게 하기 위해 고품질의 상품 생산에 안전과 신뢰성을 강조합니다.

해설 빈칸은 명사 safety and reliability를 목적어로 취하는 동사자리이다. 해석상 적절한 의미의 선택지는 (B) emphasize(강조하다)이다. emphasize safety and reliability 안전과 신뢰성을 강조하다

어휘 emphasize 강조하다 reliability 안전 manufacture 제조하다 peace of mind 마음의 안정

105

------- you find the manual to be unclear, note that there are customer support centers throughout the country where an expert can help you.
(A) Whether
(B) So that
(C) Until
(D) If

만약 매뉴얼이 불분명하다고 여긴다면, 당신을 도와주는 전문가가 있는 전국 도처의 고객 서비스센터를 기억하세요.

해설 빈칸은 두 문장 앞에 의미가 적절한 접속사가 들어갈 자리이다. 전체적인 두 문장의 해석으로 볼 때 접속사 (D) If(만약 ~면)가 정답임을 알 수 있다.

어휘 unclear 불분명한 note that ~을 명심하다 throughout 곳곳에, 전역에 expert 전문가 so that ~하기 위하여

106

Although the keynote speech has been verified for March 8 at 6:30 P.M., the rest of the conference schedule has not yet been -------.
(A) equalled
(B) announced
(C) reminded
(D) informed

기조연설이 3월 8일 오후 6시 30분으로 확인되었음에도 불구하고 나머지 회의 일정은 아직 발표되지 않았습니다.

해설 빈칸은 적절한 의미의 동사가 들어갈 자리이다. although절의 내용은 '확인되었음에도 불구하고'이고 나머지 문장에서는 '아직 ~이 되지 않았다'는 문맥이다. 따라서 정답은 (B) announced(발표하다)이다. reminded나 informed는 사람목적어를 취하므로 수동형이 되면 주어가 사람이다.

어휘 although 비록 ~ 일지라도 keynote speech 기조연설 verify 확인하다, 입증하다 the rest 나머지 remind 상기시키다 inform 알리다 equal 동일하다

107

Most candidates are ------- being reviewed for the annual staff excellence award.
(A) new
(B) now
(C) after
(D) once

연간 직원 우수상과 관련하여 대부분의 직원들이 지금 평가되고 있다

해설 be동사와 현재분사 사이의 빈칸은 부사자리이다. 문장의 시제가 현재진행이므로 어울리는 부사는 (B) now이다.

어휘 candidate 후보자 review 검토하다, 평가하다

108

Brisbane-based David Delivery Service will repay all business-related travel costs ------- three weeks of their submission.
(A) within
(B) between
(C) into
(D) when

Brisbane을 기반으로 한 David Delivery Service는 사업과 관련된 출장 경비를 제출로부터 3주 내로 상환할 것입니다.

해설 빈칸의 뒤의 기간을 나타내는 명사가 등장하므로 기간명사와 어울리는 전치사는 (A) within(~이내에)이다

어휘 repay 상환하다 travel cost 출장 경비 within ~ 이내에 submission 제출 between ~ 사이에

109

------- chooses to work in our head office must have five years of experience in a related field.
(A) Another
(B) Anyone
(C) Somebody
(D) Whoever

우리 본사에서 일하기로 선택된 사람은 누구든지 관련된 분야에서 5년의 경험을 가져야 합니다.

해설 빈칸은 주어자리에 어울리는 단어가 들어갈 자리이다. 빈칸 뒤에 동사가 두 개(chooses, must have) 있으며 빈칸부터 office까지는 문장 내에서 다시 주어가 되는 명사절이 되어야 한다. 선택지 중 절을 이끌 수 있는 단어는 (D) Whoever(누구든지)이다. 또한, whoever는 anyone who와 같은 표현으로 빈칸에 anyone who를 넣고 who부터 office까지가 관계대명사절로 앞의 anyone을 수식하는 구조이다. 그리고 whoever 뒤에는 단수동사만 올 수 있다는 점도 기억해두면 정답 확인을 쉽게 할 수 있다.

어휘 whoever 누구든지 head office 본사 related 관련된 field 분야

110

In order to continue their operation, manufacturers must satisfy the standards set ------- by regulatory agencies.
(A) along
(B) away
(C) forth
(D) in front

운영을 계속하기 위해서 제조업체는 규제력을 지닌 기관에 의해 제시된 기준을 만족시켜야 합니다.

해설 빈칸은 앞의 set과 의미가 연결되는 단어가 들어가야 한다. set forth(제시하다)를 기억해두면 해결 가능한 문제이다.

어휘 regulatory 규제력을 지닌 in order to ~하기 위하여 operation 운영, 영업 manufacturer 제조업체 satisfy 만족시키다 set forth 제시하다 standard 기준

111

Software intended for use in the diagnosis of an abnormal physical state should meet the definition of a medical device and must ------- comply with the requirements of the Medical Devices Regulations.
(A) how
(B) often
(C) sometimes
(D) therefore

비정상적인 건강상태의 진단에 사용될 목적인 소프트웨어는 의학장비의 성의를 충족시켜야 하고 그러므로 반드시 Medical Devices Regulations의 요구조건을 준수해야 합니다.

해설 빈칸은 조동사 must와 동사 comply 사이에 의미가 어울리는 부사가 들어갈 자리이다. 등위접속사 and와의 의미 관계도 고려해 볼 때 (D) therefore(따라서)가 정답이다. and ~ therefore 그리고 따라서

어휘 diagnosis 진단 abnormal 비정상적인 definition 정의 comply with ~을 지키다, 준수하다 therefore 그러므로 requirement 요구조건

112

Even though most of the computer programmers work by themselves, weekly staff meetings will give an opportunity for them to cooperate with -------.
(A) one another
(B) the same
(C) much
(D) this

비록 대부분의 컴퓨터 프로그래머들이 혼자서 일할지라도, 주간 직원미팅은 그들에게 서로서로 협력할 기회를 제공할 것입니다.

해설 문장 앞 부분(Even though ~ by themselves)의 내용이 '프로그래머들이 다른 사람 없이 혼자 일한다'이고 뒷부분은 '직원미팅이 협력할 기회를 제공한다'는 문맥이므로 '서로서로'를 뜻하는 (A) one another가 적절하다.

어휘 cooperate 협력하다 one another 서로서로 by themselves 그들 스스로

113 Celine Park ------- insisted that purchasing stationery items from another supplier could reduce operating expenses at Marc Industries.
(A) rights
(B) rightful
(C) rightly
(D) right

Celine Park 씨는 당연히 다른 제조업자로부터 문구류를 구매하는 것이 Marc Industries에서 운영경비를 줄일 수 있다고 주장했다.

해설 주어(Celine Park)와 일반동사(insisted) 사이에 빈칸이 있다. 동사 앞의 빈칸은 부사자리이므로 정답은 (C) rightly(당연히, 마땅히, 제대로)이다.

어휘 insist ~을 주장하다 stationery 문구류 supplier 제조업자 reduce 줄이다 operation expenses 운영 경비 rightly 당연히, 마땅히 right 권리, 권한 rightful 정당한, 합법적인

114 Service animals must follow all ------- laws pertaining to vaccinations as well as any registration requirements.
(A) local
(B) locally
(C) localize
(D) locals

장애인 보조 동물은 반드시 백신뿐 아니라 등록 요구조건에 관한 모든 지역의 법을 따라야 합니다.

해설 빈칸은 뒤의 명사 laws를 수식하는 형용사자리이다. 선택지 중에 형용사인 (A) local(지역의)이 정답이다.

어휘 pertaining to ~에 관계된 vaccination 예방접종 local 지역의 localize 지역화하다, 지방에 국한시키다 registration 등록

115 Workshops at the Central Convention Center will be ------- to ten people to allow for interactive discussions and Q&A sessions.
(A) remained
(B) ended
(C) limited
(D) asserted

Central Convention Center에서 워크숍은 상호 토론과 Q&A 과정을 허용하기 위하여 10명으로 제한될 것입니다.

해설 주어인 Workshops(세미나)와 빈칸 뒤의 to ten people(열 명으로) 사이에 의미가 적합한 선택지는 (C) limited이다. Workshops will be limited to ten people은 '세미나는 열 명으로 제한될 것이다'의 의미이다.

어휘 interactive 상호적인 allow 허용하다, 허락하다 discussion 토론, 논의 remain 남겨져 있다 limited 제한된 assert 주장하다

116

Corrie Kim, founder of Power Athletic Clinic, recently received an ------- for her research in the field of sports medicine.
(A) interpretation
(B) ability
(C) apology
(D) award

Power Athletic Clinic의 설립자인 Corrie Kim 씨는 스포츠의학 분야의 연구로 상을 받았다.

해설 빈칸은 동사 receive(받다)와 for her research(그녀의 연구에 대해) 사이에 어울리는 명사 목적어자리이다. receive(받다)할 수 있는 것으로 apology(사과)와 award(상)이 될 수 있겠지만 문맥상 스포츠 의학 분야의 연구에 대해 받는 것이니 받는 것은 당연히 (D) award가 될 것이다.

어휘 founder 설립자 interpretation 해석, 통역 ability 능력 apology 사과

117

Mr. Heo accepted the position of assistant financial analyst at his company, ------- he was also offered a higher position by a big bank.
(A) even though
(B) likewise
(C) whether
(D) due to

Heo 씨는 비록 큰 은행으로부터 더 높은 직급을 제의받았지만, 그의 회사에서 보조 재정분석가 직책을 수락했다.

해설 빈칸은 두 문장을 연결해주는 접속사자리이다. 접속사는 부사절을 이끄는 even though(비록 ~일지라도)밖에 없다.

어휘 accept 받아들이다, 수락하다 analyst 분석가 even though 비록 ~일지라도 a higher position 높은 직급 likewise 비슷하게, 똑같이 due to ~ 때문에

118

By consistently providing customers with high quality products and services, Omitt Corporation is able to win back clients that it had ------- lost to bigger competitors.
(A) previously
(B) behind
(C) formally
(D) ahead

고품질의 상품과 서비스를 고객들에게 지속적으로 제공함으로써, Omitt Corporation은 더 큰 경쟁사로 빼앗겼던 이전의 고객을 되찾을 수 있다.

해설 빈칸은 의미가 적절한 부사자리이다. 빈칸 앞을 보면 동사 win back(되찾다)이고, 빈칸 부분은 had lost(잃었다)이므로, 문맥상 '이전에(previously) 잃었던 고객들을 되찾다'가 자연스럽다.

어휘 consistently 일관하여, 지속적으로 previously 이전에 formally 공식적으로 competitor 경쟁사

119

Existing members of the committee should introduce ------- to new people and briefly describe their involvement with the organization.
(A) their
(B) themselves
(C) they
(D) their own

위원회의 기존의 멤버는 그들 스스로를 새로운 사람에게 소개해야 하며 간단하게 기관에 그들의 관련성을 설명해야 합니다.

해설 빈칸은 동사 introduce 뒤에 목적어가 되는 자리이다. 주어가 members로 소개의 대상이 다시 그들 자신이므로 재귀대명사인 (B) themselves가 정답이 된다.

어휘 existing 기존의 committee 위원회 describe 설명하다, 묘사하다 briefly 잠시 involvement 관련, 관여

120

Madacas Packaging ------- employees who are highly motivated to work at our manufacturing facility located in Scotia.
(A) are sought
(B) seeking
(C) have been sought
(D) is seeking

Madacas Packaging은 Scotia에 위치된 우리의 제조시설에서 근무하기 위해 대단히 의욕적인 직원들을 찾고 있다.

해설 문장에 어울리는 동사를 고르는 문제이다. 주어가 회사이름으로 단수이므로 정답은 단수동사인 (D) is seeking이다.

어휘 motivate 동기를 부여하다 manufacturing facility 제조시설 seek 찾다

121

If you are under the age of 18 at the time of application, you will also need to show ------- of your enrolment in the East Boston school system.
(A) proof
(B) process
(C) basis
(D) analysis

만약 당신이 지원할 때 18세 이하라면, 당신은 East Boston 학교시스템에 등록의 증거를 또한 보여줄 필요가 있을 것이다.

해설 빈칸은 show의 목적어(명사)자리이다. 빈칸 뒤의 of your enrollment와 의미연결이 '등록의 증거를 보여주다'가 되므로 proof가 정답임을 알 수 있다.

어휘 at the time of ~할 때 application 지원, 지원서 proof 증거 enrolment 등록 process 절차 basis 기반, 기초

122

The personnel manager had ------- forgotten that she had an appointment with the new employees until her assistant reminded her.
(A) completed
(B) complete
(C) completion
(D) completely

인사부 매니저는 그녀의 조수가 그녀에게 상기시켜줄 때까지, 신입직원과 약속이 있었다는 것을 완전히 잊었다.

해설 had와 forgotten(pp) 사이의 빈칸에는 부사(completely 완전히)가 와야 한다.

어휘 completely 완전히 forget 잊다 appointment 약속 completion 완성, 완료 complete 끝내다, 작성하다

123

As an assistant manager, Mr. Roy's main role is to facilitate cooperation ------- Syscho Corporation's numerous directors.
(A) onto
(B) among
(C) above
(D) inside

부팀장으로서, Roy 씨의 주요 업무는 Syscho Corporation의 많은 감독관들 사이에서 협조를 용이하게 하는 것입니다.

해설 빈칸은 'Syscho Corporation의 많은 감독관들'과 'cooperaton(협조)' 사이에 의미연결이 매끄러운 전치사가 들어갈 자리이다. 선택지 중 (B) among(~ 사이에)이 적절하다. cooperation among Syscho Corporation's numerous directors 많은 감독관들 사이에 협조

어휘 facilitate 가능하게 하다 main role 주요 업무 cooperation 협조, 협동 numerous 다양한 director 감독관

124

Mr. Johns suggested that I drive a company car while ------- is being repaired.
(A) mine
(B) I
(C) my
(D) myself

Johns 씨는 내 차가 수리되는 동안 회사 차량을 운전할 것을 제안했다.

해설 <접속사 + ------- + is>의 빈칸은 주어자리이다. 선택지 중 주격인 I가 눈에 띄지만 동사(is)와 어울리지 않는다. 소유격 my는 뒤에 명사 없이 쓸 수 없고, 재귀대명사 myself는 주어자리에 올 수 없으므로, '나의 것'이라는 의미의 소유대명사(mine)가 적절하다. mine은 my car를 줄여 쓴 것이다.

어휘 suggest 제안하다 repair 수리하다 mine 나의 것 while ~ 동안

125

Even employees who ------- were rather sceptical about the PEP training, afterwards appear to have accomplished improvements they did not think of as realistic.
(A) annually
(B) inadvertently
(C) initially
(D) successively

심지어 처음에는 PEP훈련에 대해서 오히려 회의적이었던 직원들도 결국엔 현실로서 그들이 생각하지 못했던 개선을 성취한 것으로 보인다.

해설 빈칸은 의미가 적절한 부사가 들어갈 자리이다. 관계대명사 who부터 training까지 선행사 employees를 수식하며 동사 afterwards appear(뒤에는 ~인 것으로 보인다)를 통해 '처음에(initially)는 PEP 훈련에 대해서 오히려 회의적이었던 직원들'이라는 의미가 적절해 보인다.

어휘 sceptical 회의적인 accomplish 성취하다, 완수하다 initially 처음에는 as realistic 현실로서 improvement 개선, 향상

126

Sales ------- has dropped dramatically despite efforts to boost recognition by increasing the marketing budget.
(A) action
(B) response
(C) appreciation
(D) revenue

마케팅 예산을 증가시킴으로써 인식을 북돋우는 노력에도 불구하고 마케팅 수익은 급격하게 떨어졌다.

해설 sales와 의미가 잘 연결되는 명사를 고르는 문제이다. 선택지 중 복합명사로 쓸 수 있는 (D) revenue(수익)가 적절하다. sales revenue 판매 수익

어휘 dramatically 극적으로 recognition 인식 revenue 수익 drop 감소하다 effort 노력 despite ~에도 불구하고 boost 북돋우다 budget 예산

127

Dr. Morgan has been involved in a car accident this morning and will be ------- to attend the seminar today.
(A) impossible
(B) doubtful
(C) remote
(D) unable

Morgan 박사는 아침에 자동차 사고가 나서 오늘 세미나에 참석할 수 없을 것이다.

해설 빈칸은 의미가 적절한 형용사가 들어갈 자리이다. 문맥상 '교통사고가 나서 세미나 참석이 불가능하다'는 의미이다. 선택지에 impossible과 unable이 '불가능한'의 의미이지만 impossible은 it is impossible~처럼 가주어를 취하는 구조이므로 오답이다. be able to의 반대의 뜻인 be unable to가 정답이다. 참고로 and 이하는 it will be impossible for him to attend the seminar로도 표현이 가능하다. 물론 이때에는 impossible 자리에 unable이 들어갈 수 없다.

어휘 be involved in ~에 연루되다 impossible 불가능한 doubtful 확신이 없는, 의심스러운 remote 먼, 가깝지 않은 be unable to ~할 수 없다

128

Even though many of our employees have lived in foreign countries, ------- few of them are fluent in another language.
(A) once
(B) hardly
(C) far
(D) very

비록 많은 직원들이 외국에 살지만, 타국어에 유창한 직원들은 거의 없다.

해설 빈칸은 문장의 앞에서 어울리는 단어가 들어갈 자리이다. 빈칸 뒤의 few of them과 의미연결을 보면, few 자체가 부정의 의미이므로 hardly(거의 ~않다)는 어울리지 않는다. once는 부사로 '한때' 또는 '한 번'의 의미이고, far는 '멀리' 또는 비교급 강조부사로 사용된다. 그래서 적다는 의미를 한층 강조하는 부사 very(매우)가 정답이다. very few of them are fluent 유창한 직원은 거의 없다

어휘 fluent 유창한 foreign country 외국 hardly 거의 ~ 않다 far 멀리 once 한때, 한 번

129

The site manager told the new worker that ------- certain kinds of construction equipment needs several years of experience.
(A) operated
(B) operate
(C) operating
(D) operates

현장 매니저는 새로운 직원에게 특정 종류의 건설장비를 작동시키는 것은 다년간의 경험을 요구한다고 말했다.

해설 빈칸은 that절의 주어자리이다. 문맥상 빈칸 뒤의 certain kinds of construction equipment(특정 종류의 건설장비)를 목적어로 취하는 동명사가 와야 하므로 (C) operating이 정답이다.

어휘 site 현장 operate 운영하다 certain 특정한 equipment 장비

130

The general manager finished his weekly report ------- schedule because his earlier presentation had been cancelled.
(A) on account of
(B) aside from
(C) ahead of
(D) far from

총지배인은 그의 이전 발표가 취소되었기 때문에, 그의 주간 보고서를 일정보다 미리 끝냈다.

해설 빈칸은 schedule과 의미연결이 어울리는 단어가 들어갈 자리이다. schedule은 on schedule 일정대로, ahead of schedule 일정에 앞서, behind schedule 예정보다 늦게 등으로 쓰인다. 그래서 정답은 (C) ahead of이다.

어휘 finish 끝내다 weekly 주간의 ahead of ~보다 일찍 on account of ~ 때문에 aside from ~ 외에는, ~을 제외하고

PART 6

Questions 131-134 refer to the following e-mail.

From: Robertnatale@cellrite.net

To: Customer Service Department (Mckinney Electronics)

Subject: Ordered Items

Date: May 17

Dear Customer Service Department:

Thank you for shipping the items earlier than I had expected.

-------. However, I would just like to inform you that the
131.
Samsung DVD player I received is not the Blu-Ray DVD player

that I ordered. I ordered the Samsung Blu-Ray DVD player

BDC 8200, but the model no. of the DVD player I received is

BDC7500. ------- they have ------- identical features, such as
132. **133.**
built-in WIFI and media sharing, I still prefer the BDC8200 since

I can record 250GB of HD videos with it.

Please let me know when you can ship the correct model so

that I can also make plans to ship the DVD player I received.

I am hoping that you can ship the unit within 48 hours, which

is earlier than your ------- shipping schedule. Thank you in
134.
advance.

발신: Robertnatale@cellrite.net

수신: 고객 서비스 부서 (Mckinney Electronics)

제목: 주문 상품

날짜: 5월 17일

고객 서비스 부서 앞:

제가 기대했던 것보다 더 빨리 제품을 배송해 주신 것에 대해 감사드립니다. 모든 것이 상태가 좋았습니다. 하지만 제가 받은 Samsung DVD 플레이어가 제가 주문했던 Blu-Ray DVD플레이어가 아니라는 것을 알려드리고 싶습니다. 저는 BDC 8200 Samsung Blu-Ray DVD 플레이어를 주문했지만 제가 받은 DVD플레이어의 제품번호는 BDC7500입니다. 비록 그것들은 내장 와이파이나 미디어 공유 같은 거의 동일한 기능을 갖고 있지만 저는 여전히 250기가의 HD비디오를 저장할 수 있기 때문에 BDC8200을 선호합니다.

언제 당신이 올바른 모델을 보내줄 수 있는지 알려주시면 제가 받은 DVD 플레이어를 보낼 계획을 짜겠습니다. 당신의 기본 배송 기간보다 빠른 48시간 이내로 상품을 보내주길 바랍니다. 미리 감사드리겠습니다.

어휘 inform 알리다 identical 동일한 sharing 공유 ship 배송하다 in advance 미리

131
(A) Unfortunately, the shipping charge cost more than we had anticipated.
(B) But the receipt I requested wasn't included.
(C) Please confirm receipt of payment for these items.
(D) Everything was in good condition.

> **해설** 빈칸 다음의 문장에 'However(하지만)'라는 접속부사를 사용한 것으로 보아 뒷문장과 반대되는 내용의 선택지를 골라야 한다. 받은 제품이 주문한 것과 다르다(is not the Blu-Ray DVD player that I ordered)는 문제점이 언급된 내용이 이어지고 있으므로 빈칸에는 '모든 것이 상태가 좋았다'는 (D)가 가장 적절한 내용이다.

(A) 불행하게도 배송비가 우리가 예상했던 것보다 더 많이 나왔습니다.
(B) 하지만 제가 요구드렸던 영수증이 포함되지 않았습니다.
(C) 이 물건들의 지불 영수증을 확인바랍니다.
(D) 모든 것이 상태가 좋았습니다.

132
(A) Although
(B) Therefore
(C) Whether
(D) Moreover

> **해설** 거의 동일한 기능을 갖고 있지만, '그럼에도 불구하고 여전히 기존에 주문했던 제품을 선호한다'는 내용이므로 양보의 접속사 (A) Although가 가장 적합하다.

133
(A) frequently
(B) intentionally
(C) previously
(D) nearly

> **해설** '동일한(identical)'을 수식하는 부사를 묻고 있다. 따라서 '거의 동일한'이라는 의미를 만들어 줄 수 있는 (D) nearly(거의)가 정답이다.

134
(A) regular
(B) regularly
(C) regularity
(D) regularness

> **해설** '배송 일정(shipping schedule)'이라는 명사의 앞자리가 비어 있으므로 명사를 수식하는 형용사가 적합하다. 따라서 정답은 (A) regular(일반적인)이다.

Questions 135-138 refer to the following e-mail.

From: Jack Clark

To: Summer Martin

Subject: RE: Phone Order

Date: March 8 15:20:35

Dear Mr. Martin,

Regarding your email today, I have no problem ------- the toy
                                              135.
cars with the transformers, so please go ahead and process my

order. I may have forgotten to mention this to your staff member,

but please make sure that in the seven sets of toy cars there is

------- one red model. Blue and green would also be nice, but
136.
they are not as ------- as the red one.
          137.

I would prefer that those items be sent to my office at this

address: Prime Holdings Co., 45 James St., New Heights, NJ.

My telephone number is (201) 836-9127. My secretary, Elena

Kirstein, will receive them if I am not in the office.

-------. That will give us some time to prepare them for a
138.
children's party that same day.

발신: Jack Clark
수신: Summer Martin
제목: RE: Phone Order
날짜: 3월 8일 15:20:35

친애하는 Martin 씨

오늘 당신의 이메일에 따라 나는 변신용 장난감 자동차로 교체하는 데 문제가 없기 때문에 주문을 진행해주시길 바랍니다. 당신의 직원들에게 이것에 대해 언급하는 것을 잊어버렸지만 7개의 장난감 자동차들 중에 적어도 하나는 빨간색 모델로 해주시길 부탁드립니다. 파란색이나 초록색도 괜찮겠지만 빨간색만큼 중요하진 않습니다.

나는 이 주소에 있는 우리 회사로 그 물건들이 배송되길 더 바랍니다: Prime Holdings Co., 45 James St., New Heights, NJ. 제 전화번호는 (201) 836-9127입니다. 제 비서 Elena Kirstein이 제가 사무실에 없다면 그것들을 받을 것입니다.

바쁜 일정 때문에 3월 14일 오후 1시 전이나 정시에 배달해주시면 좋을 것 같습니다. 그것이 우리에게 같은 날 아이들의 파티를 준비할 시간을 줄 것입니다.

어휘 regarding ~에 관하여 process 진행하다, 처리하다 mention 언급하다 prefer 선호하다

135
(A) repairing
(B) redeeming
(C) replacing
(D) recharging

해설 문제가 없으니 주문을 진행해 달라(so please go ahead and process my order)는 내용으로 보아, 편지를 받는 고객이 주문품을 다른 제품으로 '교체'해도 괜찮겠냐는 이메일을 받았던 것으로 보인다. replace A with B가 'A를 B로 교체하다'는 표현이므로 적절한 정답은 (C) replacing이다.

136

(A) at least
(B) instead of
(C) by means of
(D) so that

해설 There is 뒤에는 주어가 나와야 하고 '하나의 빨간색 모델(one red model)'이 주어의 역할을 하고 있다. 따라서 주어 앞에 전치사인 (B) instead of나 (C) by means of, 접속사인 (D) so that은 적합하지 않다. 빈칸은 one이라는 숫자형용사 앞이므로 '적어도 하나'라는 의미로 숫자를 수식해줄 수 있는 (A) at least(적어도)가 정답이다.

137

(A) importance
(B) important
(C) importantly
(D) imported

해설 원급비교표현 as~as 사이에는 형용사나 부사의 원급이 필요하다. 앞 문장에 be동사는 형용사 보어를 필요로 하는 동사이므로 정답은 (B) important이다.

138

(A) As a customer, I'm always satisfied with the quality of your product.
(B) Thank you for delivering items earlier than expected.
(C) Because of the rather tight schedule, it would be best if you could deliver them on or before 1:00 P.M. on March 14.
(D) I received an e-mail with discount coupons that can be used next time.

해설 빈칸 다음의 문장에서 '그것이 우리에게 준비할 시간을 줄 것이다(That will give us some time to prepare)'라는 표현이 사용된 것으로 보아 특정한 시간 전에 배송하여 여유시간을 갖게 해달라는 요청으로 이어지는 것이 가장 매끄러운 흐름이다.

(A) 고객으로서 저는 항상 당신의 제품의 질에 만족합니다.
(B) 예상보다 일찍 물건을 납품해줘서 감사드립니다.
(C) 바쁜 일정 때문에 3월 14일 오후 1시 전이나 정시에 배달해주시면 좋을 것 같습니다.
(D) 나는 다음에 사용할 수 있는 할인 쿠폰이 있는 이메일을 받았습니다.

Questions 139-142 refer to the following memo.

TO: All Employees FROM: Managing Director Elena Kirstein This is to ------- you that after 30 years of dedicated service to **139.** Rakestraw Industries, CEO and President Smith Barren will step down. He and his wife will be moving ------- to their summer **140.** residence in Florida, and we all wish them well. -------. Thanks **141.** to his persistence on this project, our company is now a global leader in selling baking equipment. -------, sales of the XR-800 **142.** have tripled over the last two years. We are very grateful for his dedication and commitment. We will certainly miss him.	수신: 전 직원 발신: 관리자 Elena Kirstein 이 메모는 Rakestraw Industries에 30년간의 헌신적인 노력을 한 후 CEO이자 회상인 Barren 씨가 퇴임한다는 것을 알려드리기 위한 것입니다. 그와 그의 아내는 Florida에 있는 여름 별장으로 영구적으로 이사를 갈 것이고 우리는 그들이 잘되길 바랍니다. 재임 기간 동안 Barren씨는 XR-800 시스템의 개발을 담당하고 있었습니다. 이 프로젝트에 대한 그의 고집 덕분에 우리의 회사는 이제 제빵 장비 판매에서 세계적인 선두업체가 되었습니다. 게다가 XR-800은 지난 2년간 매출이 3배 증가했습니다. 우리는 그의 헌신과 전념에 감사드립니다. 우리는 분명히 그를 그리워할 것입니다.

어휘 dedicated 바치다, 헌신하다 residence 거주지 persistence 고집 triple 3배의 commitment 전념, 헌신 certainly: 틀림없이, 분명히

139 (A) inform
(B) access
(C) announce
(D) describe

해설 빈칸 동사 뒤에 사람목적어와 that목적절이 등장한다. (B) access(접속하다)와 (C) announce(발표하다)는 사람을 목적어로 취할 수 없다. inform은 사람목적어와 that목적절을 나란히 데리고 나와서 사람에게 that 이하를 알린다는 의미이므로 정답은 (A) inform(알리다)이다.

140 (A) approximately
(B) **permanently**
(C) moderately
(D) consecutively

해설 퇴임하고 떠나는 직원에 대한 이야기를 하고 있고, 다른 지역으로 '이사할 것이다(will be moving)'를 수식해 줄 수 있는 부사를 묻고 있다. 문맥상 '영구적으로(permanently)' 이사 간다는 의미가 적절하다.

141

(A) In fact, we asked Mr. Barren to put off his retirement for two years.
(B) Throughout his presidency, Mr. Barren was in charge of the development of the XR-800 system.
(C) CEO told company shareholders that he believed the new product line would be very profitable.
(D) Mr. Barren's outstanding contribution to Rakestraw Industries over the past 30 years will be highlighted in speeches at his retirement dinner next month.

해설 빈칸 다음 문장의 '이 프로젝트(this project)'라는 지시형용사를 사용하였으므로, 프로젝트가 언급된 선택지문장을 골라야 하고, '시스템의 개발(the development of the XR-800 system)'이 언급되어 있는 (B)가 가장 적절하다.

(A) 사실상 우리는 Barren 씨에게 그의 퇴임을 2년간 미뤄 달라고 요청했습니다.
(B) 재임 기간 동안 Barren 씨는 XR-800 시스템의 개발을 담당하고 있었습니다.
(C) CEO는 주주들에게 새로운 제품라인이 아주 수익성이 좋을 것이라고 믿었다고 말했습니다.
(D) Barren 씨의 지난 30년간 Rakestraw Industries에 바친 뛰어난 공헌은 다음 달에 있을 퇴임 만찬에서 강조될 것입니다.

142

(A) In addition
(B) For example
(C) In short
(D) By comparison

해설 앞 문장에서 프로젝트 덕분에 장비 판매에서 선두가 되었다는 내용이 나와 있고 빈칸 다음 문장에서도 그 프로젝트 덕분에 매출이 증가하였다는 내용이 언급되어 있으므로, 프로젝트로 인한 이점들을 나열하고 있다는 걸 알 수 있다. 앞 문장과 관련된 두 번째 내용이 추가로 언급되어 있으므로, 가장 적절한 접속부사는 (A) in addition(게다가)이다.

Questions 143-146 refer to the following letter.

To Whom It May Concern:

Davis Lewis & Partners placed an order with your company for the book entitled Yoga for Health by Theresa Woolsley on November 27 (invoice number 394-DI).

-------. I have spoken with several customer service
143.
representatives by telephone ------- this matter, and they -------
144. **145.**
me that the Shipping Department sent the books on December 1.

I am sure that your company faithfully filled the order, but I would appreciate a replacement shipment as soon as possible so we can have the books in stock for the holiday season.

If this is not -------, then I will expect a full refund. I have
146.
enclosed a copy of the invoice for your reference. Thank you in advance for your assistance in this matter.

Sincerely,

Philip Moore
Inventory Control Manager

관계자 분께

Davis Lewis & Partners는 11월 27일에 당신의 회사에서 Theresa Wollsley의 건강에 관련된 요가책을 수분했습니다(송장번호 394–DI).

비록 우리의 기록이 그 지불이 이루어졌다는 걸 보여주더라도 우리는 아직 책들을 받지 못했습니다. 저는 이 문제에 대해 전화상담원들과 전화상담을 했고 그들은 배송부서가 12월 1일에 책을 보냈다고 확인했습니다.

저는 당신의 회사가 주문서를 신중하게 작성한 것으로 알고 있지만 가능한 한 빨리 배송을 대체해주셔서 우리가 휴가시즌에 재고를 구비할 수 있도록 해주시면 감사하겠습니다.

만약 이것이 실현 불가능하다면 저는 전액을 환불받을 것입니다. 참고하시라고 송장의 사본을 첨부했습니다. 이 문제에 대한 당신의 협조를 미리 감사드립니다.

진심을 담아

Philip Moore
재고 관리 매니저

어휘 place an order 주문을 하다 entitled ~라는 제목의 representative 대표 assure 확인하다, 보장하다 faithfully 충실히, 정확히 enclose 동봉하다 invoice 송장 for your reference 참고로

143

(A) Unfortunately, due to high demand, the item is out of stock until December 13.
(B) Although our record shows that payment was made, we have still not received the books.
(C) Because we received the defective item yesterday, I'd like to return it.
(D) The shipment is scheduled to be delivered in 2 weeks, but it's too late.

해설 빈칸 다음 문장의 '이러한 문제 (this matter)'와 어울릴 수 있도록 문제점이 언급된 문장을 골라야 한다. 선택지 모두 문제점과 관련된 내용이지만, '이 문제'에 대해 알렸을 때 배송부서에서는 책을 보냈다고 답변했으므로, 아직까지 주문한 책을 받지 못했다는 내용이 문제점으로 가장 적합하다.

(A) 불행히도 높은 수요 때문에, 그 상품은 12월 13일까지 재고가 없다.
(B) 비록 우리의 기록은 그 지불이 이루어졌다는 걸 보여주더라도 우리는 아직 책들을 받지 못했다.
(C) 우리는 어제 결함이 있는 상품을 받았기 때문에 그것을 돌려주고 싶다.
(D) 배송은 2주 후에 배달될 것으로 예정되었지만 그것은 너무 늦다.

144

(A) regard
(B) regards
(C) regarded
(D) regarding

해설 문장의 동사는 이미 앞에 나와 있으므로 빈칸에 동사의 형태는 적절하지 못하다. 어떠한 문제점에 관하여 상담전화를 했으니, 관련된 주제를 언급할 수 있는 전치사 (D) regarding(~에 관하여)이 정답이다.

145

(A) assured
(B) appointed
(C) designated
(D) directed

해설 빈칸은 '동사 + 사람 + that절'의 구조를 가지는 단어가 적절한 위치이다. 그리고 고객서비스 직원이 문제에 대한 이야기를 들었을 때 배송부서가 책을 12월 1일에 보냈다고 확실하게 이야기했다는 내용이 필요하므로 정답은 (A) assured(장담하다, 확실하게 이야기하다)이다.

146

(A) fortunate
(B) feasible
(C) urgent
(D) ultimate

해설 앞 문장에서 빠른 대체 배송을 요구하였고(I would appreciate a replacement shipment as soon as possible), '실현 가능하지' 않다면 환불을 받겠다고 하였으므로, '실현 가능한'이란 의미가 가장 적합하다.

ACTUAL TEST 01 | ACTUAL TEST 02 | ACTUAL TEST 03 | ACTUAL TEST 04 | ACTUAL TEST 05

101

Portland Airlines adopted the policy that it will no longer ------- whales and dolphins for aquariums and water parks.
(A) transported
(B) transport
(C) transporting
(D) transports

Portland Airlines는 더 이상 아쿠아리움과 워터파크를 위한 고래나 돌고래를 수송하지 않겠다는 정책을 채택했다.

해설 빈칸은 will 뒤에 어울리는 동사원형자리이다. 선택지 중 동사원형인 transport(수송하다)가 정답이다.

어휘 adopt 채택하다 policy 정책 no longer 더 이상 ~ 않다 transport 수송하다, 운반하다

102

If the order is not dispatched ------- three business days, you will be contacted to offer partial shipment or full refund.
(A) in
(B) about
(C) into
(D) until

만약 주문이 3영업일 후에 보내지지 않는다면, 당신은 부분적인 배송이나 전액환불을 받기 위해 연락받을 것이다.

해설 빈칸은 three business days(3영업일)와 어울리는 전치사자리이다. 시간과 어울리는 전치사는 선택지 중 (A) in(~ 후에)이다. until(~까지)은 기간을 나타내는 단어와 어울리지 않는다.

어휘 dispatch 보내다, 발송하다 business day 영업일 partial 부분적인 shipment 배송 full refund 전액 환불

103

The construction of gymnasium at the new State Middle School was ------- completed when we took a tour of the building Wednesday morning.
(A) nearest
(B) nearer
(C) neared
(D) nearly

새로운 State Middle School의 체육관 공사는 우리가 수요일 아침에 빌딩을 둘러보았을 때 거의 끝났었다.

해설 빈칸은 be동사 was와 과거분사 completed 사이에 어울리는 단어가 들어갈 자리이다. 형용사 앞에는 부사가 와야 하므로 정답은 (D) nearly(거의)이다.

어휘 gymnasium 체육관 nearly 거의 take a tour 둘러보다

104

In an ------- to reduce the amount of photocopier paper we use, please use recycled paper whenever possible.
(A) acceptance
(B) output
(C) account
(D) effort

우리가 사용하는 복사기 종이의 양을 줄이기 위한 노력으로, 가능할 때마다 재활용 종이를 사용해주십시오.

해설 빈칸은 의미가 적절한 명사가 들어갈 자리이다. 그러나 <in an effort to + 동사: ~하기 위한 노력으로>의 형태를 알아두면 쉽게 해결 가능한 유형이다. in an effort to reduce the amount 양을 줄이기 위한 노력으로

어휘 in an effort to ~하려는 노력으로 reduce 줄이다 recycled paper 재활용 종이 whenever possible 가능할 때마다 output 생산량, 출력

105

After 10 years of ------- the company as a business executive, Mr. Pitt decided to quit his job.
(A) donating
(B) instructing
(C) competing
(D) leading

임원으로서 회사를 이끌어온 10년 후에 Pitt 씨는 사직하기로 결정했다.

해설 빈칸은 the company를 목적어로 취하는 동명사자리이다. 문맥상 as a business executive(임원으로서)로 회사를 이끌어 왔다(leading)는 의미가 자연스럽다.

어휘 lead 이끌다 instruct 지시하다, 가르치다 compete 경쟁하다 donate 기부하다 executive 임원, 중역

106

To sum up, ------- cranes and forklifts are great ways of transporting heavy goods, but cranes are capable of lifting heavier goods.
(A) this
(B) after
(C) both
(D) once

요약해서 말하자면, 크레인과 포크리프트 둘 다 무거운 물건을 운송하기 위한 훌륭한 방법이지만, 크레인이 더 무거운 물건을 들어 올릴 수 있다.

해설 1초 안에 답을 고를 수 있는 문제이다. and를 보고 (C) both가 정답임을 알 수 있다.

어휘 to sum up 요약해서, 요컨대 heavy goods 무거운 물건 be capable of 가능하다 lift 들어 올리다

ACTUAL TEST 01 ACTUAL TEST 02 ACTUAL TEST 03 ACTUAL TEST 04 ACTUAL TEST 05

107

As a manager, ------- is important for Nicolas Janet to be able to delegate duties to subordinates rather than attempt to complete everything herself.
(A) it
(B) she
(C) there
(D) he

매니저로서, Nicolas Janet이 그녀 스스로 모든 것을 끝내려는 시도보다는 후임에게 업무를 위탁하는 것이 중요하다.

해설 빈칸은 문장의 주어가 들어갈 자리이다. 빈칸 뒤의 for와 to가 보이므로, 빈칸은 가주어 it이 들어간다는 것을 알 수 있다. it이 가주어, to 이하가 진주어, for가 to부정사에 대한 의미상의 주어이다. it ~ for ~ to구문은 'for가 to 이하를 하는 것은 ~하다'로 해석하면 된다.

어휘 delegate 위탁하다 duty 업무 subordinate 후임자, 후임 attempt 시도, 시도하다

108

Wide. R. Electronics is so ------- in the reliability of its domestic appliances that it offers a free two-year warranty on its new models.
(A) confident
(B) confidence
(C) confidential
(D) confidently

Wide. R. Electronics는 국내 가전제품의 신뢰성에 아주 자신이 있기 때문에, 회사의 새로운 모델에 대해 무료 2년의 보증기간을 제공합니다.

해설 so 앞에 be동사 is가 보이므로 일단 빈칸은 be동사 뒤에 어울리는 형용사자리이다. 선택지 중 형용사인 confident(확신하는)과 confidential(기밀의) 중에서 Wide. R. Electronics 회사가 '가전제품의 신뢰성에 대해서 아주 자신이 있다'는 의미이므로 '확신하는'의 뜻인 (A) confident가 정답이다.

어휘 confident 확신하는 confidence 자신감 confidential 기밀의 reliability 신뢰성 domestic 국내의 appliance 가전제품 warranty 보증, 보증기간

109

Please tell us about your recent experience with Brux Apparel Company ------- our web site so that we can improve our quality.
(A) on
(B) in
(C) up
(D) of

우리 회사의 품질을 개선시키기 위하여, 우리 웹사이트상에 Brux Apparel Company에서의 최근 경험에 대해 말해주세요.

해설 빈칸 뒤의 our web site와 잘 어울리는 전치사는 on이다.

어휘 so that ~하기 위하여 quality 품질 recent 최근의 improve 개선시키다

110

All researchers at Jansen pharmaceuticals must wear ------- goggles as a safety measure whenever in the workplace.
(A) protected
(B) protective
(C) protects
(D) protection

Jansen 제약사의 모든 연구자들은 작업장에 있을 때마다, 안전조치로서 보호용 고글을 착용해야 한다.

해설 빈칸은 뒤의 명사 goggles(고글)와 어울리는 품사의 단어가 들어갈 자리이다. 명사 앞은 형용사자리이므로 '보호하는, 보호용의'의 의미인 (B) protective가 정답이다. 형용사인 protected(보호된)도 고려대상이긴 하지만 '보호된 안경'은 잘못된 표현이다.

어휘 pharmaceutical 제약사 protective 보호하는 protected 보호된 protection 보호 safety measure 안전 조치 workplace 작업장

111

As soon as everyone in our tour group arrived, they were ------- served a delicious dinner in the main dining hall on the ground floor.
(A) prompting
(B) prompts
(C) promptly
(D) prompted

우리의 투어 그룹에 있는 모든 사람들이 도착하자마자, 그들은 1층에 있는 중앙 식사홀에서 맛있는 식사를 즉시 제공받았다.

해설 빈칸은 수동태 형태인 were served 사이에 어울리는 품사가 들어갈 자리이다. be동사와 pp 사이에는 부사가 어울리므로 정답은 (C) promptly(즉시, 바로)이다.

어휘 as soon as ~하자마자 promptly 즉시, 바로 prompt 즉각적인, 신속한 serve 제공하다 ground floor 1층

112

The release of Ms. Showna's building permit for her condominium was delayed because one of the documents required was filed -------.
(A) equally
(B) approximately
(C) importantly
(D) incorrectly

Showna 씨의 콘도미니움 건설허가증의 공개는 요청된 문서 중의 하나가 부정확하게 기록되었기 때문에 지연되었다.

해설 빈칸은 문장의 끝에서 의미가 어울리는 부사가 들어갈 자리이다. 문맥상 '요청된 문서 한 개가 부정확하게(incorrectly) 철해졌기 때문에 건설허가증의 공개가 지연되었다'는 의미가 자연스럽다.

어휘 release 출시, 발표 permit 허가증 delay 미루다, 연기하다 equally 동일하게 approximately 대략, 약 importantly 중요하게 incorrectly 부정확하게

113

Business owners can rent booths to promote their products at the event, allowing them to get wider ------- to thousands of potential customers.
(A) exposure
(B) expose
(C) exposing
(D) exposed

회사 대표들은 행사에서 그들의 상품을 홍보하기 위해 부스를 빌릴 수 있는데, 이는 그들을 수천 명의 잠재고객들에게 더 널리 노출시킨다.

해설 빈칸은 앞의 형용사 비교 형태인 wider 뒤에 어울리는 단어가 올 자리이다. 형용사 뒤는 명사자리이므로 정답은 (A) exposure(노출, 드러냄)이다.

어휘 promote 홍보하다 exposure 노출 potential 잠재적인 wider 더 넓은

114

Perth has flourished over the years and has ------- been named as one of the best places to live in Australia.
(A) frequenting
(B) frequently
(C) frequents
(D) frequent

Perth는 수년간 번창해왔고 호주에서 살기 좋은 장소 중 한 곳으로 자주 거명되었다.

해설 빈칸은 동사 앞에 어울리는 품사가 들어갈 자리이다. 동사 수식은 부사가 어울리므로, 선택지 중 부사형태인 (B) frequently(빈번히)가 정답이다.

어휘 flourish 번창하다 frequently 빈번하게, 자주 frequent 빈번한, 잦은 name 지명하다, 임명하다

115

We appreciate you taking time to let us know how ------- your stay was at Sunrise Edge Villa.
(A) considerable
(B) available
(C) additional
(D) enjoyable

Sunrise Edge Villa에서의 숙박이 얼마나 즐거웠는지를 알려준 당신에게 감사드립니다.

해설 빈칸은 how 뒤에 의미가 어울리는 형용사가 들어갈 자리이다. 빈칸을 포함한 문장을 살펴보면 let us know how ------- your stay was(당신의 체류가 얼마나 ~했는지를 알려 달라)는 의미이므로 빈칸에는 (D) enjoyable(즐거운)이 적절하다.

어휘 appreciate 감사하다 considerable 상당한 available 이용 가능한, 시간이 있는 additional 추가적인 enjoyable 즐거운

116

It has been more than two years since the ------- episode of Find Wolly Season 2 aired on Tooniversal Network.
(A) lasts
(B) lastly
(C) last
(D) lasted

Find Wolly Season 2의 마지막 회가 Tooniversal Network에서 방영된 이래로 2년 이상이 지났다.

해설 빈칸은 뒤의 명사 episode를 수식하는 형용사자리이다. 선택지 중 '마지막의'라는 의미의 last가 어울린다. last episode 마지막 회

어휘 more than ~이상 since ~이래로 air 방영하다, 방송하다 last 마지막의 lastly 끝으로

117

Construction is ------- 89 percent complete and the opening ceremony is scheduled for March 2nd.
(A) too
(B) quite
(C) now
(D) far

건설은 현재 89% 완공되었고 개장식은 3월 2일로 예정되어 있다.

해설 빈칸 다음 부분은 '건설은 89% 완공됐다'의 의미이므로, too(너무), quite(꽤), far(훨씬)는 의미연결이 어색하다. now(현재)를 넣어 보면 '건설은 현재 89% 완공됐다'로 의미 연결이 적절하다.

어휘 be scheduled ~로 예정되다 too 너무 quite 꽤 far 훨씬

118

Studies have shown that the media is rarely ------- of the scientific findings they report.
(A) criticize
(B) critic
(C) critically
(D) critical

연구는 미디어가 보도하는 비판적인 과학적 연구결과가 드물다는 것을 보여준다.

해설 be동사와 부사 뒤의 빈칸은 형용사자리이며 선택지 중 형용사는 (D) critical(비판적인)이다.

어휘 rarely 드물게 ~하다 findings 연구결과 criticize 비난하다, 비평하다 critic 비평가 critical 비판적인

119

After ------- a client survey, Daniel's Restaurant decided to add more international options to its lunch menu.
(A) conducts
(B) conducted
(C) conduct
(D) conducting

고객 설문조사를 실시한 후에, Daniel's Restaurant는 점심 메뉴에 좀 더 국제적으로 메뉴를 추가하기로 결정했다.

해설 빈칸 뒤에 a client survey라는 명사가 보이므로, 빈칸은 a client survey(고객 설문)을 목적어로 취하는 동명사자리임을 알 수 있다. 따라서 동사에 -ing를 붙인 (D) conducting이 정답이다.

어휘 conduct 수행하다, 실시하다 survey 설문조사 decide 결정하다 add 추가하다 international 국제적인

120

Because the company's printer on the 4th floor has been repaired, Mr. Jackey's document can be printed without -------.
(A) refund
(B) favor
(C) delay
(D) action

4층에 회사 프린터가 수리되었기 때문에, Jackey 씨의 문서는 지체 없이 출력될 수 있다.

해설 빈칸은 전치사 without과 의미연결이 적절한 명사가 들어갈 자리이다. without delay(지체 없이, 곧바로)를 알아두면 간단하게 해결된다.

어휘 refund 환불 favor 찬성 delay 지연, 지체, action 조치

121

H&D Department Store hired 12 cashiers ------- at all its branches during the busy winter season.
(A) assists
(B) have assisted
(C) to assist
(D) assisted

H&D 백화점은 바쁜 겨울 시즌 동안 모든 지점에서 돕기 위해서 12명의 출납원을 고용했다.

해설 빈칸 앞의 내용은 '백화점은 12명의 출납원을 고용했다'이고 이어서 '바쁜 겨울 시즌 동안 모든 지점에서 ~'라고 연결된다. 문맥상 '~하기 위해서'라는 표현의 to부정사가 적절하다. to assist at all its branches 모든 지점에서 돕기 위해서

어휘 assist 돕다 branch 지사 during ~ 동안 cashier 출납원

122

Ms. Magon will have to go to the Blitch office in July, so Mr. Ester will act as General Manager ------- her absence.
(A) among
(B) because
(C) during
(D) while

Magon 씨가 7월에 Blitch 사무실로 가야만 하기 때문에 그녀가 없는 동안 Ester 씨가 총지배인 역할을 할 것이다.

해설 빈칸은 her absence와 어울리는 전치사자리이다. 선택지 중 접속사인 because와 while은 먼저 탈락된다. among은 셋 이상일 때 '~사이에'라는 의미이므로, absence(부재)와는 어울리지 않는다. 정답은 '~동안'이란 뜻을 지닌 (C) during이다.

어휘 have to ~해야 한다 among ~ 사이에 absence 부재 during ~ 동안 while ~ 동안, 반면에

123

Visitors to the capital will be able to take advantage of a unique international package for tourists ------- in September 2017.
(A) start
(B) starting
(C) will start
(D) started

수도로 가는 방문객들은 2017년 9월부터 관광객들을 위한 독특한 국제 패키지를 이용할 수 있을 것이다.

해설 빈칸은 문장이 끝나고 의미를 연결해주는 단어가 들어갈 자리이다. 문장의 동사(will be able to take advantage of ~을 이용할 수 있을 것이다)가 앞쪽에 있으므로 빈칸에 동사가 들어갈 수 없다. 따라서 동사형태인 start, will start가 우선 오답이다. starting과 started 중에서 '~부터'라는 의미의 (B) starting이 적절하다.

어휘 capital 수도 visitor 방문객 take advantage of ~을 이용하다, 활용하다 unique 독특한 tourist 관광객 starting ~부터

124

------ after becoming the marketing manager of Commax Business Lenter, Jimmy Cotter expanded the market share by 20 percent.
(A) Soon
(B) Often
(C) Far
(D) Ever

Commax Business Lenter의 마케팅 매니저가 된 직후에, Jimmy Cotter는 20퍼센트까지 시장 점유율을 확장시켰다.

해설 빈칸은 바로 뒤의 after(~후에)와 의미가 어울리는 부사자리이다. 선택지 중 의미가 적절한 부사는 Soon(곧)이며, Soon after는 '~직후에'라는 의미를 가진다.

어휘 soon after ~직후에 expand 확장하다 market share 시장 점유율 by ~까지

125

The decision of the publishing company as to the number of books to be reprinted will be based on ------- many copies have been sold in the first quarter.
(A) very
(B) how
(C) as
(D) so

다시 인쇄될 책의 권수에 대한 출판사의 결정은 첫 분기에 얼마나 많은 책이 팔렸는지를 기반으로 할 것입니다.

해설 빈칸 이하의 문장을 이끌면서 many와 연결이 가능한 어휘를 고르는 문제이다. 선택지 중 두 가지 역할을 할 수 있는 단어는 how 밖에 없다. how many copies have been sold 얼마나 많은 책들이 판매되었는지

어휘 publishing company 출판사 reprint 다시 인쇄하다 based on ~를 기반으로 한 quarter 분기

126

For seven consecutive months, the National Restaurant Association has given its highest ------- in food service to Lakeview Cafe.
(A) rating
(B) personnel
(C) demonstration
(D) reliance

7개월 연속해서, National Restaurant Association은 음식서비스분야에서 Lakeview Cafe에 가장 높은 등급을 주었다.

해설 빈칸은 동사 has given(주다)과 형용사 highest(가장 높은)와 의미가 잘 연결되는 명사자리이다. 이 두 가지에 의미가 적합한 선택지는 rating(순위, 평가)이다. has given its highest rating 가장 높은 평가를 주다

어휘 rating 순위, 평가 personnel 인사부, 직원들 demonstration 증명, 시연 reliance 의존, 의지

127

Although the firm saw a 13 percent drop in revenue last year, specialists continue to express ------- in the future of Toshio Platinum.
(A) sympathy
(B) confidence
(C) challenge
(D) gratitude

비록 회사가 지난해 수익에서 13% 감소를 보였지만, 전문가들은 Toshio Platinum의 미래에 계속해서 확신을 표현한다.

해설 해설 빈칸은 동사 express(나타내다, 표하다)의 목적어자리이다. sympathy(동정), confidence(확신, 신뢰), challenge(도전, 어려움) gratitude(감사) 중에서 빈칸 뒤에 in the future of(~의 미래에)가 보이므로 미래에 대한 확신을 표현한다는 연결이 적절하다.

어휘 revenue 수익 specialist 전문가 express 표현하다 sympathy 동경, 동정 confidence 확신, 신뢰 chanllenge 도전, 어려움 gratitude 감사

128

Whole Multi Cultural Community depends on generous funding from local donors for ------- its teaching programs.
(A) maintaining
(B) maintain
(C) maintains
(D) maintenance

Whole Multi Cultural Community는 교육 프로그램 유지를 위해 지역 기부자들의 후한 자금제공에 의존한다.

해설 빈칸은 전치사 for 뒤에서 its teaching programs를 목적어로 취하는 동명사자리이다. 선택지 중에서 동명사인 (A) maintaining(유지하는 것)이 정답이다.

어휘 generous 후한, 관대한 funding 자금, 재정지원 donor 기부자 maintain ~을 유지하다 maintenance 유지, 보수

129

TF12 television station, ------- features the music of new recording artists, is expected to hold a fall concert event.
(A) which
(B) where
(C) what
(D) that

새로운 녹음 전문가의 음악을 특집으로 하는 TF12 텔레비전 방송국은 가을 콘서트 행사를 개최할 것으로 예상됩니다.

해설 빈칸은 문장 구조상 television station(TV 방송국)을 선행사로 취하는 관계대명사자리이다. where는 완전한 문장을 이끌고 what은 선행사를 포함한 관계대명사이므로 앞에 명사가 올 수 없다. 관계대명사 that은 콤마 뒤에 올 수 없으므로 정답은 사물 주격 관계대명사인 (A) which이다.

어휘 feature 특징으로 하다, 특집으로 하다 be expected to ~하기로 예상되다 hold 개최하다, 열다

130

The agreement's terms are very ------- and state that all work must be completed by July 14th.
(A) straightforward
(B) negligible
(C) accomplished
(D) immediate

합의서의 조건을 아주 간단명료하고 모든 작업은 7월 14일까지 완료되어야 한다는 것을 명시한다.

해설 빈칸은 be동사 뒤에 의미가 적절한 형용사가 들어갈 자리이다. be동사 뒤의 형용사는 주격 보어로 주어의 의미를 보충해주는 역할을 하므로, 주어인 terms(조건)와 의미가 어울리는 선택지는 (A) straightforward(간단명료한)이다.

어휘 agreement 합의서, 동의서 term 조건 straightforward 간단명료한 negligible 무시해도 될 정도의 accomplish 성취하다 immediate 즉각적인

ACTUAL TEST 01 ACTUAL TEST 02 ACTUAL TEST 03 ACTUAL TEST 04 ACTUAL TEST 05

Questions 131-134 refer to the following memorandum.

DATE: March 3

TO: Petrisha Deaze

FROM: Steven Hernandaze

SUBJECT: Earned Vacation Credits

This year, I ------- in a number of advertising projects that did
131.
not allow me to use up my vacation credits. I had hoped to use
the two weeks this month, but delays in the Cleanse Herbal
Tea project have made that impossible. -------. If we hope to
132.
finish this project by the end of the year, I will have to work on it
continuously.

I am ------- of the company's policy that vacations should be
133.
taken between January 1 and December 21 each year. -------,
134.
because of my unusual workload this year, I am requesting
permission to carry over the remaining two weeks of my
vacation time this year into the next year.

I would appreciate your favorable consideration for my request.
I look forward to receiving your answer.

날짜: 3월 3일
수신: Petrisha Deaze
발신: Steven Hernandaze
제목: 휴가일수

올해 저는 휴가를 이용할 수 없을 만큼 많은 광고 프로젝트들에 참여해 왔습니다. 이번 달에 저는 2주간의 시간을 보내고 싶어 했지만 Cleanse Herbal Tea 프로젝트의 지연이 그것을 불가능하게 했습니다. 우리는 예정보다 3주나 뒤쳐져 있습니다. 만약 우리가 올해 말에 이 프로젝트를 끝내고 싶어 한다면 저는 지속적으로 그 일을 해야 할 것입니다.

저는 매년 1월 1일과 12월 21일 사이에 휴가를 써야 한다는 회사 정책을 알고 있습니다. 하지만 올해 흔치 않은 업무량 때문에 저는 올해의 남은 2주간의 휴가를 내년으로 옮기는 것을 요청합니다.

저의 요청에 대해 호의적으로 생각해 주시면 감사하겠습니다. 답장을 기다리겠습니다.

어휘 use up ~을 다 쓰다 vacation credit 휴가일수 continuously 계속해서 workload 업무량 carry over ~을 (다른 상황까지 계속) 가져가다 acknowledge 인정하다

131 (A) **have been involved**
(B) have involved
(C) will be involved
(D) involved

해설 주어 뒤에서 동사의 형태를 고르는 문제이다. involve(연루시키다)는 타동사인데 빈칸 뒤에 목적어가 없으므로 수동태가 적절한 형태이고 '올해(this year)'라고 했으므로 미래시제인 (C) will be involved는 어울리지 않는다. 따라서 정답은 (A) have been involved 이다.

132
(A) I'm wondering what the vacation policy is.
(B) Could someone else help me with the project?
(C) Is it possible to put off the project?
(D) We are now running three weeks behind schedule.

해설 빈칸의 앞 문장에 '프로젝트의 지연(delays in the Cleans Herbal Tea project)'이 있다는 내용이 있으므로 지연에 대해 구체적인 설명을 덧붙여주는 (D)가 가장 적절하다. (B)와 (C)는 프로젝트와 관련된 이야기를 하고 있긴 하지만 도움을 요청한다거나 지연을 요구하는 내용이므로 휴가 사용에 관한 문의를 하고 있는 전체글의 중심내용에서 벗어나므로 적절하지 못하다.

(A) 저는 휴가 정책이 어떤 것인지 궁금합니다.
(B) 누군가가 이 프로젝트에 대해 저를 도와줄 수 있습니까?
(C) 그 프로젝트를 연기하는 것이 가능한가요?
(D) 우리는 예정보다 3주나 뒤쳐져 있습니다.

133
(A) proposed
(B) known
(C) aware
(D) confident

해설 회사의 정책에 대해서 '잘 알고 있다'는 의미가 필요하다. 빈출표현인 be aware of(~를 알고 있다)를 꼭 암기해두자.

134
(A) However
(B) Additionally
(C) Thus
(D) Otherwise

해설 '휴가는 1월~12월 중에 가져야 한다는 걸 알고 있다'는 문장이 앞에 있고, 뒤에는 정책과는 어긋나지만 올해의 '남은 2주의 휴가(remaining two weeks of my vacation time)'를 내년으로 미루고 싶다는 문장이 이어진다. '반대'의 의미를 나타내주는 (A) However(그러나)가 정답이다.

To: Adam Eastbourne <adam@mmedia.com>

From: Rosalin Hopes <hope@mmedia.com>

C.C: Richard Wagner <rich@mmedia.com>

Subject: Tardiness

Attach: Februarysummary.doc

Date: March 10

This is to call your attention to the excessive tardiness you ------- **135.** last month. ------- **136.** our records, there were five instances when you came in beyond the normal start of office hours.

Because you have accumulated more than 60 minutes of tardiness, your monthly pay for March will reflect a deduction ------- **137.** to the time in question. -------. **138.** Otherwise, we will have no alternative but to put you on suspension should the same thing happen again in the future.

We look forward to seeing an improvement in your record soon.

수신: Adam Eastbourne 〈adam@mme-dia.com〉

발신: Rosalin Hopes 〈hope@mmedia.com〉

참조: Richard Wagner 〈rich@mmedia.com〉

제목: 지각

첨부: Februarysummary.doc

날짜: 3월 10일

이것은 지난달에 당신이 초래한 과도한 지각에 주의를 환기시키기 위한 것입니다. 기록에 근거하면, 당신이 정규 근무시간을 지나서 출근한 사례는 5번입니다.

지각이 60분 이상 누적되었기 때문에 3월 급여는 문제의 시간에 상당하는 공제를 반영할 것입니다. 만약 9시 이전이나 정시 출근하는 데 어려운 문제가 있다면 매니저와 그 문제에 대해 상의하시길 바랍니다. 그렇지 않을 경우, 앞으로도 같은 일이 발생할 수 있기 때문에 정직 처리 이외에 다른 대안이 없습니다.

우리는 당신의 출근 기록이 곧 개선되기를 기대합니다.

어휘 excessive 지나친, 과도한 tardiness 지연 instance 사례, 경우 beyond 지나, 이후 accumulate 축적하다 deduction 공제 alternative 대안 suspension 보류, 유예

135
(A) to incur
(B) incurring
(C) incurred
(D) incur

해설 '과도한 지각(the excessive tardiness)'를 수식하기 위해 목적격 관계대명사가 생략된 문장이 이어지고 있고, 주어 you 뒤에서 사용될 동사를 고르는 문제이다. 빈칸 뒤의 '지난달(last month)'을 통해 과거시제가 적절하다는 것을 알 수 있다.

136
(A) Regarding
(B) In spite of
(C) Based on
(D) Owing to

> 해설 우리의 기록을 근거로 하여 5번의 지각이 있었다는 것을 알 수 있으므로 (C) Based on(~에 근거하여)이 가장 적절하다. '우리의 기록(our records)'이 뒤 문장의 근거가 될 수 있지만 원인이 될 수는 없으므로 (D) Owing to(~ 때문에)는 적절하지 않다.

137
(A) equivalent
(B) official
(C) intended
(D) outstanding

> 해설 지각한 시간에 '상응하는' 만큼의 급여 삭감이 있을 것이므로 (A) equivalent(상응하는)가 정답이다. equivalent to N(N에 상응하는)을 꼭 암기해두자.

138
(A) This action of a monthly salary cut was also notified to your direct supervisor.
(B) If there are any problems that make it difficult for you to be here on or before 9 A.M., please discuss those issues with your manager.
(C) If this happens repeatedly, there will be a cut in salary for six months.
(D) New regulations about tardiness have been implemented since last year.

> 해설 빈칸 다음 문장에 '그렇지 않을 경우(otherwise)' 정직에 처하겠다는 내용이 이어지고 있다. 따라서 만약 지각할 수밖에 없는 문제가 있다면 매니저와 논의하라는 내용이 적절하다.

(A) 이 월급 삭감은 당신의 직속상관에게도 역시 알려졌습니다.
(B) 만약 9시 이전이나 정시 출근하는 데 어려운 문제가 있다면 매니저와 그 문제에 대해 상의하시길 바랍니다.
(C) 만약 이 일이 지속적으로 일어난다면 6개월분의 월급이 삭감될 것입니다.
(D) 지각에 대한 새로운 규정이 작년부터 시행되어 왔습니다.

Questions 139-142 refer to the following information.

New Policy at the Palo Alto Public Library -------. However, due to a significant increase in the number of **139.** overdue books, cardholders from outside the Palo Alto area will now have to pay an annual membership fee in order to use the library. -------, the lending of books outside the library will no **140.** longer be allowed for non-Palo Alto area residents. This new policy will go into ------- on May 3. **141.** To obtain a non-resident library card, simply fill out the required form and pay the $ 40 annual fee at the library's front desk. Your card ------- within three business days. **142.** Although we regret to introduce this policy, we feel it is a necessary measure that must be taken to protect our library's valuable resources.	Palo Alto 공공도서관의 새로운 정책 1995년 개관 이후, Palo Alto 공공도서관은 근처의 지역주민들에게도 공짜로 책 대여를 허용하고 있습니다. 하지만 연체된 책의 양이 눈에 띄게 증가해서 Palo Alto지역 외의 회원들은 도서관 이용을 위해 연간 멤버십 요금을 지불해야 합니다. 게다가 도서관 밖으로 책을 빌리는 것은 더 이상 Palo Alto지역에 거주하지 않은 사람들에게는 불가능합니다. 이 새로운 정책은 5월 3일에 시행될 것입니다. 비거주자 도서관 카드를 발급받기 위해서는 도서관 안내데스크에서 간단히 요구되는 서류를 작성하고 40달러의 연회비를 지불하면 됩니다. 카드는 영업일 3일 이내에 발급될 것입니다. 비록 이러한 정책을 알리는 것이 유감이지만, 우리는 이것이 우리 도서관의 가치 있는 자료들을 보호하기 위해 시행되어야 하는 필요 정책이라고 생각합니다.

어휘 significant 눈에 띄게 overdue 기한이 지난 cardholder 회원 fee 비용 in order to 위하여 no longer 더 이상 ~ 않다 regret to 유감스럽게도 measure 조치, 정책 valuable 가치 있는

139 (A) The Palo Alto Public Library is conveniently located near both the bus stop and the subway station.
(B) Information on using the library is available on the website or at the front desk.
(C) The Palo Alto Public Library was founded by the mayor Peter Adams 30 years ago.
(D) Since its opening in 1995, the Palo Alto Public Library has always allowed the lending of books for free to residents of neighboring communities.

해설 빈칸 다음 문장에 접속부사 However(하지만)가 나오고 멤버십 요금을 지불해야 한다(will now have to pay an annual membership fee)는 내용이 이어진다. 빈칸에는 이와 반대로 '공짜로 책을 빌려준다(the lending of books for free)'는 내용이 가장 어울리므로 정답은 (D)이다.

(A) Palo Alto 공공도서관은 버스 정류장과 지하철 역 근처에 편리하게 위치해 있습니다.
(B) 도서관 이용정보는 홈페이지나 안내데스크에서 확인할 수 있습니다.
(C) Palo Alto 공공도서관은 30년 전 Peter Adams 시장에 의해 설립되었습니다.
(D) 1995년 개관 이후, Palo Alto 공공도서관은 근처의 지역주민들에게도 공짜로 책 대여를 허용하고 있습니다.

140

(A) Specifically
(B) Instead
(C) In addition
(D) As a result

해설 앞 문장에서 멤버십 요금을 지불해야 한다는 내용이 있고, 빈칸 뒤의 문장에서는 그 지역의 거주자가 아닌 사람들에게는 대여가 허락되지 않는다는 내용이 있으므로, 요금 지불 이외에도 거주지를 기준으로 하는 또 다른 정책이 있다는 걸 추가적으로 알려주고 있다. 따라서 (C) in addition(게다가)이 정답이다.

141

(A) creation
(B) effect
(C) practice
(D) composition

해설 새로운 정책들이 5월 3일에 '시행되다'라는 의미가 필요하므로 정답은 (B) effect(효력)이다. go into effect가 '시행되다, 효력을 발생하다'의 표현이라는 것을 기억하자.

142

(A) is issued
(B) has issued
(C) will issue
(D) will be issued

해설 '발행하다(issue)'는 타동사인데 빈칸 뒤에 목적어가 없으므로 수동형이 필요하고, 앞 문장에서 카드를 얻기 위해서 신청서를 작성하고 요금을 지불하면 된다는 안내를 하고 있고 그런 절차를 따르게 되면 카드가 발급될 것이라는 미래의 의미가 가장 적절하다.

ACTUAL TEST 01 | ACTUAL TEST 02 | ACTUAL TEST 03 | ACTUAL TEST 04 | ACTUAL TEST 05

Questions 143-146 refer to the following letter.

Dear Wells,

-------143.-------. Over the past few years, we have organized fun runs, which -------144.------- enthusiastic responses from kindhearted people like you. As you know, our organization is -------145.------- to raising awareness of the disease, educating the public about its signs and symptoms, and raising money for more effective detection and treatment methods.

I hope you will join us on October 30 at Midtown Park for this year's fun run. If you can't be there but would like to contribute, please make your check -------146.------- to the American Diabetes Society and mail it to our office address. If you want to register for the race or pledge online, please go to www.diabetes.org.

Thank you for your support.

Sincerely,

Matthew Saltmarsh
President, ADA

Wells 앞

저는 당신에게 당뇨병을 앓고 있는 아이들을 위한 돈을 모금하는 것을 돕기 위해 기부 서약을 해주거나 직접 참여를 요청하기 위해서 이 글을 쓰고 있습니다. 지난 몇 년간 우리는 당신처럼 친절한 사람들로부터 열광적인 반응을 얻은 재미있는 달리기 경주를 준비해왔습니다. 이미 알고 있듯이, 우리 단체는 그 질병에 대한 인식을 높이고, 대중들에게 그 질병의 초기 신호와 증상을 알리고, 더 효과적인 발견과 치료 방법에 대한 자금을 모으는 것에 대해 전념하고 있습니다.

저는 당신이 10월 30일, Midtown공원에서 열리는 올해의 펀 레이스에 참가하기를 바랍니다. 만약 당신이 올 수 없지만 기부를 하고 싶다면 American Diabetes Society에 지불 가능한 수표를 써서 그것을 우리 사무실 주소로 보내주세요. 만약 당신이 레이스나 서약에 온라인으로 등록하고 싶다면 홈페이지 www.diabetes.org를 방문해주세요.

당신의 지원에 감사드립니다.

진심을 담아

Matthew Saltmarsh
ADA 대표

어휘 enthusiastic 열정적인 kindheart 친절한 awareness 인식, 관심 detection 발견, 감지 treatment 치료 contribute 기부, 기증하다 register for 등록하다 pledge 서약

143

(A) I am writing to express my gratitude for helping us finish the event successfully.
(B) According to the expert, the number of diabetes patients is increasing dramatically.
(C) Diabetes can be prevented by eating healthily and exercising regularly.
(D) I am writing to invite you to participate in person or through a cash pledge to help raise money for children with diabetes.

해설 빈칸 다음의 내용들을 보면 질병의 신호와 증상을 알리고 치료법 개발을 위한 자금모금에 전념하고 있는 단체에서 글을 쓰고 있고, 두 번째 문단에서 올해의 행사에 참가해달라는 내용이 이어지고 있으므로, 자금 모금에 참가해달라고 요청하는 내용이 가장 적합하다. (A)는 행사가 끝난 상황에서 전달할 수 있는 내용이므로 시제가 맞지 않다.

(A) 저는 이 행사를 성공적으로 끝마칠 수 있게 도와주셔서 고맙다는 말을 전하려고 이 글을 쓰고 있습니다.
(B) 전문가에 따르면 당뇨병환자들의 수는 극적으로 증가하고 있습니다.
(C) 당뇨병은 몸에 좋은 음식을 먹고 운동을 규칙적으로 하는 것으로 예방할 수 있습니다.
(D) 저는 당신에게 당뇨병을 앓고 있는 아이들을 위한 돈을 모금하는 것을 돕기 위해 기부 서약을 해주거나 직접 참여를 요청하기 위해서 이 글을 쓰고 있습니다.

144

(A) draw
(B) draws
(C) have drawn
(D) drew

해설 '지난 몇 년 동안(Over the past few years)'이라 하였으므로 과거부터 지금까지 계속해서 달리기 행사를 조직해오고 있다는 걸 알 수 있다. 따라서 현재완료시제인 (C) have drawn이 정답이다.

145

(A) expressed
(B) scheduled
(C) designed
(D) committed

해설 질병에 대한 인식을 높이고, 대중들에게 그 질병의 초기 신호와 증상을 알리고, 더 효과적인 발견과 치료 방법에 대한 자금을 모으는 것에 '전념하고 있다'는 의미가 가장 어울리므로 정답은 (D) committed(전념하는)이다. 빈출표현인 be committed to -ing(~하는 것에 전념하고 있다)를 암기해두자.

146

(A) pay
(B) to pay
(C) payable
(D) payment

해설 '~한 수표를 작성해 달라'고 했으므로 payable(지불 가능한)이 적절하다.

101

Because it has so many skilled mechanics, Jimmy's Repair Shop has ------- the fierce competition from other repair shops in the region.
(A) withstands
(B) withstood
(C) withstanding
(D) to withstand

너무 많은 숙련된 정비공이 있기 때문에, Jimmy's Repair Shop은 그 지역이 다른 수리 가게로부터 심한 경쟁을 견뎌왔다.

해설 빈칸은 동사 has 뒤에 어울리는 형태의 단어가 올 자리이다. 우선 has to는 '~ 해야 한다'는 must의 의미이고, has pp는 현재완료형태로 '~해왔다'라는 의미이다. 앞부분의 해석을 보면 '많은 숙련된 정비공들을 보유하기 때문에'이므로 has to withstand the fierce competition(심한 경쟁을 견뎌야 한다)보다는 has withstood the fierce competition(심한 경쟁을 견뎌왔다)이 더 적절하다.

어휘 skilled 숙련된 mechanic 정비공 withstand 견디다 fierce 심한 competition 경쟁 region 지역

102

The development costs of the new product exceeded the budget, ------- it was still profitable because of the unexpected increase in sales.
(A) perhaps
(B) instead
(C) but
(D) next

신제품의 개발비용이 예산을 능가했지만, 여전히 판매량에서 예상치 못한 증가 때문에 수익성이 좋다.

해설 빈칸은 두 문장을 연결하는 등위접속사자리이며 선택지 중에 등위접속사는 (C) but밖에 없다.

어휘 exceed 능가하다 budget 예산 profitable 수익성 있는 unexpected 예상치 못한

103

That television commercial was part of the advertising campaign ------- main goal was to promote tourism of the country.
(A) that
(B) who
(C) whose
(D) which

TV 광고는 홍보 캠페인의 일부였고, 홍보 캠페인의 주요 목적은 그 나라의 관광업을 증진시키는 것이었다.

해설 앞의 명사 advertising campaign을 선행사로 취하고 뒤에 명사 goal이 다시 보이므로 소유격 관계대명사 whose가 유력해 보인다. 다시 한 번 정답인지 확인하기 위해 앞의 명사에 '~의'를 붙여 뒤의 명사와 연결해보면, '광고 캠페인의 주요 목적'이라고 의미연결이 매끄럽다. 빈칸에는 소유격 관계대명사 (C) whose가 들어갈 자리임을 알 수 있다.

어휘 commercial 광고 advertising campaign 광고 캠페인 goal 목표 promote 증진시키다, 촉진시키다 tourism 관광업

104

Holyfield Ltd. has hired an international advertising agency in an effort to strengthen its ------- in South Canada.
(A) description
(B) presence
(C) treatment
(D) purchase

Holyfield 사는 캐나다 남부에서 입지를 강화시키려는 노력으로 국제 광고 에이전시를 고용했다.

해설 빈칸은 동사 strengthen(강화시키다)의 목적어자리이다. 선택지 중 강화할 수 있는 대상은 (B) presence(입지, 존재)이다.

어휘 in an effort to ~하려는 노력으로 strengthen 강화시키다 presence 입지 description 설명 treatment 치료 purchase 구매

105

It is their top ------- to make sure that client information and transaction reports are kept safe at all times.
(A) priority
(B) summary
(C) variety
(D) segment

고객정보와 거래보고서가 항상 안전하게 있다는 걸 확실히 하는 게 그들의 최고 우선순위이다.

해설 빈칸은 top(최고의)과 어울리는 명사가 들어갈 자리이다. 선택지 중 적절한 의미의 단어는 (A) priority(우선순위)이다. top priority 최고 우선순위

어휘 top priority 최고 우선순위 transaction 거래 at all times 항상 summary 요약, 요약본 variety 다양성 segment 부분

106

Completion of next quarter's marketing proposals on time ------- hard work and dedication of the managers and team members.
(A) requiring
(B) is required
(C) require
(D) requires

다음 분기의 마케팅 제안서의 정시 작성은 매니저와 팀 멤버의 노고와 헌신을 요구합니다.

해설 빈칸은 문장의 동사자리이다. 주어가 단수이고 뒤에 목적어가 있으므로, 단수동사형태인 (D) requires가 정답이다.

어휘 quarter 분기 proposal 제안서 on time 정시 require 요구하다 hard work 노고 dedication 헌신

107

Employees are reminded to put away their belongings and office supplies neatly ------- leaving for the day.
(A) before
(B) beside
(C) between
(D) behind

직원들은 퇴근하기 전에 깔끔하게 그들의 소지품과 사무용품을 치우라고 상기됩니다.

해설 빈칸은 의미가 적절한 전치사 또는 접속사자리이다. 빈칸 뒤의 의미를 보면 leave for the day가 '퇴근하다'이므로, '퇴근하기 전에'와 의미연결이 되는 전치사 (A) before가 정답이다.

어휘 put away ~을 치우다 belongings 소지품 supply 사무용품 neatly 깔끔하게 leave for the day 퇴근하다

108

In order to make sure that all recently promoted managers deal with every problem properly, a ------- training program should be passed.
(A) spacious
(B) various
(C) rigorous
(D) considerate

최근에 승진된 매니저들이 모든 문제를 제대로 다루는 것을 확실히 하기 위하여, 엄격한 훈련 프로그램이 통과되어야 합니다.

해설 빈칸은 뒤의 training program(훈련 프로그램)을 수식하는 형용사자리이다. spacious(넓은), various(다양한), rigorous(엄격한), considerate(배려하는) 중에, various와 rigorous가 적절하다. 단, various는 복수명사와 어울리며, (C) rigorous가 문맥상 자연스럽다. a rigorous training program 엄격한 훈련 프로그램

어휘 in order to ~하기 위하여 deal with ~을 다루다, 처리하다 properly 제대로 spacious 공간이 넓은 various 다양한 rigorous 엄격한 considerate 사려 깊은

109

Please ------- Ms. Caitlin's e-mail dated June 2 to schedule the date of our following seminar on the new safety regulations.
(A) consult
(B) inquire
(C) invest
(D) look

새로운 안전규정에 관한 다음 세미나의 날짜 일정을 잡기 위하여, 6월 2일에 보내진 Caitlin 씨의 이메일을 참조하십시오.

해설 빈칸은 email을 목적어로 취하는 동사자리이다. inquire(문의하다), look(보다)은 자동사로 오답이다. invest는 '투자하다'의 의미로 이메일과는 의미연결이 적절하지 않다. consult는 '참조하다(사물목적어), 상담하다(사람목적어)'로 쓰이며, consult Ms. Caitlin's e-mail은 Caitlin 씨의 이메일을 참조하다'라는 의미이다.

어휘 inquire 문의하다 consult 상담하다, 참조하다 invest 투자하다 safety regulation 안전 규정

110

Ms. Gao has ------- for several days before making her decision to accept the other company's job offer.
(A) collaborate
(B) deliberated
(C) established
(D) designated

Gao 씨는 다른 회사의 일자리 제안을 수용하는 결정을 하기 전에 며칠을 심사숙고했다.

해설 빈칸 뒤의 for several days(며칠 동안)를 통해 빈칸은 목적어가 필요 없는 자동사자리라는 것을 알 수 있다. collaborate(협력하다), deliberate(심사숙고하다), establish(설립하다), designate(지정하다) 중에, 자동사는 collaborate와 deliberate이다. 이 둘 중 전체적인 해석이 어울리는 선택지는 deliberate(심사숙고하다)가 정답이다.

어휘 collaborate 협동하다 deliberate 심사숙고하다 establish 설립하다 designate 지정하다 make decisions 결정하다 accept 수락하다 job offer 일자리 제안

111

The KMDH Electronic Company will begin production of its new line as soon as the necessary equipment ------- at the plant in Busan.
(A) arrive
(B) arrived
(C) arrives
(D) will arrive

KMDH Electronic Company는 필수적인 장비가 Busan 공장에 도착하자마자 새로운 라인의 생산을 시작할 것입니다.

해설 빈칸은 as soon as로 시작하는 문장에 적절한 동사형태가 들어갈 자리이다. as soon as는 시간을 나타내는 부사절을 이끄는 접속사로, 나머지 문장의 시제가 미래라도 as soon as 부사절의 시제는 현재 또는 현재완료가 되어야 한다. 그래서 나머지 문장이 will begin(시작할 것이다)으로 미래시제이지만, 빈칸은 현재시제를 나타내는 arrives가 정답이다. 주어가 equipment(장비)로 셀 수 없는 명사(불가산명사)이므로 동사 arrive와 수일치되지 않는다.

어휘 production 생산 as soon as ~하자마자 necessary 필수적인 equipment 장비 plant 공장

112

Free blood testing by the local Physical Center will ------- in the community center from 3:30 P.M. until 6:00 P.M. this Friday.
(A) be holding
(B) have held
(C) hold
(D) be held

지역 Physical Center에 의한 무료 혈액검사는 이번 주 금요일 오후 3시 30분부터 저녁 6시까지 문화회관에서 열릴 것입니다.

해설 빈칸은 문장의 동사가 들어갈 자리이다. hold는 타동사로 '개최하다, 주최하다'의 의미가 있으며 빈칸 뒤에 목적어가 없으므로 수동형태가 되어야 한다. 그래서 선택지 중 수동형태인 (D) be held가 정답이다.

어휘 blood testing 혈액 검사 be held 개최되다, 열리다 community center 문화회관

ACTUAL TEST 01 ACTUAL TEST 02 ACTUAL TEST 03 ACTUAL TEST 04 ACTUAL TEST 05

113

We can offer you a complete refund as long as you return the
------- product along with a copy of the purchase receipt.
(A) defective
(B) high
(C) underlying
(D) untrue

구매영수증과 함께 결함 있는 제품을 반품하는 한, 우리는 당신에게 전액 환불을 해 드릴 수 있습니다.

해설 빈칸은 뒤의 product(제품)와 의미연결이 적절한 형용사가 들어갈 자리이다. 선택지 중 defective(결함 있는)가 의미상 적절하다.

어휘 as long as ~ 하는 한 return 반납하다, 반품하다 defective 결함 있는 underlying 근본적인 untrue 사실이 아닌, 허위의

114

Malcolm Tech Inc. has announced that it will relocate its
company offices from San Francisco to Chicago ------- April.
(A) with
(B) in
(C) on
(D) at

Malcolm Tech 회사는 4월에 San Francisco에서 Chicago로 사무실을 옮긴다고 발표했다.

해설 빈칸은 뒤의 April(4월)과 의미연결이 어울리는 전치사가 들어갈 자리이다. '월'과 어울리는 전치사는 in임을 알면 쉽게 해결 가능하다.

어휘 announce 발표하다 relocate 옮기다, 이전하다

115

My family and I would like to give our thanks to you for -------
to our request so quickly.
(A) responding
(B) responds
(C) respond
(D) responded

우리 가족과 나는 아주 빠르게 요청을 해준 당신에게 감사를 표현하고 싶습니다.

해설 빈칸은 전치사 뒤에 어울리는 형태의 단어가 들어갈 자리이다. 자동사인 respond는 전치사 뒤에 동명사로 쓰이더라도 전치사 to를 가질 수 있다. 그래서 정답은 (A) responding이다.

어휘 respond to ~에 응답하다 request 요청 quickly 빠르게

120

116

Please contact the network administrator since many people have ------- that they cannot access their e-mail accounts.
(A) compensated
(B) complained
(C) collected
(D) complimented

많은 사람들이 그들의 계정에 접근할 수 없다고 불평했기 때문에, 네트워크 관리자에게 연락해주십시오.

해설 문장 구조상 바로 뒤에 that절을 받아야 하므로, 선택지 중 that절을 받는 단어는 complain이다. <complain that S V> that 이하를 불평하다

어휘 administrator 관리자 compensate 보상하다 complain 불평하다 collect 모으다 compliment 칭찬하다 account 계정

117

Reimbursements will not be processed ------- a signed expense form and valid receipt showing that the amount has been paid.
(A) without
(B) across
(C) besides
(D) oxcopt

금액이 지불되었다는 것을 보여주는 유효한 영수증과 서명된 경비양식 없이는 상환은 처리되지 않을 것입니다.

해설 빈칸은 a signed expense form and valid receipt(서명된 비용 양식서와 유효한 영수증)와 will not be processed(처리되지 않을 것이다)를 적절하게 연결해주는 전치사자리이다. 이 두 부분의 의미연결에는 without(~없이)이 적절하다. across ~맞은편에 besides ~뿐만 아니라 except ~ 제외하고

어휘 reimbursement 상환, 환불 process 처리하다 signed 서명된 valid 유효한

118

A review article on the ------- aspects of Chia seed was recently published in the magazine Healthy Life.
(A) benefited
(B) beneficial
(C) benefit
(D) beneficially

Chia 씨앗의 유익한 측면의 후기가 잡지 La Fourchette에 최근에 출판되었다.

해설 빈칸은 명사 aspects(측면)와 의미가 어울리는 형용사자리이다. benefited(혜택을 받은), beneficial(유익한) 중에 의미 연결이 적절한 선택지는 beneficial이다. the beneficial aspects 유익한 측면

어휘 beneficial 유익한 benefit 혜택, 이익, 편익 recently 최근에 publish 출판하다 aspect 측면

ACTUAL TEST 01 ACTUAL TEST 02 ACTUAL TEST 03 ACTUAL TEST 04 ACTUAL TEST 05

119

Unfortunately, the construction is not moving forward
------- the proposal for the footbridge between the two
terminal buildings was rejected by the Portland Airport
Administration.
(A) while
(B) unless
(C) until
(D) because

불행하게도, 두 개의 터미널 빌딩 사이의 징검다리를 위한 제안서가 Portland Airport Administration에 의해서 거절되었기 때문에, 건설은 더 이상 진척되지 않았다.

해설 빈칸은 앞뒤 문장을 매끄럽게 연결해줄 접속사자리이다. 빈칸 앞 문장은 '공사가 진행되지 않고 있다'이고, 뒤 문장은 '제안서가 거절되었다'이므로 '제안서가 거절되었기 때문에 공사가 진행되지 못하고 있다.'가 의미 연결이 자연스럽다.

어휘 unfortunately 불행하게도 move forward 진행하다 proposal 제안서 footbridge 징검다리 reject 거절하다 while ~동안, 반면에 unless 만약 ~하지 않는다면

120

According to today's press release, Bio Cosmetics ------- to
open a plant in Toronto within the next three years.
(A) intends
(B) initiates
(C) considers
(D) previews

오늘자 일간지에 따르면, Wii Cosmetis는 3년 내로 Toronto에 공장을 개장할 작정이다.

해설 빈칸의 뒤의 to부정사를 목적어로 취하는 동사자리이다. 선택지 중 intend가 대표적으로 to부정사를 목적어로 취하는 동사이다. consider는 동명사를 목적어로 가지는 대표적인 동사이이다.

121

------- an elementary school and then a women's health club,
the red brick building will be completely renovated before
opening as Victory High School.
(A) Directly
(B) Before
(C) Formerly
(D) Since

이전에 초등학교와 여성 체육관과 벽돌 건물은 Victory High School로서 개장 전에 완전히 개조될 것입니다.

해설 빈칸은 뒤의 '학교와 체육관'과 의미연결이 적절한 단어가 들어갈 자리이다. 문맥상 '이전에(formerly) 초등학교 그리고 체육관이었던, 벽돌 건물이 개조될 것이다'가 의미 연결이 매끄럽다.

어휘 formerly 이전에 directly 직접적으로 brick 벽돌 renovate 개조하다 opening 개장

122

------- of a central apartment building where fire broke out on Thursday night have been allowed to return to their units.
(A) Resided
(B) Resides
(C) Residing
(D) Residents

목요일 밤에 화재가 발생했던 중앙 아파트 거주민들은 그들의 아파트로 돌아오라고 허락되었다.

해설 빈칸은 문장의 앞에 주어로 올 명사자리이다. 동사가 have been이기 때문에 복수주어가 와야 하므로 Residents(거주민들)이 정답이다.

어휘 resident 거주민 break out 발생하다 reside 살다, 거주하다

123

The White Pages lists addresses and telephone numbers of business establishments in the city, including ------- outside the city limits.
(A) their
(B) that
(C) them
(D) those

White Pages는 도시 경계 밖을 포함하여 도시 내에 있는 회사들의 주소와 전화번호를 나열한다.

해설 빈칸은 한 문장에서 같은 어구가 반복될 때 다른 것을 대신해서 받는 지시대명사가 들어갈 자리이다. 단수이면 that, 복수이면 those를 쓴다. 본문에서는 앞의 '회사들의 주소와 전화번호들'을 받는 의미로 복수이므로 (D) those가 정답이다.

어휘 list 나열하다 establishment 회사 including ~을 포함하여 city limit 시 경계

124

Please ------- the maintenance crew that repairs of the equipment must be done no later than next Monday.
(A) confirm
(B) inform
(C) neglect
(D) refer

유지보수 직원에게 장비 수리가 늦어도 다음 주 월요일까지는 완료되어야 한다는 것을 알려주십시오.

해설 빈칸은 사람목적어를 취하고 뒤에 that절의 구조를 갖는 동사자리이다. 다행히 선택지 중 inform이 이러한 구조를 취한다. <inform + 사람 + that + 주어 + 동사> 사람에게 that 이하를 알리다

어휘 confirm 확인하다 inform 알리다 neglect 방치하다, 등한시하다 refer 참조하다 crew 직원 no later than 늦어도 ~까지

125

As soon as all passengers board the ferry, they must show their tickets ------- keep their ticket stubs as proof of payment.
(A) so
(B) as
(C) and
(D) both

승객들이 여객선에 탑승하자마자, 그들은 티켓을 보여주어야 하고 구매의 증거로서 입장권의 반쪽을 보관해야 한다.

해설 빈칸은 앞의 show their tickets와 뒤의 keep their ticket stubs를 나란히 연결하는 등위접속사인 and가 정답이다.

어휘 board 탑승하다 ferry 여객선 stub 반쪽 proof 증거

126

If Ms. Elliot had not filled in the new agreement completely, the landlord of the property ------- back to the old agreement.
(A) have reverted
(B) will revert
(C) would have reverted
(D) being revert

만약 Elliot 씨가 새로운 합의서를 완전히 작성하지 않았다면, 부동산 집주인은 이전의 합의서를 돌이켜 보지 않았을 것이다.

해설 빈칸은 가정법의 어울리는 동사형태가 들어갈 자리이다. 앞의 if절을 보면 had not filed로 <if + 주어+ had pp>의 가정법 과거완료임을 알 수 있다. 가정법 과거완료는 <if + 주어 + had pp, 주어 + would [could, should, might] have pp>의 형태이다.

어휘 fill in ~을 작성하다 completely 완전히 landlord 집주인 property 부동산 revert 되돌아가다

127

The advertising team worked ------- over the weekend to complete the project by the deadline.
(A) hardly
(B) heavily
(C) diligently
(D) repeatedly

광고 팀은 마감일까지 프로젝트를 마치기 위하여 주말 동안 근면 성실하게 일했다.

해설 문맥상 주말 동안 근면 성실하게 일했다는 내용이 어울리므로 정답은 (C)이다.

어휘 hardly 거의 ~않다 heavily 상당히 diligently 근면 성실하게 repeatedly 반복적으로 deadline 마감일

128

The Institute of Arts and Sciences ------- $ 35,000 to the Public Broadcasting corporation this quarter.
(A) is donated
(B) was donated
(C) has donated
(D) has been donated

Institute of Arts and Sciences는 이번 분기에 Public Broadcasting corporation에 35,000달러를 기부했다.

해설 빈칸은 문장에서 형태가 적절한 동사가 들어갈 자리이다. 빈칸 뒤에 금액을 나타내는 목적어($ 35,000)가 있으므로 능동의 구조가 되어야 하므로 정답은 (C) has donated이다.

어휘 donate 기부하다 corporation 회사 quarter 분기

129

Mr. Richards was ------- to start his managerial research because he had not yet received enough funding for it.
(A) hesitantly
(B) hesitant
(C) hesitated
(D) hesitation

Richards 씨는 그가 아직 충분한 자금을 받지 못했기 때문에, 그의 경영상의 조사를 시작하는 것을 망설였다.

해설 빈칸은 be동사 was 뒤에 들어갈 적절한 단어가 와야 한다. be동사 뒤에 형용사가 올 수도 있고, 수동형이 올 수도 있다. 그러나 선택지의 단어 hesitate(주저하다)는 자동사로 수동태가 될 수 없으므로, 형용사인 hesitant(망설이는, 머뭇거리는)이 정답이다.

어휘 hesitantly 머뭇거리며, 우물거리며 hesitant 주저하는 hesitation 주저, 망설임 managerial 경영의 not yet 아직 ~ 않다 enough 충분한 funding 자금

130

Phil McKnight's ability to increase revenue through team coaching and training is well known ------- the business world.
(A) throughout
(B) regarding
(C) aboard
(D) toward

팀 코칭과 훈련을 통해 수익을 증가시키는 Phil McKnight의 노력은 업계 전반에 걸쳐 잘 알려져 있다.

해설 빈칸은 뒤의 the business world(업계)와 의미가 어울리는 전치사가 들어갈 자리이다. 빈칸 앞부분은 is well known(잘 알려져 있다)이므로, '업계 전반에 걸쳐 잘 알려져 있다'는 의미로 (A) throughout이 정답이다.

어휘 ability 능력 be well known ~으로 유명하다 throughout 곳곳에, 도처에, 전반에 regarding 관하여 toward 향하여, 쪽으로

Questions 131-134 refer to the following advertisement.

CERN Medical Service has begun to ------- our new services **131.** and longer opening hours to help better serve our customers. We have added 5 new locations ------- the city, where our **132.** patients can access our full range of services. -------. However, **133.** we have added more laboratory space to handle patient blood analysis from our new locations. All locations will now be ------- **134.** from 7 A.M. until 10 P.M. Monday to Friday, and Saturday and Sundays from 11 A.M. to 3 P.M. For more information on all our services, along with the addresses to the new locations, please visit us on the web at www.medical-service.com.

CERN Medical Service는 더 좋은 고객 서비스를 제공하기 위해 새로운 서비스와 업무시간 연장을 시작했습니다. 우리는 도시 전역에 5개의 새로운 지점을 추가하였고 그곳에서 환자들이 우리의 서비스를 이용할 수 있습니다. 우리 본사 건물은 여전히 Orface Road에 있습니다. 하지만 우리의 새로운 지점에서 온 환자들의 혈액 분석을 위해 더 많은 실험공간을 추가했습니다. 모든 지점은 월요일부터 금요일에는 아침 7시부터 밤 10시, 토요일과 일요일에는 아침 11시부터 오후 3시까지 문을 열 것입니다. 새로운 지점의 주소와 우리 서비스에 대해 더 정보가 필요하시다면 홈페이지 www.medical-service.com을 방문해주십시오.

어휘 serve 제공하다, 봉사하다 patient 환자 range 범위 laboratory 실험실 analysis 분석

131
(A) find out
(B) roll out
(C) agree with
(D) meet with

해설 '새로운 서비스(new services)'를 목적어로 취할 수 있는 동사는 (B) roll out(출시하다)이다.

132
(A) among
(B) onto
(C) off
(D) across

해설 도시 전역에 5개의 지점을 추가했다는 의미가 가장 적절하므로 장소를 이야기해줄 수 있는 (D) across(전체에 걸쳐)가 정답이다.

133
(A) CERN Medical Service has been continually trying to provide better service.
(B) Our main building is still on Orface Road.
(C) These new locations are conveniently located.
(D) Our patients will be more satisfied with this service.

해설 빈칸 다음 문장에서 '그러나(However)'라는 역접부사를 사용하여 실험실 공간을 추가했다는 변경사항을 언급하고 있으므로 빈칸에는 그와 반대의 의미를 나타내도록 본사는 여전히(still) 기존의 지역에 위치하고 있다는 문장이 가장 적절하므로 정답은 (B)이다.

(A) CERN Medical Service는 더 나은 서비스를 제공하기 위해 지속적으로 노력해왔다.
(B) 우리 본사 건물은 여전히 Orface Road에 있습니다.
(C) 새로운 위치들은 편리한 곳에 위치해 있습니다.
(D) 우리 환자들은 이 서비스에 더 만족할 것입니다.

134
(A) progress
(B) open
(C) potential
(D) limited

해설 모든 지점들에서의 근무시간을 언급하고 있으므로 지점들이 '열리다'는 의미가 가장 적절하므로 정답은 (B) open(열린)이다.

Hostile Takeover Brings Judicial Review

California (27 November) - Since Sam Cleaning ------- Waste
135.
Removal Service last week in a hostile takeover, Washington
lawmakers have been ------- watching the court case developing
136.
against Sam Cleaning and the U.S. government. If the takeover
is allowed to go on, -------. The government is concerned that
137.
the lack of competition could ------- a 30% increase in bills for
138.
hospital waste within the next 5 years.

적대적 인수는 사법 심사를 초래했다

California (11월 27일) – Sam Cleaning
이 지난주에 적대적인 기업인수로 Waste
Removal Service를 취득한 후 워싱턴의
입법자들은 Sam Cleaning과 미국 정부에
대한 소송 사건을 주의 깊게 주시해왔다.
만일 인수가 진행하도록 허용된다면, Sam
Cleaning은 남서쪽 해안에 있는 의료 폐기
물 시장에 남아 있는 유일한 회사가 될 것
이다. 정부는 경쟁 부족으로 인해 향후 5
년 이내에 병원 폐기물에 대한 청구금액이
30프로 증가로 이어질 수 있을 것으로 염
려하고 있다.

어휘 hostile 적대적인 takeover 인수, 탈취 lawmaker 입법자 concern 염려하다 lack of 부족, 결핍 competition 경쟁

135 (A) generated
(B) informed
(C) acquired
(D) merged

해설 San Diego가 Waste Removal Service를 '인수[취득]했다'는 의미가 필요하다. 비슷한 의미 같아 보이겠지만 (D)의 merged(
합병했다)는 자동사라서 목적어를 바로 데리고 나올 수 없어 전치사 with와 함께 사용하는 동사이므로 적절하지 않다. 따라서 정답은
(C) acquired(인수했다)이다.

136 (A) closed
(B) close
(C) closing
(D) closely

해설 watching이라는 형용사의 앞자리가 비어 있으므로 형용사를 수식할 수 있는 부사를 골라야 한다. (B) close도 부사로의 쓰임이
있지만 '가깝게'의 의미이므로 어울리지 않고, 면밀하게 주시하고 있다는 의미를 만들어주는 (D) closely가 정답이다.

137
(A) Sam Cleaning will be the best medical waste disposal company in the region.
(B) Jobs and salaries of Waste Removal Service's employees will remain same.
(C) The processing procedure of a takeover will start immediately.
(D) Sam Cleaning will be the only company left in the market of medical waste disposal on the southwest coast.

해설 빈칸 다음의 문장에서 '경쟁의 부족(the lack of competition)'이 폐기물 처리 금액에서의 증가를 야기할 수 있을 것'이라고 했으므로, '남서쪽 해안에 있는 의료 폐기물 시장에 남아 있는 유일한 회사(the only company left in the market of medical waste disposal on the southwest coast)'가 될 거라는 문장이 가장 적절하다. 따라서 정답은 (D)이다.

(A) Sam Cleaning은 지역에서 최고의 의료 폐기물 처리 회사가 될 것이다.
(B) Removal Service 직원들의 업무와 봉급은 똑같이 유지될 것이다.
(C) 인수의 처리 절차는 즉시 시작될 것이다.
(D) Sam Cleaning은 남서쪽 해안에 있는 의료 폐기물 시장에 남아 있는 유일한 회사가 될 것이다.

138
(A) lead to
(B) retrieve
(C) grant
(D) comment on

해설 주어인 '경쟁의 부족(the lack of competition)'이 빈칸 뒤의 목적어인 '청구금액에서의 30프로의 증가(a 30% increase in bills)'의 원인이 되므로. 증가라는 결과로 '이어지게 되다'라는 의미가 가장 어울린다. 따라서 정답은 (A) lead to(~로 이어지다)이다.

Questions 139-142 refer to the following letter.

Alabama Ski and Sports Club Dear Mr. Radnor, This is to ------- receipt of your membership check for $65 **139.** last July 20 and to welcome you to ASSC. -------. We are **140.** also allocating 5% of your membership fee to our designated beneficiary, the Boys and Girls Club of Alabama. In a recent meeting with our travel agency partners, however, we ------- that they can no longer afford to extend the 30% **141.** discount to our members. Instead, they are willing to grant a 25% discount to anyone who presents their ASSC card. Other than this slight change, all other membership benefits still hold. Rest assured that we are ------- trying to develop **142.** partnerships with other service providers for the benefit of our members. Again, thanks for joining ASSC and we look forward to seeing you at our events. Sincerely, Jim Cassidy	Alabama 스키 앤 스포츠 클럽 Radnor 씨께, 이것은 지난 7월 20일 당신의 65달러 회원증의 영수증을 인정하기 위한 것과 ASSC로의 환영을 위한 것입니다. 새로운 회원으로서 당신은 우리가 공지했던 모든 특권을 누릴 자격이 있습니다. 우리는 또한 회비의 5%를 우리 지정 수익자인 Boys and Girls Club of Alabama에 할당하고 있습니다. 하지만 최근 저희 여행사와의 회의에서 회원들에게 더 이상 30%의 할인 혜택을 줄 수 없다고 들었습니다. 대신에 그들은 누구든지 자신의 ASSC 카드를 제시하는 사람들에게 25% 할인을 기꺼이 제공할 것입니다. 이 약간의 변화 외에 모든 다른 회원들의 이익은 여전히 남아 있습니다. 우리는 우리의 회원님들의 복지를 위해 다른 서비스 제공자들과 협력 관계를 개발하려고 지속적으로 노력하고 있으니 안심하시기 바랍니다. 다시 한 번, ASSC에 합류해 주셔서 감사드리고 우리 행사에서 뵙기를 기대합니다. 진심을 담아 Jim Cassidy

어휘 receipt 영수증 allocate 할당하다 designated beneficiary 지정된 수령인 recent 최근의 be willing to 기꺼이 ~하다 grant 승인하다 slight 약간의 assure 장담하다

139
(A) revlew
(B) submit
(C) acknowledge
(D) publish

해설 '멤버십 수표(your membership check)'를 목적어로 취할 수 있는 동사를 골라야 한다. 따라서 가장 적절한 동사는 (C) ac-knowledge(인정하다)이다. acknowledge receipt of는 '~를 받았음을 알리다'는 표현이다.

140
(A) Our annual membership fee increased nearly 10 percent this year.
(B) If your friend decides to join the ASSC, you will be eligible for additional membership benefits.
(C) As a new member, you are entitled to all the privileges we mentioned in our notice.
(D) ASSC has added new equipment and upgraded the facility.

해설 빈칸 앞의 문장에 멤버십 수표를 받았음을 알리면서 'ASSC에 가입한 걸 환영하다(welcome you to ASSC)라고 했으므로, 가입한 신규멤버에게 보내는 편지글이고 빈칸 다음의 문장에 당신의 멤버십 요금을 특정 단체에 기부한다는 내용이 이어지고 있다. 따라서 '새로운 회원으로서 우리가 공지했던 모든 특권을 누릴 자격이 있다(As a new member, you are entitled to all the privileges we mentioned in our notice)'는 내용이 가장 적절하므로 정답은 (C)이다.

(A) 우리의 연간 회원비는 올해 거의 10퍼센트 증가하였습니다.
(B) 만약 당신의 친구가 ASSC에 가입하기를 결정했다면, 당신은 추가회원 혜택을 받을 자격이 있습니다.
(C) 새로운 회원으로서 당신은 우리가 공지했던 모든 특권을 누릴 자격이 있습니다.
(D) ASSC는 새로운 창비를 추가했고 시설들을 업그레이드 했습니다.

141
(A) tells
(B) are telling
(C) were told
(D) told

해설 여행사 파트너와의 최근 미팅에서 더 이상 30프로의 할인을 제공할 수가 없다는 that 이하의 내용을 우리가 '듣게 되었다'는 것을 고객에서 알려주고 있으므로, 수동태이자 과거시제인 (C) were told가 정답이다.

142
(A) continuously
(B) continuous
(C) continuity
(D) continue

해설 be동사의 보어로 사용된 trying이라는 형용사의 앞자리가 비었으므로 형용사를 수식해 줄 수 있도록 부사를 골라야 한다. 따라서 정답은 (A) continuously이다.

Questions 143-146 refer to the following e-mail.

To: Colin Falconer <colin@aol.com>

From: David Faber <davidfaber33@buckhead.com>

Date: Sept. 8

Subject: Your inquiry

Dear Mr. Falconer,

Thank you for your inquiry about our ongoing promotion. Based on the details you have provided, we are pleased to recommend a package ------- of three family-sized pizzas, five plates of
143.
pasta, and three servings of Chicken Marsala with bottomless servings of our popular iced tea. The total bill would ------- cost
144.
you $200, but with our ongoing promotion, that will go down to $160 after the 20% discount.

Your preferred date of September 15 falls on a Friday, which is a busy day for Buckhead Diner. More so, you plan to come in at 7 P.M. which is the peak time of our operations. -------. Please call
145.
us two hours before your arrival so that we can ------- the seats
146.
for your party of seven. We look forward to seeing you and your friends at Buckhead Diner.

Sincerely yours,

David Faber
General Manager
Buckhead Diner

수신: Colin Falconer ⟨colin@aol.com⟩
발신: David Faber ⟨davidfaber33@buckhead.com⟩
날짜: 9월 8일
세목: 귀하의 요청

Falconer 씨께

우리의 진행 중인 할인 행사에 대한 문의에 감사드립니다. 당신이 제공한 세부 사항에 근거하여 우리는 기꺼이 패밀리 사이즈 피자 3판, 파스타 5개 그리고 아이스티가 무한으로 제공되는 Chiken Marsala3인분을 추천해 드리고 싶습니다. 총 가격은 원래는 200달러이지만 행사 중이기 때문에 20프로 할인되어 160달러가 될 것입니다.

당신이 원하시는 날짜는 Buckhed Diner의 바쁜 날인 9월 15일 금요일입니다. 더욱이 당신은 우리의 주문이 가장 바쁜 피크시간인 7시에 오기를 계획하고 있습니다. 그러므로 우리는 당일에 당신의 예약을 확인할 것을 권고드립니다. 도착하기 2시간 전에 전화를 주시면 우리는 7시 파티를 위해 자리를 준비해 둘 수 있습니다. 우리는 당신과 당신의 친구 분들을 Buckhead Diner에서 뵙기를 기대하고 있습니다.

진심을 담아

David Faber
총지배인
Buckhead Diner

어휘 inquiry 문의 ongoing 계속 진행 중인 be pleased to 기꺼이 ~하다 bottomless 무한한 look forward to ~을 기대하다

143
(A) consisting
(B) consist
(C) consisted
(D) to consist

해설 빈칸 앞에 있는 목적어를 수식해 줄 수 있는 단어가 필요하다. (D) to consist는 '구성되기 위해서'는 '구성될'이라는 의미이고 (A) consisting은 '~로 구성된'이므로 정답은 (A) consisting이다.

144
(A) recently
(B) fairly
(C) openly
(D) normally

해설 빈칸 뒤의 동사 'cost(비용을 들게 하다)'를 수식할 부사를 골라야 한다. (A) recently(최근에)는 과거나 과거완료를 수식할 수 있으므로 적절하지 못하다. '보통(일반적으로)은 200달러의 비용이 들지만 진행 중인 행사로 인해 160달러로 할인된다'는 의미가 가장 적절하므로 정답은 (D) normally(보통, 일반적으로)이다.

145
(A) The usual peak time for Buckhead Diner is between 6 P.M.-9 P.M.
(B) In peak times, our restaurant may be very busy.
(C) Therefore, we request that you confirm your reservation on the same day.
(D) Buckhead Diner is the most popular restaurant in the area.

해설 앞 문장에는 고객이 예약한 시간이 피크시간대라는 내용이 있고, 피크시간대에 예약을 했으니 '그래서 당일에 다시 한 번 예약을 확실하게 확인해 달라'는 요청과 두 시간 전에 미리 전화해달라는 요청이 이어지는 것이 가장 적절한 흐름이다. 따라서 정답은 (C)이다.

(A) Buckhead Diner의 보통 피크 타임은 6시부터 9시까지입니다.
(B) 피크타임에 우리 레스토랑은 매우 바쁠 것입니다.
(C) 그러므로 우리는 당일에 당신의 예약을 확인할 것을 권고드립니다.
(D) Buckhead Diner는 그 지역에가 가장 유명한 레스토랑입니다.

146
(A) keep up with
(B) take on
(C) deal with
(D) set aside

해설 7명의 일행을 위해서 자리를 따로 마련할 수 있도록 미리 전화를 달라고 했으므로, 정답은 (D) set aside(확보하다, 따로 챙겨두다)

101

Suzan Fridley was offered the human resources director position last Thursday ------- has not yet accepted it.
(A) while
(B) unless
(C) but
(D) even if

Suzan Friedley 씨는 지난 목요일에 인사부장 직책을 제안받았지만 아직 수락하지 않았다.

해설 앞부분은 was offered(제안을 받았다), 뒷부분 has not yet accepted(승낙하지 않았다)이다. 문맥상 '그러나'라는 의미의 (C) but이 적절하다.

어휘 position 직책 while ~동안, 반면에 unless 만약 ~하지 않는다면 even if 비록 ~하지 않는다면

102

------- the lanes of St. Anthony Street should result in a 15 minutes decrease in commuting hours for traffic in and out of the city.
(A) Expanding
(B) Expansive
(C) Expand
(D) Expansion

St. Anthony거리의 도로 확장은 도시의 안과 밖에 몇 시간 동안 통근 시간을 15분 정도 줄여주는 결과를 초래해야 합니다.

해설 빈칸은 문장의 주어자리이다. 빈칸 뒤에 명사 the lanes가 바로 나오므로, 뒤의 명사를 목적어로 취하면서 주어 역할을 해야 하므로 동명사인 (A) Expanding이 정답이 된다.

어휘 expand 확장하다 result in ~을 초래하다 decrease 감소하다 commute 통근하다 expansive 포괄적인, 광범위한 expansion 확장, 확대

103

The vehicle manufacturer ------- that the filter be changed every year or 25,000 miles.
(A) recognizes
(B) remembers
(C) registers
(D) recommends

차량 제조업체는 필터가 매년 또는 25,000마일마다 변경되어야 한다고 권고합니다.

해설 빈칸은 that절을 목적어로 취하고 뒤에 the filter (should) be의 형태가 될 수 있는 동사가 들어갈 자리이다. 이 두 가지 요건을 충족시키는 단어는 recommend(권유하다)이다.

어휘 recognize 인정하다, 인지하다 register 등록하다 recommend 추천하다, 권유하다 vehicle 차량

104 The latest spring collection designed by Charles Elster is available for a ------- time only.
(A) limited
(B) limit
(C) limiting
(D) limits

Charles Elster에 의해 디자인된 최근 봄 컬렉션은 제한된 시간 동안만 이용 가능합니다.

해설 빈칸은 명사 time 앞에 어울리는 형용사가 들어갈 자리이다. 선택지 중 '제한된'의 의미인 (A) limited가 정답이다.
어휘 latest 최신의 limited 제한된

105 All new employees preparing their first report are encouraged to help ------- by writing together.
(A) whichever
(B) each
(C) either
(D) one another

첫 보고서를 준비하는 모든 신입직원들은 함께 작성함으로써 서로서로 도울 것으로 권고됩니다.

해설 빈칸은 동사 help의 목적어자리이다. 문맥상 '서로서로'라는 의미의 (D) one another가 적절하다.
어휘 prepare 준비하다 encourage 권고하다 whichever 무엇이든지 each 각각 one another 서로서로

106 In the first quarter of 2017, Norwich Kitchenware Company reported a 30 percent increase ------- profits despite the fact that domestic sales declined.
(A) off
(B) in
(C) up
(D) at

2017년의 첫 분기에, Norwich Kitchenware 회사는 국내 판매가 감소된다는 사실에도 불구하고 30퍼센트 수익 증가를 보고했습니다.

해설 빈칸은 앞의 명사 increase와 어울리는 전치사가 들어갈 자리이다. '~에서의 증가'라는 의미로 increase in을 알아두면 쉽게 해결된다.
어휘 profit 수익 despite ~에도 불구하고 the fact that ~라는 사실 domestic sales 국내 판매 decline 감소하다

ACTUAL TEST 01 ACTUAL TEST 02 ACTUAL TEST 03 ACTUAL TEST 04 ACTUAL TEST 05

107

All clients in the waiting room are ------- to use an outlet to charge their laptop computer batteries or any other electronic device they may have with them.
(A) pending
(B) expectant
(C) customary
(D) welcome

대기실에 있는 모든 고객들은 그들이 소지하고 있을 수도 있는 노트북 배터리나 다른 전자 장비를 충전하기 위하여 콘센트를 사용해도 됩니다.

해설 빈칸은 앞의 be동사 are에 의미연결이 적절한 형용사가 들어갈 자리이다. be welcome to(마음대로 ~하다)를 알아두면 해결이 간단하다.

어휘 outlet 콘센트 charge 충전하다 pending 미확정의 expectant 기대하는 customary 관례적인, 습관적인

108

This free web site is of use to those ------- familiar with the Korean and Chinese language.
(A) less
(B) little
(C) fewer
(D) none

이 무료 웹사이트는 한국어와 중국어에 능숙하지 않은 사람들에게 유용합니다.

해설 빈칸은 뒤의 형용사 familiar와 의미가 어울리는 부사자리이다. less는 '덜'이라는 의미로 연결이 적절해 보인다. little, fewer는 형용사로 뒤에 명사가 필요하고, none은 단독으로 쓰이는 단어이다.

어휘 familiar with ~와 익숙한 of use to ~에게 유용한

109

Downpours over the last two weeks ------- the city government from reinforcing patrolling along riverbanks.
(A) will prevent
(B) has prevented
(C) prevented
(D) have prevented

지난 2주간의 폭우는 시 정부가 강둑을 따라 순찰을 강화하는 것을 막았다.

해설 빈칸은 적절한 형태의 동사가 들어갈 자리이다. 빈칸 앞에 over the last two weeks(지난 2주 동안)는 현재완료와 어울린다. 주어가 복수이므로 has prevented는 수일치가 맞지 않으며, 정답은 (D) have prevented이다.

어휘 downpour 폭우 prevent N from 명사가 ~하는 것을 막다 reinforce 강화하다 patrol 순찰을 돌다 riverbank 강둑

110

It Is ------- for people to raise concerns about the way we are extracting certain kinds of natural resources.
(A) reasoning
(B) reasonable
(C) reasoned
(D) reasonably

사람들이 특정한 종류의 천연자원을 추출하는 방법에 대한 우려를 제기하는 것은 합리적입니다.

해설 be동사 뒤의 빈칸은 형용사자리이므로 정답은 (B) reasonable이다.

어휘 reasonable 합리적인 raise concern 우려를 일으키다 extract 추출하다 certain 어떠한, 특정 natural resources 천연 자원

111

The latest developments in navigation systems allow drivers to know where there is congestion ------- in advance.
(A) nor
(B) well
(C) ever
(D) now

최근 내비게이션 시스템의 발전은 운전자들이 훨씬 미리 어디에서 교통 혼잡이 있는지 알도록 해줍니다.

해설 빈칸은 뒤의 전치사구 in advance와 어울리는 단어가 들어갈 자리이다. well은 '훨씬'이라는 의미로 연결이 적절하다. well in advance 훨씬 미리

어휘 latest 최신의 development 발전 congestion 혼잡 in advance 미리, 사전에

112

Sommet Mattresses provides its customers ------- only the best quality at incredibly low prices.
(A) over
(B) onto
(C) with
(D) for

Sommet Mattresses는 고객들에게 엄청나게 낮은 가격으로 최고 품질만을 제공합니다.

해설 빈칸은 동사 provide와 어울리는 전치사자리이다. 목적어로 사람이 왔으므로 전치사 with가 어울린다. <provide + 사람 + with + 사물>, <provide + 사물 + to [for] + 사람>의 구조이다.

어휘 provide 제공하다 quality 품질 incredibly 믿을 수 없을 정도로, 엄청나게

113

The exact date of completion for Anne's software installation has yet to be announced, but it will be ------- between September 20 and October 10.
(A) current
(B) tomorrow
(C) sometime
(D) there

Anne 소프트웨어 설치를 위한 완료의 정확한 날짜는 아직 발표되지 않았지만, 9월 20일과 10월 10일 사이쯤 발표될 것입니다.

해설 빈칸은 뒤의 9월 20일과 10월 10일 사이에 막연한 시간을 나타내는 단어가 들어갈 자리이다. sometime은 '쯤'의 의미로 미래의 막연한 시간을 나타내는 부사이다.

어휘 exact 정확한 installation 설치 announce 알리다, 발표하다 current 현재의 sometime (미래에) 언젠가

114

With over 15 years experience in the field, we are capable of ------- roads, houses, and bridges.
(A) designs
(B) design
(C) designed
(D) designing

이 분야에서 15년 이상의 경험으로, 우리는 도로와 집과 다리를 설계할 수 있습니다.

해설 빈칸은 뒤의 도로, 주택, 다리를 목적어로 취하는 동명사자리이다. 정답은 (D) designing이다.

어휘 over 이상 field 분야 be capable of ~할 수 있다 bridge 다리

115

Richard was selected for the lead patent attorney position because his educational background was very -------.
(A) knowledgeable
(B) impressive
(C) qualified
(D) pleased

Richard 씨는 학력이 매우 인상적이기 때문에, 특허 변리사 직책으로 선정되었습니다.

해설 주어인 educational background(학력)와 어울리는 형용사는 impressive(인상적인)이다. 나머지 단어들은 사람 주어와 어울리는 형용사들이다.

어휘 patent attorney 특허 변리사 educational 교육적인 background 배경 knowledgeable 해박한 impressive 인상적인 qualified 자격 있는 pleased 기쁜

116

After you complete the ------- permit applications, please detach the pages from the booklet and bring them to the Public Service Center.
(A) relevantly
(B) relevance
(C) relevancies
(D) relevant

관련 있는 허가 지원서를 작성한 후에, 책자로부터 그 페이지를 떼서 Public Service Center로 가져오세요.

(해설) 빈칸은 명사 앞에 어울리는 형용사(relevant)자리이다.
(어휘) relevance 관련, 연관 relevant 관련 있는 permit 허가증 detach 떼다 booklet 소책자

117

It is imperative you do not attempt to ------- items that are too heavy for you, whether you are on your own or with someone else.
(A) draw
(B) select
(C) lift
(D) damage

당신이 스스로 하든 다른 누군가와 함께하든지 간에, 너무 무거운 물건을 들어 올리려고 하지 않는 게 필수적입니다.

(해설) 빈칸은 뒤의 명사 item을 목적어로 취하는 동사자리이다. 뒤의 items는 관계대명사 that절의 수식을 받는다. 문맥상 '당신에게 너무 무거운 물건을 ~'이 되므로 '들어 올리다'라는 뜻의 (C) lift가 정답이다.
(어휘) imperative 필수적인 attempt 시도 whether A or B A이든 B이든 draw 그리다, 끌다 select 선택하다 lift 들어 올리다 damage 손상을 입히다

118

The most ------- way to get motivated to exercise is to make it a part of your everyday routine.
(A) practically
(B) practice
(C) practicing
(D) practical

운동을 하기 위하여 동기부여를 받는 가장 실용적인 방법은 운동을 일과의 한 부분으로 만드는 것입니다.

(해설) 빈칸은 명사 way와 어울리는 형용사자리(practical)이다.
(어휘) practically 사실상, 현실적으로 practical 실용적인 motivate 동기부여하다 routine 일과

119

In Canada, new teacher's salaries differ ------- according to which province they are teaching in.
(A) great
(B) greatest
(C) greater
(D) greatly

캐나다에서, 새로운 선생님의 월급은 어느 지역에서 가르치는지에 따라서 매우 다르다.

해설 빈칸은 자동사 differ 뒤에 어울리는 단어가 들어갈 자리이다. 자동사 뒤에는 부사가 어울리므로, 정답은 (D) greatly(대단히, 매우)이다.

어휘 salary 월급 differ 다르다 greatly 매우 according to ~에 따르면 province 지역, 지방

120

You can change the departure date of your flight without any extra charge, ------- seats are available.
(A) will assume
(B) assume
(C) assuming
(D) assumed

당신은 좌석이 존재한다는 가정 하에, 추가 요금 없이 비행기의 출발 날짜를 변경할 수 있습니다.

해설 빈칸은 뒤 문장을 받는 접속사자리이다. 선택지 중에서 (C) assuming이 assuming that S V의 구조에서 that이 생략되어 정답이다.

어휘 without ~ 없이 assume 가정하다 departure 출발

121

The Board Charter describes the ------- of the responsibilities between the Chairman and the Chief Executive Officer.
(A) division
(B) support
(C) statement
(D) enforcement

Board Charter 씨는 회장과 CEO 사이의 책임의 분할을 설명하고 있다.

해설 빈칸은 of the responsibilities(책임의)와 의미연결이 어울리는 명사자리이다. 문맥상 '회장과 최고경영자 사이의 책임의 ~'라고 해석이 되므로, (A) division(분할)이 정답이다.

어휘 describe 설명하다, 묘사하다 division 분할 support 지원 statement 성명서 enforcement 시행, 집행 chairman 의장

122

Complete the form below with the required information and we will send you a ------- that you have been successfully added to our system.
(A) notifies
(B) notify
(C) notification
(D) notifying

요구된 정보로 아래에 있는 양식을 작성하면 당신에게 우리 시스템에 성공적으로 추가되었다는 공지를 보낼 것입니다.

해설 빈칸은 관사 뒤에 어울리는 품사가 들어갈 자리이다. 관사 뒤에는 명사가 와야 하므로, 정답은 (C) notification이다.

어휘 complete 작성하다 below 아래에 required 요구된 notify 알리다 notification 알림 add 추가하다

123

All new employees are on a probationary period when their performance is ------- monthly by managers.
(A) experimental
(B) built
(C) evaluated
(D) understood

모든 신입사원들은 수습기간을 거칠 것이고 그때 성과가 관리자들에 의해 매달 평가될 것이다.

해설 빈칸은 주어인 their performance(그들의 성과)와 의미 연결이 적절한 단어가 들어갈 자리이다. 의미상 적절한 단어는 evaluate(평가하다)이다.

124

Tickets are not ------- under any circumstances other than cancellation of the event.
(A) refunding
(B) refund
(C) refunds
(D) refundable

티켓은 행사 취소 이외에 그 어떤 경우에라도 환불이 불가능합니다.

해설 빈칸은 be동사 뒤의 빈칸은 형용사(refundable 환불이 가능한)자리이다.

어휘 refundable 환불이 가능한 circumstance 상황 other than ~외에, cancellation 취소

125

Mr. Lim asked ------- Ms. Hwang would be available to photograph the food for the party in July.
(A) although
(B) whether
(C) whenever
(D) either

Lim 씨는 Hwang 씨가 7월에 파티용 음식 사진을 찍을 수 있는지 없는지를 물었다.

해설 빈칸은 동사 ask의 목적어로 명사절을 이끌 수 있는 접속사가 들어갈 자리이다. 선택지 중 명사절을 이끄는 접속사는 (B) whether(~인지 아닌지)가 정답이다.

어휘 although 비록 ~일지라도 photograph 사진을 찍다 whenever 언제든지 available 이용 가능한, 시간이 있는

126

It would be hard for ------- who has watched the movie to deny that Mr. Neo's performance is the best of his career.
(A) some
(B) you
(C) anyone
(D) those

영화를 봤던 사람들이 Neo 씨의 공연이 그의 경력에서 최고였음을 부인하기는 어렵다.

해설 빈칸은 who has와 연결이 가능한 선행사자리이다. who 뒤의 동사가 has이기 때문에 선행사 역시 단수가 되어야 하므로 정답은 (C) anyone이다. those who 뒤에는 복수동사가 와야 한다.

어휘 those who ~하는 사람들 watch 보다 deny 부인하다 performance 공연 career 경력

127

All applicants for a two-wheeled vehicle license are asked to pass a driving test ------- by the National Police Agency.
(A) exchanged
(B) administered
(C) occupied
(D) exceeded

이륜차 면허지원자들은 National Police Agency에 의해 관리되는 운전시험을 통과할 것을 요구합니다.

해설 빈칸은 명사 driving test(운전시험)를 수식하는 형용사자리이다. 선택지 중 test와 의미연결이 적절한 단어는 administer(시행하다, 관리하다)이다.

어휘 applicant 지원자 pass 통과하다 exchange 교환하다 administered 관리된 occupy 차지된 exceed 초과하다

128

The committee members visited Mumbai last month to inspect the ------- site for the new airport.
(A) propose
(B) proposing
(C) proposer
(D) proposed

위원회 멤버들은 새로운 공항을 위해 제안된 장소를 점검하기 위하여 지난달에 Mumbia를 방문했습니다.

해설 빈칸은 명사 site 앞에 어울리는 형용사자리이다. site(부지, 장소)는 '제안된'의 의미로 proposed와 어울린다.

어휘 committee 위원회 inspect 점검하다 proposed 제안된

129

Of the ten members of the marketing team, Ms. Chi is the ------- about the new marketing strategy.
(A) most knowledgeable
(B) knowledgeable
(C) knowledge
(D) more knowledge

마케팅 팀의 10명 중에서, Chi 씨가 새로운 마케팅 전략에 가장 해박합니다.

해설 빈칸은 the 뒤에 어울리는 형태의 단어가 올 자리이다. 앞에서 '10명의 직원 중에서'라고 범위를 한정해 주므로, 최상급이 어울린다. 따라서 정답은 (A) most knowledgeable이다.

어휘 knowledge 지식 knowledgeable 해박한 strategy 전략

130

Jack and Associates provides a three-dimensional, ------- version of its full-scale interior designs.
(A) major
(B) fierce
(C) eager
(D) miniature

Jack and Associates는 실물 크기의 인테리어 디자인의 3차원 축소 버전을 제공합니다.

해설 빈칸은 version과 의미연결이 적절한 형용사가 들어갈 자리이다. 빈칸 뒤를 보면 '실물 크기의 내부 디자인의'라고 되므로, 축소를 나타내는 (D) miniature(소형의)가 정답이다.

어휘 three-dimensional 3차원의 miniature 소형의 full-scale 실물 크기의 major 주요한 fierce 격렬한, 극심한 eager 열렬한

Questions 131-134 refer to the following announcement.

Mendoza Engines, the largest ------- of civilian aviation jet engines in Europe, will unveil its new website on Wednesday. The biggest change ------- our older site is the targeting of actual passengers rather than airline companies. Due to the recent number of accidents involving engines on commercial flights, we want to make clear the 99.98% safety record our engineers and technicians have achieved. -------. The CEO, George Mendoza, explains, "If we can make people confident in our business partner products, it will lead to larger sales for us in the future." Please visit www.mendozaengineandturbine. com to learn more about ------- Mendoza Engines has become a leader in jet engine safety and reliability.

131.

132.

133.

134.

유럽에서 가장 큰 민간 항공기 제트엔진 제조업체인 Mendoza Engines는 수요일 새 홈페이지를 공개할 것입니다. 우리의 구 홈페이지에 비해 가장 큰 변화는 항공사들보다 실제 승객들을 대상으로 삼은 것입니다. 상업 항공편에 관련된 최근의 사고 건수 때문에 우리의 엔지니어들과 기술자들이 달성한 99.98% 안전기록을 분명히 알리고 싶습니다. 또한, 우리 비행사의 사업 파트너들은 비행기 엔진에 대한 어떠한 작은 문제도 갖고 있지 않습니다. George Mendoza의 CEO는 '만약 우리의 사업 파트너 제품에 대한 신뢰도를 높일 수 있다면 그것은 미래에도 더 큰 매출을 올릴 수 있게 이끌어 줄 것입니다.'라고 설명했습니다. Mendoza Engines가 안전하고 신뢰성 있는 제트엔진계의 리더가 되었는지 www.mendozaengineandturbine.com에 방문하셔서 어떻게 더 알아보시기 바랍니다.

어휘 civilian 민간 aviation 항공 unveil 공개하다 rather than ~라기보다 due to 때문에 involve 관련시키다 confident 자신하는, 확신하는 reliability 신뢰할 수 있음

131
(A) manufacturer
(B) manufactured
(C) manufacturing
(D) manufacture

해설 Mendoza Engines라는 명사주어와 동격이 될 수 있는 명사는 (A) manufacturer(제조업체)이다.

132
(A) at
(B) by
(C) from
(D) between

해설 빈칸 앞에 있는 '변화(change)'를 수식해 줄 수 있고 뒤에 전치사를 골라야 한다. '우리의 예전 사이트(our older site)'에서부터 생겨난 변화를 뜻하는 단어를 고르는 것이 적합하므로 정답은 (C) from이다.

133
(A) There Is a range of ways to get our flight tickets at a reduced price.
(B) An awarded artist, Kathy Anderson designed the engine cowl to match our aircraft body.
(C) Plus, our airline business partners have not had a single problem with an aircraft engine.
(D) Our business partners have renewed their yearly contract with us for 10 years in a row.

해설 빈칸 앞의 문장에서 우리의 엔지니어들과 기술자들이 달성한 99.98프로의 안전기록을 분명히 알리고 싶다고 했고 뒷문장에서는 사업 파트너 상품의 신뢰도를 높이는 게 좋다고 하므로, 우리의 안전기록은 뛰어나고 '또한 우리의 파트너들은 엔진에 대한 문제가 없다'는 내용이 자연스러운 흐름이 된다. 따라서 정답은 (C)이다.

(A) 우리의 할인된 비행기 표를 얻기 위한 여러 가지 방법이 있습니다.
(B) 상을 받았던 예술가 Kathy Anderson은 우리의 비행기 동체와 어울리는 엔진 카울을 디자인했습니다.
(C) 또한, 우리 비행사의 사업 파트너들은 비행기 엔진에 대한 어떠한 작은 문제도 갖고 있지 않습니다.
(D) 우리의 사업 파트너는 법적으로 10년간 우리와 연간 계약을 갱신했습니다.

134
(A) how
(B) what
(C) each
(D) during

해설 빈칸 앞에 전치사가 있고 빈칸 뒤에는 문장이 이어지고 있으므로 명사절 접속사를 골라주어야 한다. 명사절 접속사는 (A) how와 (B) what이 있다. 그중 어떻게 '리더가 되었는지'를 홈페이지에서 확인해 보라'는 내용이 들어가는 것이적절하므로 정답은 (A) how(어떻게)이다.

ACTUAL TEST 01 ACTUAL TEST 02 ACTUAL TEST 03 ACTUAL TEST 04 ACTUAL TEST 05

Questions 135-138 refer to the following letter.

Dear Ms. Sheridan, Enclosed in this letter is the report about the camera you brought to us for free repair service. As stated in the report, we could not do any repairs due to a ------- of the terms and **135.** conditions of your warranty. Our technician discovered that the camera shutter had been altered by someone so that it works at a lower speed than normal. When the ------- to the shutter was carried out, it seems **136.** to have been damaged. Our guarantee clearly says that any damage that is the result of alterations or repairs by the owner cannot be covered. -------. **137.** Otherwise, you should pick it up within seven days. Please let us know as ------- as possible what you would like to do. We **138.** look forward to hearing from you soon. Thanks. Sincerely, Sarah Lipinski, Customer Service Supervisor Enclosure	Sheridan 씨께 이 편지에는 당신이 우리에게 무료 수리서 비스를 받기 위해 가져왔던 카메라의 보고 서가 동봉되어 있습니다. 이 보고서에 명시 된 것과 같이 당신이 보증 조건에 대한 약 관을 위반했기 때문에 어떤 수리도 할 수 없었습니다. 우리 정비사는 카메라 셔터가 이미 누군가 에 의해 변경되어서 정상적인 속도보다 느 리게 작동한다는 것을 발견하였습니다. 그 셔터가 변경이 되었을 때 손상을 입은 것으 로 보입니다. 우리의 보증약관은 소유자에 의한 수리나 변경에 의한 결과로 입은 손상 에는 보상을 할 수 없다고 정확히 명시되 어 있습니다. 그러므로 아마 당신이 카메라 를 우리 가게에서 수리하고 싶어 한다면 우 리는 85달러의 수리비를 청구해야 합니다. 그렇지 않으면 당신은 7일 이내에 그것을 가지고 가셔야 합니다. 무엇을 원하는지 저 희에게 될 수 있는 한 빨리 알려 주세요. 당 신으로부터 빨리 답변을 듣길 바랍니다. 감 사합니다. 진심을 담아 Sarah Lipinski, 고객 서비스 담당자 동봉

어휘 enclosed 동봉된 term 조건 warranty 보증서 carry out ~을 실행하다, 이행하다 guarantee 품질보증 alteration 변경 look forward to ~을 기대하다

135
  (A) experiment
  (B) courtesy
  (C) violation
  (D) perspective

해설 빈칸의 명사를 수식하기 위해 뒤에 of the terms(조항들의 ~)가 나와 있고, 내용상 보증서의 조항을 위반했기 때문에 수리해 줄 수가 없다는 의미가 필요하므로 정답은 (C) violation(위반)이다.

136

(A) alteration
(B) alternating
(C) alternatives
(D) alternatively

해설 관사 the 뒤에 명사가 필요하고 (A) alteration은 '개조, 수선', (C) alternatives는 '대안들'을 뜻한다. '셔터에 가해진 개조가 시행되었을 때 손상을 입은 것으로 보인다'는 내용이 적절하므로 정답은 (A) alteration이다.

137

(A) Additionally, if you buy one camera battery by ordering from our website, you will get one for free.
(B) Therefore, if you would like to repair your camera, we have to charge you a fee of $85.
(C) With the exception of the product's manufacturing defect, the refund request is not approved.
(D) Please take extra care not to immerse the camera body into any liquid when cleaning.

해설 (A) 추가적으로 만약 당신이 우리의 홈페이지에서 카메라 배터리를 하나 산다면 하나를 공짜로 더 받을 것입니다.
(B) 그러므로 아마 당신이 카메라를 수리하고 싶어 한다면 우리는 85달러의 수리비를 청구해야 합니다.
(C) 상품의 오작동의 결함을 제외하고는 환불 요청은 승인되지 않습니다.
(D) 세척할 때 배터리의 본체를 어떠한 액체에도 담그지 않도록 각별히 주의하세요.

앞 문장의 내용이 '개조나 수리의 결과로 인한 손상은 보증서에 의해 보상되지 않는다(Our guarantee clearly says that any damage that is the result of alterations or repairs by the owner cannot be covered)'는 의미였으므로, '그래서 수리를 원한다면 수리비를 청구해야 한다'는 (B)가 가장 적절하다.

138

(A) sooner
(B) soon
(C) soonest
(D) the soonest

해설 해설 as ~ as 사이에는 형용사나 부사의 원급이 들어가야 하므로 정답은 (B) soon이다. as soon as possible(가능한 한 빨리)라는 표현을 반드시 암기해두자.

Questions 139-142 refer to the following e-mail.

To: swhite@doverengineering.com

From: sschaefer@doverengineering.com

Subject: Approval of the Order

Attachment: Materials required for training

Dear Mr. Sandra,

I have ordered ------- of the materials that you require for the
139.
training sessions for summer interns. I have attached a copy of

the purchase order I made.

However, our regular supplier has informed us that they -------
140.
produce the folders with the client's logo on them. After I

contacted several companies, I found that Conoco Marketing

produces the folders with the logo. -------.
141.

Please confirm at your earliest convenience the purchase of

the folders. Once you authorize this transaction, I will order the

items -------.
142.

Also, I have been informed that we will have all items no later

than June 10.

Sincerely,

Steve Schaefer

수신: swhite@doverengineering.com

발신: sschaefer@doverengineering.com

제목: 주문 승인

첨부: 트레이닝에 필요한 물품

Sandra 씨께

저는 당신이 여름 인턴들의 트레이닝 기간 동안 필요한 대부분의 필요한 물품들을 주문했습니다. 제가 주문했던 구매내역을 첨부했습니다.

하지만 기존의 우리 공급업자들은 그들이 더 이상 고객 로고가 붙어 있는 폴더를 생산하지 않는다고 우리에게 알려왔습니다. 다른 몇몇 회사들과 연락을 취한 후 저는 Conoco Marketing이 로고를 부탁한 폴더를 생산하는 것을 확인했습니다. 그들의 폴더는 이전의 폴더보다 좀 더 비싸지만 Conoco Marketing 폴더가 좀 더 좋다고 생각합니다.

가급적 빨리 폴더 구매에 대한 것을 확인 바랍니다. 당신이 이 거래를 허가하면 저는 즉시 물품들을 주문하겠습니다.

또한 저는 우리가 모든 물품들을 늦어도 6월 10일까지는 다 준비해야 한다고 들었습니다.

진심을 담아

Steve Schaefer

어휘 materials 재료 supplier 공급업자 confirm 확인하다 convenience 편리한 상태 authorize 허가하다 transaction 거래 no later than 늦어도 ~까지는

139
(A) every
(B) these
(C) anyone
(D) most

해설 order의 목적어자리에 명사를 골라야 한다. 문맥상 '자재들의 대부분을 주문했다'라는 의미가 적절하므로 정답은 (D) most(대부분)이다.

140
(A) no longer
(B) any more
(C) no later than
(D) not only

해설 문맥상 '대부분의 물품을 주문했지만, 제조업체가 폴더들을 더 이상 제조하지 않는다'는 의미이므로 정답은 (A) no longer(더 이상 ~하지 않다)이다.

141
(A) The logo has been created by our in-house designer and received many compliments for its originality.
(B) Their folders are a bit more expensive than the previous folders, but I think the Conoco Marketing folder is better.
(C) Our folders are made of the highest quality and we guarantee that you will be satisfied with it.
(D) Since its foundation, our company has never changed its logo, so this is a good opportunity to do so.

해설 기존의 공급업체가 클라이언트의 로고가 새겨진 폴더를 더 이상 제작하지 않아서 다른 회사들에 연락을 해보니 Conoco Marketing이 로고가 새겨진 폴더들을 만든다는 것을 알게 되었다며 대안으로써 다른 회사를 언급하고 있다. 따라서 '그들의 폴더는 이전의 폴더보다 좀 더 비싸지만 Conoco Marketing 폴더가 좀 더 좋다고 하는 내용이 자연스럽다.

(A) 그 로고는 사내 디자이너들에 의해서 만들어졌고 독창성 때문에 많은 칭찬을 받았습니다.
(B) 그들의 폴더는 이전의 폴더보다 좀 더 비싸지만 Conoco Marketing 폴더가 좀 더 좋다고 생각합니다.
(C) 우리 폴더는 높은 품질로 만들어졌고 그것으로부터 안전할 것이라고 보장합니다.
(D) 설립 이래로 우리 회사는 로고를 바꾸지 않았고 이것이 그렇게 할 수 있는 좋은 기회입니다.

142
(A) immediately
(B) impartially
(C) meticulously
(D) positively

해설 '주문하다(order)'를 수식해줄 수 있는 부사어휘를 고르는 문제이다. 거래를 승인해준다면 즉시 주문하겠다는 내용이 가장 적절하므로 정답은 (A) immediately이다.

ACTUAL TEST 01 | ACTUAL TEST 02 | ACTUAL TEST 03 | ACTUAL TEST 04 | ACTUAL TEST 05

Questions 143-146 refer to the following e-mail.

To: jsparshott@unam.com

From: sbean@ewdf.com

Subject: Response to the Inquiry

Dear Ms. Sparshott,

I appreciate the inquiry you made recently. As the host of the
European World Dance Festival, European World Arts Center
welcomes members of the news media, ------- freelance writers
143.
on commission, to come to report on special events held in
our facilities since both Spanish and international media have
a high ------- in the event, passes for journalists will be given
144.
on a first-come, first-served basis, except for some passes
secured in advance. -------. The form is available through our
145.
website. All credentials attached must be written on official
company letterhead. Successful applicants will receive an email
notification, and their passes will be sent to them ------- mail.
146.

Sincerely,

Star Bean

Public Relations Office, EWDF

수신: jsparshott@unam.com
발신: sbean@ewdf.com
제목: 문의에 대한 응답

Sparshott 씨께,

최근에 문의해주신 사항에 대해 감사드립니다. European World Dance Festival의 주최자로써 European World Art Center는 스페인과 국제 매체들의 행사에 대한 높은 관심 때문에 우리 시설에서 열리는 특별한 행사를 보고하기 위해 참여하신 위원회의 프리랜서 작가들을 포함한 뉴스 매체를 환영하고 기자들에게 제공되는 출입증은 사전에 보증된 몇 개를 제외하고 선착순으로 제공됩니다. 기자 출입증을 받고 싶은 지원자들은 반드시 그들의 요청을 서면으로 댄스 축제 위원회에 제출해야 합니다. 양식은 우리 홈페이지를 통해서 확인할 수 있습니다. 모든 부착되는 자격 인증서들은 반드시 회사이름이 윗부분에 쓰여진 회사 공식 편지지에 기록되어야 합니다. 승인된 신청자는 이메일을 통해 알려드리고 출입증은 우편으로 보내집니다.

진심을 담아

Star Bean
홍보부, EWDF

어휘 inquiry 문의 freelance 프리랜서 commission 위원회 credential 자격인증서 letterhead 편지 윗부분에 인쇄된 회사 이름과 주소 applicant 신청자 notify 알리다

143
(A) included
(B) was including
(C) to include
(D) including

해설 welcome이라는 동사가 있었으므로 빈칸에 동사는 들어갈 수 없다. 문맥상 '프리랜서를 포함한 뉴스미디어 멤버들을 환영한다'는 내용이 어울리므로 정답은 (D) including(~를 포함하여)이다.

144 **(A) Interest**
(B) emphasis
(C) fragile
(D) impact

해설 스페인미디어와 전 세계적인 미디어들이 이벤트에 높은 '관심'을 가지고 있기 때문에 선착순으로 통행권을 받게 될 거라는 의미의 문장이므로 정답은 (A) interest(관심)이다.

145 (A) To successfully host this festival, admission into the arena is restricted to the dancers and their family members.
(B) The Spanish media has a reputation for its impartial reporting and the full confidence of the public.
(C) Applicants who want to have a journalist pass must submit their request in writing to the dance festival committee.
(D) Secured passes are for disabled people, pregnant women, and the elderly.

해설 페스티벌 행사에의 기자들의 출입에 대한 내용을 알려주고 있는 글이다. 빈칸 뒤 문장에서 그 양식(The form)이라는 단수명사가 사용되었다는 것을 유념하여, 홈페이지에서 이용할 수 있는 문서양식이 적절하게 사용된 문장을 골라야 한다.

(A) 이 축제를 성공적으로 개최하기 위해서, 경기장으로의 입장은 댄서들과 그들 가족들로 제한됩니다.
(B) 스페인 언론은 공정한 보도와 대중들의 온전한 신뢰에 대한 평판을 가지고 있습니다.
(C) 기자 출입증을 받고 싶은 지원자들은 반드시 그들의 요청을 서면으로 댄스 축제 위원회에 제출해야 합니다.
(D) 보안 출입증들은 장애인들, 임신부들, 그리고 노인들을 위한 것입니다.

146 **(A) by**
(B) during
(C) from
(D) across

해설 통행증은 그들에게 우편이라는 수단에 '의해서' 보내지게 되므로 정답은 (A) by(~에 의해)이다.

101 Heavy machinery engineers at ------- check the fluid levels of the forklifts and bulldozers.
(A) regularize
(B) regular
(C) regularly
(D) regular

중장비 기술자는 정기적으로 지게차와 불도저의 유체 레벨을 확인합니다.

해설 빈칸은 동사 앞에 어울리는 부사(regularly)자리이다. ·
어휘 heavy machinery 중장비 fluid 액체, 유체 forklift 지게차 bulldozer 불도저

102 Thanks to technological innovation online, the future of mass media is less ------- than ever.
(A) predictable
(B) predicting
(C) predicts
(D) predict

온라인에서 기술적인 진보 덕문에, 대중매체의 미래는 어느 때보다 덜 예측 가능하다.

해설 빈칸은 be동사 뒤에 어울리는 품사가 와야 하는 위치이다. be동사 뒤에는 형용사를 보어로 가질 수 있으므로 정답은 (A) predictable이다.

103 Savings banks ------- the country are expected to recover from the recent economic downturn in two months.
(A) behind
(B) despite
(C) across
(D) among

나라 전역에 저축은행들은 최근의 경제적인 침체로부터 2달 후에 회복할 것으로 예상됩니다.

해설 빈칸은 뒤의 명사 the country와 의미연결이 적절한 전치사가 와야 하므로, 장소를 나타내는 전치사인 across(~ 전역에)가 정답이다.
어휘 saving bank 저축은행 downturn 침체

104 Please be reminded that checks ------- at the National Australia Bank no later than 5 P.M. on weekdays will be credited to an account the next morning.
(A) deposited
(B) amounted
(C) borrowed
(D) coined

주중에 늦어도 5시까지 National Australia 에서 입금되는 수표는 다음날 아침 계좌로 입금된다는 것을 상기해주십시오.

해설 빈칸은 앞의 명사 checks(수표)를 수식하는 적절한 의미의 단어가 들어갈 자리이다. 빈칸 뒤의 해석은 '늦어도 5시까지 National Australia Bank에 ~되는 수표'라는 의미이므로 deposited가 정답이다.

어휘 check 수표 no later than 늦어도 credit 입금하다 amount 합계가 되다 borrow 빌리다

105 The Zenga Beauty ------- introduced new cosmetics products for the teenage market that include colorful eye and lip products.
(A) recently
(B) rather
(C) very
(D) still

Zenga Beauty는 눈, 입술을 위한 다채로운 상품을 포함하는 10대 시장을 위해 새로운 화장품을 최근에 소개했습니다.

해설 빈칸은 문장 전체적인 의미가 적절한 부사자리이다. 동사 introduce(소개하다, 발표하다, 출시하다)와 내용상 연결이 매끄러운 부사는 (A) recently이다.

어휘 introduce 소개하다 cosmetics 화장품 teenage 10대 rather 다소

106 The delivery fee listed on our website is an ------- and varies depending on the weight of items.
(A) estimate
(B) attempt
(C) objective
(D) omission

웹사이트에 목록된 배달 요금은 추정치이고 물건의 무게에 따라서 다르다.

해설 빈칸은 be동사 뒤의 명사자리로, be동사 뒤의 명사는 주어와 동격관계이므로 주어인 delivery fee(배송비)와 적합한 동격관계의 선택지는 (A) estimate이다.

어휘 vary 다르다 depending on ~에 따라 estimate 예상치, 추정치 attempt 시도 objective 목적, 목표 omission 생략, 누락

107

Tus Airways is happy to provide all the necessary services to ensure that passengers ------- special needs enjoy a comfortable flight in a perfect safety.
(A) over
(B) with
(C) of
(D) from

Tus Airways는 특별한 도움이 필요한 승객들이 완전 안전하게 편안한 비행을 즐기는 것을 보장하기 위해 모든 필요한 서비스를 기꺼이 제공할 것입니다.

해설 빈칸 앞의 passengers(승객들)과 뒤의 special needs(특별한 필요)를 연결하기에 어울리는 전치사는 (B) with(~을 가진)이다.

어휘 be happy to 기꺼이 ~하다 comfortable 안락한

108

Requests from clients for ------- our office hours are positively being considered by executives.
(A) submitting
(B) offering
(C) reaching
(D) extending

우리의 사무실 업무 시간을 연장하기 위한 고객들로부터의 요청은 중역진에 의해서 긍정적으로 고려되는 중입니다.

해설 빈칸은 뒤의 office hours(업무 시간)를 목적어로 취하는 적절한 의미의 동명사자리이다. extend(연장하다)의 동명사 형태가 의미 연결이 매끄러운 정답이다.

어휘 office hours 업무 시간 positively 긍정적으로 executives 중역, 임원 reach 도달하다 extend 연장하다

109

Though Nature Organic introduced a new line of luxurious bed clothing made of organic cotton, its revenue has ------- the same.
(A) remained
(B) determine
(C) announced
(D) resulted

비록 Nature Organic은 유기농 솜으로 만들어진 호화로운 침구류의 신제품을 출시했을지라도, 수익은 동일하다.

해설 빈칸은 the same과 의미 연결이 적절한 동사가 들어갈 자리이다. 선택지 동사 중 remain이 the same과 연결되어 remain the same(같은 상태를 유지하다)의 표현을 만든다.

어휘 luxurious 고급스러운 bed clothing 침구류 organic cotton 유기농 솜 revenue 수익 remain the same 같은 상태를 유지하다

110

A guest speaker advised participants that rewarding outstanding performance is good way to increase employee -------.
(A) productively
(B) produce
(C) productivity
(D) to produce

초청연사는 참가자들에게 뛰어난 성과를 보상하는 것은 직원 생산성을 증가시키는 좋은 방법임을 조언했습니다.

해설 빈칸은 명사 employee와 연결이 적절한 단어가 들어갈 자리이다. employee는 셀 수 있는 명사인데 관사가 없으므로 빈칸까지 명사가 들어가야 increase에 대한 목적어가 될 수 있다. 그래서 employee productivity(직원 생산성)라는 복합명사의 형태가 적절하다.

어휘 guest speaker 초청연사 reward 보상하다 productively 생산적으로 produce 농산물 productivity 생산성

111

Ms. Hwang's excellent managerial skills resulted in her being ------- as the general manager of the Taipan group of hotels.
(A) designated
(B) appealed
(C) processed
(D) conducted

Hwang의 뛰어난 관리능력은 그녀가 Taipan 호텔 그룹의 총괄 매니저로서 지정되도록 했습니다.

해설 빈칸은 as the general manager(총괄 관리자로서)와 의미 연결이 적절한 단어가 들어갈 자리이다. 관리자의 자리로 승진되거나(promoted), 고용되거나(hired), 임명되거나(appointed) 등의 의미연결이 적절하므로, 선택지 중 (A) designated(지정된)가 적절하다.

어휘 result in ~를 야기하다, 초래하다 designate 지정하다 appeal 호소하다, 간청하다 process 처리하다 conduct 시행하다

112

After adopting a new marketing strategy, Woolworths made big profits this year, ------- surpassing last year's gains.
(A) easy
(B) easily
(C) easing
(D) ease

새로운 마케팅 전략을 채택한 후에, Woolworths 싸는 작년의 수익을 쉽게 능가하면서, 올해 큰 수익을 내었다.

해설 빈칸은 분사 형태인 surpassing 앞에 어울리는 형태의 단어가 들어갈 자리이다. 동사는 부사를 수식하므로 동사에서 모양이 바뀐 분사도 부사가 수식한다. 그래서 정답은 (B) easily(쉽게)이다.

어휘 adopt 채택하다 strategy 전략 make profits 수익을 내다 surpass 능가하다 gain 수익 easily 쉽게

113

After thoughtful consideration, United Electronics -------
accepted Myer Construction's bid to renovate its Sydney
plant.
(A) finally
(B) hardly
(C) previously
(D) seldom

심사숙고 후에, Unite Electronics는 시드니
공장을 개조하기 위하여 Myer Construc-
tion의 입찰을 마침내 수락했습니다.

해설 빈칸은 동사 accept(승낙하다)와 의미가 잘 어울리는 부사자리이다. finally(마침내)가 after thoughtful consideration(신중한 고려 뒤에)과 연결이 적절하다.

어휘 thoughtful 신중한 consideration 고려 bid 입찰 finally 마침내 hardly 거의 - 않다 previously 이전에 seldom 거의 ~ 않다

114

------- manager responds to the customer's inquiries just
depends on the area the customer lives in.
(A) Each
(B) Which
(C) Something
(D) Either

어떠한 매니저가 고객들의 문의에 응답할
지는 고객들이 거주하는 지역에 따라 다
릅니다.

해설 빈칸은 문장에서 주어가 되는 명사절을 이끌 수 있는 단어가 들어갈 자리이다. 선택지 중 명사절을 취하는 선택지는 (B) Which(어떠한)뿐이다.

어휘 respond to 응답하다 inquiry 문의 사항 depend on 의존하다

115

Should your payment details be incorrect, the delivery will
be postponed ------- the correct information is received from
you.
(A) within
(B) from
(C) around
(D) until

만약 지불 세무사항이 부정확하다면, 당신
으로부터 정확한 정보를 받을 때까지 배달
이 지연될 것입니다.

해설 빈칸은 뒤의 문장을 받을 수 있는 접속사자리이다. 선택지 중 접속사는 (D) until(~까지)이다. 나머지는 전치사이다.

어휘 incorrect 부정확한 correct 정확한

116

Every stay at the Comfort Hotel ------- a free buffet-style breakfast each morning.
(A) inclusive
(B) including
(C) to include
(D) includes

Comfort Hotel에서 모든 숙박은 매일 아침 무료 뷔페 아침식사를 포함합니다.

해설 빈칸은 문장에 필요한 동사가 들어갈 자리이다. 선택지 중 동사는 (D) includes뿐으로 정답이 된다.

117

To purchase a weekly ------- monthly pass, you will need to register on the website and pay by credit card.
(A) or
(B) out
(C) after
(D) still

주간 또는 월간 통행권을 구매하기 위하여, 웹사이트에 등록하고 신용카드로 지불할 필요가 있습니다.

해설 빈칸은 앞의 weekly와 뒤의 monthly를 적절하게 연결하는 단어가 들어갈 자리이다. 선택지 중 등위접속사인 (A) or가 정답이다.
어휘 pass 통행권 register 등록하다

118

Jin Airlines ------- a nonstop flight between Seoul and Osaka later this week.
(A) being announced
(B) announcing
(C) will announce
(D) announced

Jin Airlines는 이번 주말에 Seoul과 Osaka 사이를 왕복하는 직항 비행기를 발표할 것입니다.

해설 빈칸은 동사자리이다. being announced와 announcing은 동사형태가 아니므로 오답이다. 문장의 끝에 later this week(이번 주 후반에)라는 미래를 나타내는 단어가 보이므로, 미래시제인 (C) will announce가 정답이다.
어휘 nonstop flight 직항 비행기 later this week 이번 주 후반에

119

If you would like expedited shipping please contact us ------- you have placed your order at info@aco.com
(A) so that
(B) in fact
(C) as soon as
(D) meanwhile

만약 빠른 배송을 원한다면, 주문하자마자 우리에게 info@aco.com로 연락 주십시오.

해설 빈칸은 뒤의 문장을 연결하는 접속사가 들어갈 자리이다. 선택지 중 접속사인 so that(~하기 위해서)과 as soon as(~하자마자) 중에서 의미가 적절한 것은 (C) as soon as이다.

어휘 expedited shipping 빠른 배송 contact 연락하다 place an order 주문하다 in fact 사실 meanwhile 그동안, 그사이에

120

Prior to booking any appointments, it will be ------- to send medical information related to the problem along with any imaging reports.
(A) necessarily
(B) necessities
(C) necessitating
(D) necessary

약속을 잡기 전에, 영상보고와 더불어 어떤 문제에 관련된 의학 정보를 보내는 것은 필수적입니다.

해설 be동사 뒤는 형용사가 와야 하므로 (D) necessary(필수적인)가 정답이 된다.

어휘 prior to ~에 앞서 related to ~와 관련된 along with ~와 함께 imaging report 영상 보고서 necessarily 반드시, 필수적으로

121

Red Printing is a firm that ------- in printing business cards and resumes, using the latest laser technology.
(A) specializes
(B) special
(C) specialization
(D) specially

Red Printing은 최신식의 레이저 기술을 사용하여 명함과 이력서를 인쇄하는 것을 전문으로 하는 회사입니다.

해설 빈칸은 관계대명사 that 뒤에 형태가 적절한 단어가 들어갈 자리이다. 관계대명사절에는 반드시 동사가 있어야 하는데, that절에 동사가 없으므로 빈칸은 동사인 (A) specializes가 정답이다.

어휘 firm 회사 specialize in ~을 전문으로 하다 business card 명함 resume 이력서

122

Compensation paid to workers must ------- with all applicable wage laws, including those related to minimum wages, overtime hours and legally mandated benefits.
(A) achieve
(B) authorize
(C) comply
(D) regulate

근로자들에게 지불되는 급여는 반드시 최저 시급, 초과근무 시간, 법적으로 지정된 복리후생과 관련된 것들을 포함하여 해당되는 임금 법률을 준수해야 합니다.

해설 빈칸은 뒤의 전치사 with와 어울리는 자동사가 들어갈 자리이다. 선택지 중 이에 적절한 동사는 (C) comply(준수하다)이다.

어휘 compensation 급여 applicable 적용 가능한 related to ~에 관련한 minimum wage 최소 임금 overtime hour 초과 근무 시간 mandated 정해진 benefits 복지혜택 achieve 성취하다 authorize 허가하다 comply with 준수하다 regulate 규제하다

123

After ------- review the terms and conditions of the contract, please sign in the appropriate space below.
(A) yours
(B) yourself
(C) your
(D) you

계약서의 조건을 검토한 후에, 아래 적절한 공간에 서명을 하세요.

해설 빈칸은 문장의 주어자리이다. 주격인 (D) you가 정답이다.

어휘 review 검토하다 terms and conditions 조건들 sign 서명하다 appropriate 적절한

124

One of the general complaints from apartment residents is that the volume of unwanted mail which they receive has become too -------.
(A) overwhelm
(B) overwhelmed
(C) overwhelming
(D) overwhelmingly

아파트 거주민들 일반적인 불평 중 하나는 그들이 수령하는 스팸메일의 양이 너무 압도적으로 많다는 것입니다.

해설 빈칸은 동사 become과 어울리는 형태의 단어가 들어갈 자리이다. become(~이 되다)은 형용사 보어를 취하므로 선택지 중 overwhelmed(압도된) 또는 overwhelming(압도하는)이 빈칸에 적절하다. become 뒤의 형용사는 주격보어 역할을 하므로 다시 주어와의 관계를 살펴보면, 주어는 the volume of unwanted mail(원치 않는 우편물의 양)이고, 우편물의 양이 압도적으로 많다는 뜻이므로 (C) overwhelming이 정답이 된다.

어휘 general 일반적인 resident 주민 volume 양 overwhelmed 압도된 overwhelming 압도하는 overwhelmingly 압도적으로

125

This letter is to ------- you that your subscription to Chronicle Science magazine ends with next month's issue.
(A) inform
(B) recommend
(C) persuade
(D) invite

이 편지는 당신에게 Chronicle Science의 정기구독이 다음 달호로 끝난다는 것을 알려주기 위함입니다.

해설 빈칸은 뒤의 <사람 + that절>을 받을 수 있는 동사가 들어가야 하는 자리이다. 선택지 중 이 형태를 충족시키는 동사는 (A) inform이다.

어휘 subscription 정기구독 end 끝나다 issue (잡지) 호 inform 알리다 persuade 설득하다 invite 권유하다

126

Anyone ------- in receiving a box of food and care items has to get a voucher in advance by calling Neo Partners at (808) 569-2785.
(A) interest
(B) interested
(C) to interest
(D) interesting

음식 한 박스나 관리용품을 받는 것에 관심이 있는 누구든지 (808) 569-2785로 Neo Partners에게 전화함으로써 미리 바우처를 받아야 합니다.

해설 빈칸은 앞의 anyone을 수식하는 적절한 형태의 단어가 들어갈 자리이다. anyone 뒤에 who is가 생략된 구조(anyone who is ------- in)로 be interested in으로 연결된다.

어휘 voucher 증서, (숙박, 식사)권 in advance 미리, 사전에

127

The Surrey Delicatessen is very famous in the West Beach area for its quality of service and reasonable ------- on its delicious selection of baked sandwiches.
(A) priced
(B) price
(C) to price
(D) prices

Surrey Delicatessen은 맛있게 구워진 샌드위치들과 수준 높은 서비스와 합리적인 가격으로 West Beach 지역에서 아주 유명합니다.

해설 빈칸은 형용사 reasonable 뒤에 어울리는 명사가 들어갈 자리이다. 선택지의 명사 price는 셀 수 있는 명사이므로, (D) prices가 정답이다.

어휘 famous 유명한 reasonable 적절한

128

BNK Financial Group will ------- its financial support so we must look for another major investor for the development project.
(A) detach
(B) withdraw
(C) correspond
(D) write

BNK Financial Group은 재정지원을 중단할 것이고, 우리는 개발 프로젝트를 위하여 또 다른 주요 투자자를 찾아야 합니다.

해설 빈칸은 뒤의 financial support(재정적인 지원)를 목적어로 취하는 적절한 의미의 동사가 들어갈 자리이다. 선택지 중 (B) withdraw(중단하다, 취소하다)가 의미상 적절하다.

어휘 financial support 재정지원 look for ~을 찾다 detach 떼다, 분리하다 withdraw 중단하다, 취소하다, 철회하다, 인출하다 correspond 해당하다, 일치하다, 서신 연락하다

129

Due to our advanced technologies, we have increased the number of customers by ------- 15 percent.
(A) approximately
(B) approximate
(C) approximated
(D) approximating

진보된 기술 때문에, 우리는 고객 수를 대략 15%만큼 증가시켰다.

해설 빈칸은 숫자 앞에 어울리는 품사가 들어갈 자리이다. percent는 명사, 15라는 숫자는 형용사로 볼 때, 빈칸은 부사자리이다.

어휘 due to ~ 때문에 advanced 향상된, 진보된 approximately 대략

130

Miterran State Library is not in charge of items left ------- in the reading room.
(A) unattended
(B) discounted
(C) ineligible
(D) nonrefundable

Miterran State Library는 독서실에 방치된 물건에 대해서는 책임이 없습니다.

해설 빈칸은 items left(방치된 물건)와 의미연결이 적절한 형용사가 들어갈 자리이다. 이 문장은 items which are left -----의 구조로 which 앞의 선행사인 items는 which와 같으므로, items are left -----의 형태로 볼 수 있다. 이 구조를 다시 능동으로 보면 leave items -----이 된다. 즉 '물건들을 빈칸의 상태로 두다'라고 되므로, 이에 어울리는 의미는 형용사인 (A) unattended(방치된)이다.

어휘 discounted 할인된 ineligible 자격 없는

PART 6

Questions 131-134 refer to the following announcement.

Beginning next month, the Manchester Science and Technology Center will ------- its latest exhibition on the history of lighting.
131.
Beginning Saturday, June 1st, come and learn how humans first learned to harness flame for ------- use, and later refined it in the
132.
form of candles, whale oil lanterns and gas fired street lights.
As we approach the modern age, you will see how electricity transformed night to day with the ------- of the incandescent
133.
light bulb. The Manchester Science and Technology Center address is 4587 Park View Drive, across the street from the court house. -------. To learn more, call 543-2341-6582.
134.

나음 달부터 Manchester Science와 Technology Center는 조명의 역사에 관한 가장 최신의 전시회를 공개합니다. 6월 1일 토요일을 시작으로 사람들이 어떻게 그들 스스로 불꽃을 이용하는 방법을 최초로 알게 됐는지 그리고 후에 초나 고래기름 랜턴과 가스 점화 가로등을 어떻게 개선시켰는지 알아보러 오시기 바랍니다. 현대 시대에 접어들면서 백열전구의 도래로 어떻게 전기가 밤을 낮으로 바꾸는지 보게 될 것입니다. Manchester Science and Technology Center의 주소는 법원청사 길 건너편인 4587 Park View Drive입니다. 이 전시회는 영구적이며 자주 업데이트될 것입니다. 더 많이 알고 싶으면 543-2341-6582로 전화 주세요.

어휘 exhibition 전시회 lighting 조명 harness 이용, 활용하다 flame 불꽃 refine 정제하다 approach 접근하다 incandescent 백열성의 bulb 전구 court house 법원청사

131 (A) undo
(B) redeem
(C) recall
(D) unveil

해설 다음 달에 최신 전시회를 '열 것이다'는 내용을 발표하고 있는 글이므로 선택지 중에서 가장 적절한 정답은 (D) unveil(공개하다, 발표하다)이다.

132 (A) ourselves
(B) our own
(C) ours
(D) we

해설 대명사의 격을 묻는 문제이다. 빈칸 앞에는 전치사가 있고 빈칸 뒤에는 명사가 있으므로 소유격인 (B) our own(우리의)이 정답이다.

133
(A) arrive
(B) to arrive
(C) arrival
(D) arriving

해설 빈칸 앞에 관사 the가 있으므로 명사형이 필요하다. 따라서 정답은 (C) arrival(도착)이다.

134
(A) You can watch a video about how a steam train was developed.
(B) This exhibition will be permanent and will be updated every so often.
(C) Whale oil sale is prohibited by animal protection law.
(D) We have to continue our efforts to reduce the amount of electricity used.

해설 조명의 역사에 대한 전시회를 개최한다는 내용이다. 전시회의 내용과 주제에 대한 것들을 언급한 후 빈칸 바로 앞에서는 전시회의 장소를 알려주고 있다. 따라서 이번 전시회가 영구적이며 자주 업데이트될 것이라는 (B)가 가장 적절한 문장이다.

(A) 당신은 증기 기관차가 어떻게 개발되었는지에 관한 영상을 볼 수 있습니다.
(B) 이 전시회는 영구적이며 자주 업데이트될 것입니다.
(C) 동물 보호법에 의해 고래 기름은 금지되어 있습니다.
(D) 우리는 전기사용량을 줄이는 데에 노력을 계속해야 합니다.

ACTUAL TEST 01 ACTUAL TEST 02 ACTUAL TEST 03 ACTUAL TEST 04 ACTUAL TEST 05

Sandy's mountain Equipment

We make sure our products are of the ------- quality and tested
135.
in the outdoor environment before making them available to
our customers. Your satisfaction is our number one goal. -------
136.
you feel that any of our merchandise does not meet your exact
needs, please feel free to return it. -------.
137.

Simply place your item to be returned in the package we
included with your shipment, and we will ------- the shipping
138.
expense. We guarantee to process your return immediately on
arrival and will have your replacement item sent back out on the
same day.

Sandy's 산악 장비

우리의 상품은 가장 품질이 좋고 고객들이 상품을 사용하기 전에 야외 환경에서 테스트됩니다. 당신의 만족이 우리의 첫 번째 목표입니다. 우리의 물건들 중 어떤 것이라도 당신을 만족시키지 않는다면 언제든 돌려주세요. 우리는 기꺼이 교환이나 전액 환불을 해드릴 것입니다.

물건을 배송 시에 포함되었던 상자에 그냥 넣어서 돌려주시면 되고 배송비는 우리가 책임지겠습니다. 도착 즉시 반품처리를 하고 교환 물품을 같은 날에 발송해 드릴 것을 보장해드립니다.

어휘 satisfaction 만족 merchandise 상품 simply 그냥(간단히) shipping fee 배송비 guarantee 보장하다 replacement 대체, 교체물

135
(A) highly
(B) high
(C) highest
(D) higher

해설 <the + ------ + 명사> 형태이므로 빈칸은 형용사자리이다. '가장 높은 품질의 상품'이라는 것을 강조하고 있으므로 최상급인 (C) highest(가장 높은)가 정답이다.

136
(A) Should
(B) Would
(C) Had
(D) Could

해설 빈칸 뒤의 문장은 전체 문장에서 부사절 역할을 하고 있다. 부사절(if + 주어 + should + 동사원형)에서 if가 생략되고 주어와 동사가 도치되므로, <Should + 주어 + 동사원형(만약 주어가 동사한다면)>이라는 표현이 만들어지게 된다. 따라서 정답은 (A) Should이다.

137
    (A) We also supply our products to professional climbers.
    (B) You can personally see our product at our showroom.
    (C) We will gladly offer you an exchange or a complete refund.
    (D) Delivery takes normally 2 business days from the purchase.

해설 빈칸 앞 문장에서 만족스럽지 못하다면 '반품해도 된다(please feel free to return it)'는 내용이 있고, 빈칸 뒤에는 반품의 방법에 대한 안내를 하는 것으로 보아, 만족하지 못한다면 기꺼이 교환이나 환불을 해주기 때문에 패키지에 넣어서 보내면 된다는 흐름이 가장 적절하다.

(A) 우리는 또한 우리의 제품을 전문 등반가에게 공급합니다.
(B) 당신은 전시장에서 우리 제품을 직접 보실 수 있습니다.
(C) 우리는 기꺼이 교환이나 전액 환불을 해드릴 것입니다.
(D) 배송은 보통 구매 후 영업일 2일 이내가 걸립니다.

138
    (A) use
    (B) cover
    (C) persist
    (D) tend

해설 배송비(the shipping expense)라는 목적어와 어울리는 동사를 골라야 한다. 우리 회사 측에서 배송비를 책임지므로 부담 없이 환불이 가능하다는 내용이 자연스럽다.

Questions 139-142 refer to the following letter.

MILO-Kurata Credit Services

Mr. Maria Shurn

84b Trilling Road

Calgarly, AB

Dear Mr. Shurn,

After ------- **139.** two years of negotiations, MILO Asset Management and Kurata Holdings have finally merged to become MILO-Kurata Credit Services. Two successful financial product companies have now become the industry leader in the finance sector. We promise to continue honoring our previous commitments to you, a ------- **140.** customer. However, we are also pleased to be able to offer you a range of new and exciting financial products to ------- **141.** your portfolio and lower your risk exposure. -------. **142.** Please look over the brochure we've included with this letter regarding our products. If you have any questions, a friendly and knowledgeable associate will be only too pleased to help at any of our branches. We look forward to serving you better.

Sincerely,

Graham Carter

Asset Advisor

MILO-Kurata Credit Services

Maria Shurn 씨

84b Trilling Road

Calgarly, AB

Shurn 씨께,

2년이 넘는 협상 끝에 MILO Asset Management와 Kurata Holdings는 마침내 MILO-Kurota Credit Service로 합병되었습니다. 두 성공적인 금융 상품 회사들은 이제 금융 분야에서 업계 선두가 되었습니다. 우리는 소중한 고객인 당신께 이전의 약속을 계속해서 명예롭게 지켜 나갈 것을 약속드립니다. 하지만 우리는 또한 당신의 투자자산구성을 넓히고 위험으로의 노출을 줄이기 위한 다양한 새롭고 흥미로운 금융 상품들을 제공하게 되어 기쁩니다. 9월 17일을 시작으로 우리의 모든 고객들에게 이 서비스들은 사용 가능하게 될 것입니다. 이 편지에 동봉된 상품 소책자를 살펴보세요. 만약 질문이 있으시다면 다정하고 아는 것이 많은 직원이 우리 지사들을 친절하게 안내해줄 것입니다. 우리는 당신을 더욱 잘 모시게 되길 바랍니다.

진심을 담아,

Graham Carter

자산 고문

어휘 negotiation 협상 merge 합병하다 financial 재정적인 sector 분야 previous 이전의 commitment 약속 be able to 할 수 있다 a range of 다양한 portfolio 투자 자산 구성, 포트폴리오 exposure 노출 associate 동료 branch 지사, 분점

139
(A) following
(B) more than
(C) very
(D) much more

'2년(two years)'에서 숫자 two를 수식하는 부사는 (B) more than(~ 이상의)이다.

140
(A) first
(B) referred
(C) temporary
(D) valued

회사가 합병했다는 이야기를 고객에게 알리고 있다. 이전의 헌신과 노력을 계속해 나가겠다고 하므로, 당신과 같은 '소중한' 고객이라는 표현이 가장 적절하다. 따라서 정답은 (D) valued(가치 있는, 소중한)이다.

141
(A) broaden
(B) extend
(C) excel
(D) forecast

합병을 통해서 더욱 다양한 금융상품들을 제공할 수 있게 되었다는 내용이 앞에 있고, 투자자산구성(portfolio)이라는 목적어와 어울리는 동사를 골라야 하므로, 자산 구성을 넓혀줄 다양한 재정상품들을 제공한다는 의미가 가장 적절하다. 따라서 정답은 (A) broaden(넓히다)이다.

142
(A) After we used this service for 3 months, we decided to cancel our contract.
(B) Beginning September 17, these services will become available to all our customers.
(C) We are an awarded financial advisor and we are confident that our service will exceed your expectation.
(D) Making a huge profit through investing needs experts'insight from many year's experience.

빈칸 앞에 '당신의 투자자산구성을 넓히고 위험으로의 노출을 줄이기 위한 다양한 새롭고 흥미로운 금융상품들을 제공하게 되어 기쁘다(we are also pleased to be able to offer you a range of new and exciting financial products to broaden your portfolio and lower your risk exposure)'는 문장이 있고, '이러한 서비스들(these services)은 9월 17일부터 이용 가능하다'는 내용이 가장 적절한 흐름이므로 정답은 (B)이다.

(A) 이 서비스를 3개월 동안 이용하고 난 후 우리는 계약을 취소하기로 결심했습니다.
(B) 9월 17일을 시작으로 모든 고객들에게 사용 가능하게 될 것입니다.
(C) 우리는 수상경력이 있는 금융자문기관이며 우리의 서비스가 당신의 기대치를 넘을 것이라고 자신합니다.
(D) 투자를 통해 큰 수익을 만드는 것은 오랜 경험을 통한 전문가의 견해가 필요합니다.

Questions 143-146 refer to the following e-mail.

To: Kolnas@stanfordcom.net

From: customerservice@zonacomcenter.com

Date: March 30

Subject: Invoice # 346750

Dear Ms. Kolnas,

As I mentioned in our conversation over the phone, we finished

------- your laptop on March 15, and we shipped it to you

143.

through Fedex on March 16. ------- you have notified us that

144.

you have not yet received the laptop, our only assumption

is that it was lost in transit. Right after receiving your letter,

we informed the shipping agency about the loss, and one of

its representatives is now trying to locate the shipment. We

expect a report from them within two days. -------. If it cannot

145.

be found within seven days, you will be refunded for the exact

amount you paid for the laptop by Fedex. We apologize for the

inconvenience you -------, and look forward to doing business

146.

with you again in the future.

Sincerely,

Quincy Bishop

Customer Service, Zona Computer Center

수신: Kolnas@stanfordcom.net

발신: customerservice@zonacomcenter.com

날짜: 3월 30일

제목: 송장 # 346750

Kolnas 씨께,

제가 전화로 이미 언급했듯이 우리는 노트북 수리를 3월 15일에 마쳤고 그것을 3월 16일에 Fedex를 통해 배송을 했습니다. 당신이 아직 노트북을 받지 못했다는 것을 우리에게 알려주었기 때문에 우리의 유일한 추측은 그것을 운송 도중에 잃어버렸다는 것입니다. 당신의 편지를 받은 직후 우리는 배송업체에 분실을 알렸고 그 직원 중 한 명이 수송품의 정확한 위치를 찾아내기 위해 노력 중입니다. 우리는 이틀 이내에 그들로부터 보고받을 걸로 예상합니다. 만약 Fedex 직원이 노트북을 찾는다면 바로 배송해 드리겠습니다. 만약 그것이 일주일 이내로 찾아지지 않는다면 Fedex로부터 노트북을 사기 위해 지불했던 정확한 금액을 환불받을 것입니다. 당신이 겪었던 불편함에 대해 사과드리고 향후에 다시 우리 회사를 이용해 주시길 기대합니다.

진심을 담아

Quincy Bishop

고객 서비스, Zona Computer Center

어휘 notify 알리다 assumption 추측 transit 수송 representative 대표, 직원 locate ~의 정확한 위치를 찾아내다 shipment 수송품 inconvenience 불편

143
(A) to repair
(B) repairs
(C) repairing
(D) repair

해설 동사 finish 뒤에 들어갈 목적어를 고르는 문제이다. finish는 to부정사를 목적어를 취하지 못하므로 (A) to repair는 정답이 될 수 없다. 빈칸 뒤에 '너의 노트북(your laptop)'이라는 명사목적어기 있기 때문에 너의 노트북을 수리하는 것을 끝냈다는 의미가 적절하므로 정답은 동명사인 (C) repairing이다.

144
(A) Since
(B) While
(C) Though
(D) Due to

해설 해설 빈칸 뒤에 문장이 있으므로 빈칸은 부사절 접속사자리이다. 전치사인 (D) Due to(~때문에)는 답이 될 수 없다. 문맥상 아직 노트북을 받지 못했다는 것을 우리에게 알려주었기 때문에 운송 도중에 잃어버렸다고 추측한다는 내용이 가장 적절하므로, 정답은 (A) Since(~때문에)이다.

145
(A) After talking with one of the delivery staff, we concluded that your shipment has successfully arrived.
(B) The manufacturer informed us that the item will be included in our next regular shipment.
(C) If the Fedex representative can find your laptop, it will be delivered to you right away.
(D) The items left in baggage claim area will be kept in our lost & found office for 90 days.

해설 빈칸 앞에는 직원이 수송품의 위치를 찾는 중이고, 곧 보고가 올 것이라는 내용이 있고, 빈칸 뒤에는 찾아지지 않는다면 환불을 해드리겠다는 내용으로 연결된다. 이 사이에 '만약 찾게 된다면 바로 배송해 드리겠다'는 문맥이 자연스럽다.

(A) 배달직원 중 한 명과 얘기한 후 당신의 선적물이 성공적으로 도착했다고 결론 내렸습니다.
(B) 제조업체는 우리에게 다음 정기 선적에 포함될 품목에 대해서 알려주었습니다.
(C) 만약 Fedex 직원이 노트북을 찾는다면 당신에게 바로 배송해 드리겠습니다.
(D) 수하물 찾는 곳에 남겨진 물건들은 분실물 보관소에 90일간 보관될 것입니다.

146
(A) will be experienced
(B) are experienced
(C) have experienced
(D) will have experienced

해설 '고객이 경험했을 불편함에 대해 사과드린다'는 내용이므로 정답은 (C) have experienced이다.

169

101

------- the goods have been delivered at the delivery address, the risk concerning the products is the purchaser's responsibility.
(A) In addition to
(B) Even so
(C) As soon as
(D) Other than

제품이 배송 주소로 배송되자마자, 제품에 대한 위험은 구매자의 책임이다.

해설 빈칸은 의미가 적절한 접속사가 들어갈 자리이다. 전치사인 in addition to(~뿐만 아니라)와 other than(~외에)은 구조가 안 맞는 오답이다.

어휘 goods 상품 concerning ~에 관한 other than ~ 외에

102

------- four months, the management committee of Gold West Corporation checks if their policies are moving toward the right direction.
(A) Every
(B) Only
(C) During
(D) About

4개월마다, Gold West Corporation의 경영위원회는 그들의 정책이 올바른 방향으로 가고 있는지 아닌지를 확인합니다.

해설 빈칸은 뒤의 four months(4개월)와 연결이 적절한 단어가 들어갈 자리이다. every(매 ~마다), during(~동안), about(대략)이 들어갈 수 있지만 뒤 문장의 내용으로 볼 때 every four months(4개월마다)가 적절하다.

어휘 committee 위원회 move toward 방향으로 진행하다 right 적절한 direction 방향

103

All employees who were hired last month must submit their first report to Mr. Stich's office ------- 5:30 P.M. on Friday.
(A) by
(B) within
(C) onto
(D) until

지난달에 고용된 모든 직원들은 금요일 오후 5시 30분까지 Stich 씨의 사무실에 그들의 첫 보고서를 제출해야 합니다.

해설 빈칸은 시간과 어울리는 전치사가 들어갈 자리이다. 시간과 어울리는 by(~까지), within(~ 이내에), until(~까지) 중에, 일단 기간과 어울리는 within은 오답이다. by와 until은 둘 다 '~까지'의 의미이지만, by는 정해진 시점까지 한 번이라는 의미로 complete, submit 등과 어울리고, until은 정해진 시점까지 계속 진행하는 의미로 wait, postpone, stay 등과 어울린다. 본 문장에서는 must submit(반드시 제출하다)를 통해 (A) by를 정답으로 고른다.

어휘 hire 고용하다 submit 제출하다

104

The Melbourne City Council will take its citizens' preferences into -------when choosing a location for the new community center.
(A) construction
(B) participation
(C) account
(D) registration

Melbourne 시 의회는 새로운 시민 문화회관을 위해 새로운 장소를 선택할 때, 시민들의 선호도를 고려할 것입니다.

해설 빈칸은 앞의 단어 take into와 연결되는 명사자리이다. take sth into account (consideration)는 '~을 고려하다'로 기억해 두면 쉽게 해결된다.

어휘 take sth into account ~을 고려하다 preference 선호도 community center 지역회관 participation 참여 registration 등록

105

The delegation ------- at ten in the morning tomorrow, so please go to the airport to meet them.
(A) arrived
(B) will be arrived
(C) is arriving
(D) have arrived

대표단이 내일 아침 10시에 도착한다. 그래서 그들을 만나러 공항으로 가길 바란다.

해설 빈칸은 문장의 시제가 일치하는 동사가 들어갈 자리이다. '내일 아침 10시'이므로 가까운 미래를 나타내는 진행형인 (C) is arriving이 정답이다.

어휘 delegation 대표단

106

Since adopting non-toxic paint last year, Bridge Home Improvement Service has ------- doubled its profit margin.
(A) after
(B) until
(C) almost
(D) during

작년에 무독성 페인트를 채택한 이래로, Bridge Home Improvement Service는 거의 두 배의 이익을 남겼다.

해설 빈칸은 뒤의 동사 double(두 배로 만들다)와 의미연결이 적절한 부사가 들어갈 자리이다. 문맥상 '거의 두 배의 이익을 남겼다'는 의미가 자연스럽다.

어휘 adopt 채택하다 non-toxic 무독성의 double 두 배로 만들다 profit margin 수익

107

Only those who have the ------- to travel abroad for business are considered for the position of the overseas sales division head.
(A) commission
(B) flexibility
(C) relative
(D) destination

해외로 출장을 가는 데 융통성 있는 사람만이 해외영업 담당부장의 직책에 고려됩니다.

해설 빈칸은 have에 대한 목적어자리로 의미가 적절한 명사가 올 자리이다. 앞 부분을 보면 only those(단지 그러한 사람들)이고, 뒷부분은 are considered for the position of the overseas sales division head(해외 영업부장의 직책에 고려된다)이므로, '융통성 있는 사람만이 고려된다'는 의미이다.

어휘 abroad 해외로 overseas sales 해외 영업 division 부문, 부서 commission 수수료 flexibility 유연성 relative 친척 destination 목적지, 장소

108

By the time this item is launched in the market, Big Chase Supplies ------- a new advertisement.
(A) is published
(B) will be published
(C) will have published
(D) had published

이 상품이 시장에 출시될 때쯤이면, Big Chase Supplies는 새로운 광고를 출판했을 것입니다.

해설 빈칸은 적절한 형태의 동사가 들어갈 자리이다. 앞 문장에서 by the time이 보인다. by the time은 접속사로 쓰여 <By the time + 현재, 미래완료> 또는 <By the time + 과거, 과거완료>의 형태로 쓰인다. By the time의 시제가 현재이므로, 빈칸은 미래완료시제인 (C) will have published가 정답이다.

어휘 by the time ~할 무렵, ~때까지 launch 출시하다 advertisement 광고 publish 발행하다

109

Make sure to avoid covering the item's bar code when ------- new price stickers to books on sale.
(A) applies
(B) applying
(C) apply
(D) applied

할인 중인 책에 새로운 가격표를 붙일 때, 상품의 바코드를 덮는 것을 확실하게 피하세요.

해설 빈칸은 접속사 when 뒤에 적절한 형태의 단어가 들어갈 자리이다. 이 문장은 when (주어 + be동사) ------- new price stickers이다. be동사 뒤이고 빈칸 뒤에 목적어가 있으므로 빈칸은 동사의 -ing형태가 들어가야 한다.

어휘 make sure ~을 확실히 하다 avoid 피하다 cover 덮다 apply 붙이다 on sale 할인 중인

110

The new tax policy is intended ------- local growth and development, but its effects may not be seen for a couple of years.
(A) facilitating
(B) to facilitate
(C) facilitate
(D) to be facilitated

새로운 세금 정책은 지역 성장과 개발을 위한 것이지만 이것의 효과는 몇 년 동안 보이지 않을지도 모른다.

(해설) 빈칸은 앞의 is intended와 연결이 적절한 단어 형태가 들어갈 자리이다. be intended는 be intended to V의 패턴으로 쓰인다. 그리고, 뒤에 local growth and development라는 목적어가 보이므로 능동의 형태가 되어야 한다. 이 두 가지를 충족시키는 선택지는 to facilitate이다.

(어휘) be intended to ~하기를 의도하다 development 개발 effect 효과 facilitate 용이하게 하다

111

Mr. Chan will announce the idea ------- has come up with to market our soap line.
(A) him
(B) his
(C) he
(D) himself

Chan 씨는 비누라인을 시장에 판매하기 위하여 고안해냈던 생각을 발표할 것입니다.

(해설) 빈칸은 has come이라는 동사형태 앞에 어울리는 대명사자리이다. 우선 명사 the idea와 빈칸 사이에 목적격 관계대명사 that이나 which가 생략된 것을 알아야 한다. 빈칸은 주어자리이므로 주격대명사인 (C) he가 정답이다.

(어휘) announce 발표하다 come up with 생각해 내다, 고안하다 market 판매하다 soap 비누

112

------- is willing to apply for the sales manager position must submit their resume and previous employer's references.
(A) Another
(B) Someone
(C) Whoever
(D) Anyone

판매 매니저 직책에 기꺼이 지원하려는 사람은 누구든지 그들의 이력서와 이전 고용주의 추천서를 제출해야 합니다.

(해설) 빈칸은 문장의 주어가 되는 자리이다. 빈칸 뒤에 is라는 단수동사가 보이고 뒤쪽에 must submit이라고 동사가 보인다. 이 두 가지를 충족시키는 선택지는 anyone who를 줄여놓은 (C) Whoever(누구든 ~하는 사람)이다.

(어휘) be willing to 기꺼이 ~하다 apply for ~을 신청하다 reference 추천서

ACTUAL TEST 06 ACTUAL TEST 07 ACTUAL TEST 08 ACTUAL TEST 09 ACTUAL TEST 10

113

------- working for the department store, Mr. Han had to handle about 20 complaints from customers per week.
(A) While
(B) During
(C) Meanwhile
(D) For

백화점에서 일하는 동안, Han 씨는 일주일에 대략 20건 정도의 고객들로부터의 불만 사항을 처리해야 했다.

해설 빈칸은 뒤의 working과 연결이 적절한 단어가 들어갈 자리이다. 의미상 During과 While이 적절해 보이지만, During은 동명사를 취할 수 없는 전치사이다. 그래서 정답은 (A) While이 된다. 이 문장은 While (he was) working for의 구조이다.

어휘 department store 백화점 handle 다루다 per ~당, 마다

114

Ms. Oh will be transferred to the marketing department, in ------- she will take charge of web advertising.
(A) which
(B) what
(C) where
(D) that

Oh 씨는 마케팅 부서로 전근될 것이고 그 부서에서 그녀는 인터넷 광고를 책임질 것입니다.

해설 빈칸은 명사 marketing department를 선행사로 받는 관계대명사자리이다. 먼저 전치사 뒤에는 that이 올 수 없기 때문에 오답이 되고, where 같은 관계부사 역시 전치사와 함께 쓸 수 없는 오답이다. what은 선행사를 포함한 관계대명사이므로 앞에 명사가 올 수 없다. 정답은 사물을 선행사로 받는 (A) which이다.

어휘 transfer 전근시키다 take charge of ~을 맡다 web advertising 인터넷 광고

115

Residents of Festival Tower and employees at Lakeview Manufacturing Company worked ------- to lessen water pollution in the area.
(A) collaboratively
(B) collaborative
(C) collaborating
(D) collaboration

Festival Tower의 거주민들과 Lakeview 제조회사의 직원들은 그 지역에서 수질 오염을 줄이기 위하여 협동적으로 일했습니다.

해설 빈칸은 자동사인 work 뒤에 적절한 형태의 단어가 들어갈 자리이다. 자동사 뒤의 빈칸은 부사자리이므로 정답은 (A) collaboratively(협동적으로)이다.

어휘 resident 주민 lessen 줄이다 water pollution 수질 오염 collaboratively 협동적으로

116

The president of Hussy company commissioned Corrle Vernard to create a ------- designed company logo.
(A) profession
(B) professional
(C) professionals
(D) professionally

Hussy 사의 사장은 Corrie Vernard 씨에게 전문적으로 디자인된 회사 로고를 제작하도록 의뢰했다.

해설 빈칸은 분사 형태의 형용사인 deigned(고안된) 앞에 어울리는 단어가 들어갈 자리이다. 형용사 앞의 빈칸은 부사자리이므로, 정답은 (D) professionally(전문적으로)이다.

어휘 commission 위임하다, 의뢰하다 designed 고안된, 디자인된 profession 직업 professional 전문적인, 전문가 professionally 전문적으로

117

I-plan, a new mobile phone application, can help you organize your calendar schedule -------.
(A) yours
(B) you
(C) yourself
(D) your own

새로운 휴대폰 응용프로그램인 I-plan은 당신이 직접 달력 일정을 정리하는 것을 돕는다.

해설 빈칸은 문장 성분상 없어도 되는 자리이다. 대명사 중 강조의 의미로 들어가는 재귀대명사가 적절해 보인다. 그래서 정답은 (C) yourself이다.

어휘 application 응용 프로그램 organize 정리하다

118

Our Engine Clean machine has been manufactured in Australia and delivers ------- results on your car engine parts.
(A) exceptional
(B) exceptions
(C) exceptionally
(D) exception

우리의 Engine Clean기계는 호주에서 제조되었고 당신의 자동차 엔진 부품에 뛰어난 결과를 초래합니다.

해설 빈칸은 뒤의 명사 results 앞에 어울리는 단어가 들어갈 자리이다. 명사 앞에 올 수 있는 품사는 형용사이므로 정답은 (A) exceptional(뛰어난)이다.

어휘 manufacture 제조하다 part 부품 exceptional 뛰어난

119

In honor of ------- achievements, Mr. Hwang was given the lifetime achievement award.
(A) perceptive
(B) noteworthy
(C) interested
(D) satisfied

주목할 만한 성취에 경의를 표하여 Hwang 씨는 공로상을 수상했다.

해설 빈칸은 achievement와 의미가 어울리는 형용사자리이다. perceptive(지각하는), noteworthy(현저한), interested(관심 있는), satisfied(만족스러운) 중에 noteworthy가 의미 연결이 가장 매끄럽다.

어휘 in honor of ~에 경의를 표하여 achievement 성취 lifetime achievement award 평생 공로상 perceptive 인식하는 noteworthy 현저한 interested 관심 있는 satisfied 만족스러운

120

The document attached in the file contains essential information about your newly ------- car insurance policy.
(A) issued
(B) expected
(C) expressed
(D) influenced

파일에 첨부된 문서는 당신의 새롭게 발행된 자동차 보험에 대한 필수적인 정보를 포함합니다.

해설 빈칸은 뒤의 car insurance policy(자동차 보험)와 연결이 적절한 형용사가 들어갈 자리이다. 보험과 관련된 선택지는 issue(발행하다)이다.

어휘 attach 첨부하다 contain 포함하다 essential 필수적인 newly 새롭게 insurance policy 보험 issue 발행하다 express 표현하다 influence 영향을 미치다

121

Since its founding fifteen years ago, Jamie's Kitchen ------- customer satisfaction to be a top priority.
(A) consider
(B) has been considered
(C) has considered
(D) considered

15년 전 설립 이래로, Jamie's Kitchen은 고객 만족을 최고 우선순위로 여겨왔습니다.

해설 since(~이래로)를 통해 현재완료가 들어감을 알 수 있고, 뒤에 '고객 만족'이라는 목적어가 있으므로 능동임을 알 수 있다. 이 두 가지를 충족시키는 선택지는 (C) has considered이다.

어휘 founding 설립 customer satisfaction 고객 만족 top priority 최고의 우선순위

122

Please help us provide better service to our customers by taking a few moments to ------- to this short and simple written questionnaire.
(A) announce
(B) respond
(C) fill
(D) sign

이 짧고 간단한 서면 설문조사에 응답하기 위해 시간을 내 주심으로써, 고객들에게 더 좋은 서비스를 제공하도록 도와주십시오.

해설 빈칸은 전치사 to와 어울리는 동사자리이다. 선택지 중 자동사인 (B) respond가 전치사 to를 받는다. respond to ~에 응답하다

어휘 take a few moments 잠시 시간을 보내다 respond to ~에 응답하다 written 서면 questionnaire 설문지 announce 발표하다 fill 채우다

123

Paul Gouguin faced many difficulties in his life, but he used them as ------- for his art.
(A) inspiration
(B) constructions
(C) suspicions
(D) apprehensions

Paul Gouguin 씨는 일생에서 많은 어려움에 직면했지만, 그것들을 예술을 위한 영감으로써 사용하였다.

해설 빈칸은 as 뒤에 의미가 어울리는 명사자리이다. 빈칸 앞을 보면 used them(그것들을 이용하다) as(~로서)이고, 뒤는 for his art(그의 예술에 대해)인데, 대명사 them은 앞의 many difficulties(많은 어려움)를 받는다. 이런 진행을 볼 때 '인생의 많은 어려움들을 예술에 대한 영감으로 이용하다'라는 의미가 적절하므로 (A) inspiration이 정답이 된다.

124

If your passport is set ------- soon and you have travel plans, it will be a good idea to renew it as soon as possible.
(A) to expire
(B) expired
(C) expiring
(D) will have expired

만약 당신의 여권이 곧 만료되고 여행갈 계획이 있다면, 가능한 한 빨리 여권을 갱신하는 것이 좋을 것입니다.

해설 빈칸은 앞의 is set과 연결이 적절한 형태의 단어가 들어갈 자리이다. be set to(~할 예정이다)를 알아두면 쉽게 해결되는 유형이다.

어휘 passport 여권 be set to ~할 예정이다 renew 갱신하다 expire 만료되다

125 Most specialists ------- with the construction market predict that construction of buildings will decrease over the next two years.
(A) familiar
(B) usual
(C) normal
(D) recognizable

건설시장을 아주 잘 아는 대부분의 전문가들은 빌딩의 건설이 2년에 걸쳐 감소할 것이라고 예상합니다.

해설 빈칸은 뒤의 전치사 with와 어울리는 형용사자리이다. 선택지 중 이에 맞는 형용사는 (A) familiar(익숙한)이다.

어휘 specialist 전문가 construction 건설 decrease 감소하다 familiar 익숙한 recognizable 인식 가능한

126 Four years ago, at the age of 32, Kike Alfredo ------- to Tokyo to work in the financial sector.
(A) moved
(B) has moved
(C) would move
(D) moves

32살, 4년 전에, Kike Alfredo는 금융분야에서 일하기 위하여 도쿄로 이사했다.

해설 빈칸은 동사자리이며 앞에서 four years ago라고 하므로 과거동사인 (A) moved가 정답이다.

어휘 financial sector 금융 분야

127 On behalf of the management and staff at Mega Mart, we would like to thank all of our loyal customers for their ------- and support.
(A) item
(B) backup
(C) usage
(D) patronage

Mega Mart에서의 경영진과 직원을 대신하여, 우리는 그들의 애용과 지원에 대한 충성스러운 고객들에게 감사함을 전하고 싶습니다.

해설 빈칸은 support와 연결이 적절한 명사가 들어갈 자리이다. patronage and support(애용과 지원)라는 의미 연결이 해석상 가장 적절해 보인다.

어휘 on behalf of ~을 대신하여 loyal customer 단골 patronage 애용 support 지원 item 항목 usage 사용

128
Over the years, we have been ranked not just ------, but repeatedly by the Arizona Business Journal as the best Law Firm throughout North Carolina.
(A) still
(B) about
(C) so
(D) once

수년에 걸쳐서, 우리는 Arizona Business Journal에 의해 North Carolina 전역에서 최고의 법률 회사로서 한번이 아니라 반복적으로 순위에 올랐다.

해설 빈칸은 not과 but 사이에 의미가 적절한 부사가 들어갈 자리이다. not just once but repeatedly(단지 한 번이 아니라 반복적으로)가 적절하다.

어휘 rank 평가하다, 등급을 매기다 throughout 전역에 once 한 번, 한 차례 repeatedly 반복적으로

129
------ among the reasons Victoria is a favored city to live in are the city's strong educational system, growing economy, and temperate climate.
(A) Proper
(B) Adept
(C) Similar
(D) Chief

Victoria가 살기에 가장 선호되는 도시라는 많은 이유들 중 주된 것은, 도시의 강력한 교육시스템, 성장하는 경제, 기후 조건 때문입니다.

해설 빈칸은 의미가 적절한 형용사가 들어갈 자리이다. 이 문제는 도치문장으로 주어는 be동사(are) 이하이다. 내용을 살펴보면, '강한 교육 시스템, 성장하는 경제, 온화한 기후들이 빅토리아가 인기를 받는 도시라는 이유로 주된 것이다'라는 의미로 (D) Chief(주요한, 주된)가 정답이다.

어휘 favored 인기 있는, 선호되는 growing 성장하는 temperate 온화한 proper 적절한 adept 숙련된 similar 유사한 chief 주요한

130
Vancouver police are implementing a new model to train officers and are hoping to ------ the results of their research with other Canadian law-enforcement agencies.
(A) share
(B) split
(C) suggest
(D) taste

Vancouver 경찰은 경찰관들을 훈련시키는 새로운 모델을 실시하고 다른 캐나다 법 집행기관과 연구결과를 공유하기를 희망합니다.

해설 빈칸은 적절한 형태의 동사가 들어갈 자리이다. 뒤의 전치사 with와의 연결도 고려해 볼 때, share A with B(A를 B와 공유하다) 형태가 적절하다.

어휘 implement 시행하다 law-enforcement 법 집행 agency 기관 share 공유하다 split 분할하다 taste 맛보다

Questions 131-134 refer to the following memo.

To: All Employees

From: Lance Alvarez, Manager of Facilities

Date: March 20

Subject: Access card

On April 15, our company will install card-access systems ------- **131.** to the gates of the two parking areas. Parking Lot A, just behind the Golden View Building, and Parking Lot B, adjacent to the Calipso Building. -------. **132.** Nevertheless, employees in the maintenance and security departments who will be reporting to work on that day should be aware that they cannot enter the parking lot while the installation -------. **133.** On Friday, a memo will be sent out about ------- parking spaces for staff members who **134.** will be at work on April 15.

수신: All Employees

발신: Lance Alvarez, Manager of Facilities

날짜: 3월 20일

제목: 출입카드

4월 15일, 우리 회사는 두 주차장 입구 가까이에 카드-통과 시스템을 설치할 것입니다. Golden View Building 바로 뒤에 있는 주차장 A와 Calipso Building과 가까운 주차장 B에 설치됩니다. 설치가 하루 만에 완료되면 설치 과정이 대부분의 제조업체 직원들에게 영향을 미치지 않을 것입니다. 그럼에도 불구하고 그날 근무할 예정인 유지 관리팀과 보안팀 직원들은 설치를 하는 동안 주차장에 들어갈 수 없다는 것을 알아야 합니다. 금요일에 4월 15일에 일하게 되는 직원들에게 대안의 주차 장소에 관한 메모를 보낼 것입니다.

어휘 behind ~뒤에 adjacent 인접한, 가까운 maintenance 유지 관리 (보수) be aware ~을 감지하다 enter 들어가다

131
(A) nearby
(B) nearly
(C) close
(D) proximity

해설 완전한 문장 이후에 수식어 자리이므로 명사 (D)는 오답이다. 문맥상 '입구 가까이에 카드-통과 시스템을 설치할 것이다'라는 의미가 자연스럽다. 빈칸 뒤에 있는 전치사 to와 함께 쓰이는 close to(~가까이에)를 기억해두자.

132
(A) This newly Installed system has been revealed to have a serious defect and will be replaced.
(B) The security workers will inspect this system on a monthly basis to find any error.
(C) This new system will help increase customer satisfaction by helping them access our building more easily.
(D) As the installation will be completed in a single day, the installation process will not affect most Manufacturing workers.

133
(A) is taking place
(B) will be taken place
(C) was taking place
(D) will have taken place

134
(A) alternative
(B) alternate
(C) alternatively
(D) alternation

Questions 135-138 refer to the following e-mail.

To: All employees

From: Floyd Mitchum

Date: April 1

Subject: Next Week's Assignment

Thank you, everyone, for finishing all of your tasks for this week efficiently. I will go on rotating you weekly so that the tasks are ------- distributed to all of us, in addition to our regular work.
135.

On April 4, Ela will take charge of ordering coffee, tea and other supplies from Superior Taste Coffee Supplies. She will also ------- the kitchen cabinets when items we have ordered arrive.
136.
Excess supplies must be stored in the closet in our storage room. Mariposa ------- the filing cabinets on the third floor.
137.
-------. There is also a request from the payroll department to
138.
help them organize their files. It should take about two hours to finish this job each day.

If you have any questions, please contact me in my office.

Floyd Mitchum

수신: 전 직원

발신: Floyd Mitchum

날짜: 4월 1일

제목: 다음 주 업무

모든 분들께 이번 주 여러분의 업무를 효율적으로 끝내준 것에 대해 감사드립니다. 저는 우리 모두에게 정규 업무 외에도 일을 공평하게 분배되도록 주별로 교대 근무를 계속할 것입니다.

4월 4일, Ela는 Superior Taste Coffee Supplies에서 커피와 차, 그리고 다른 물품들을 주문하는 것을 맡게 될 것입니다. 그녀는 또한 우리가 주문한 물건들이 도착하면 부엌 찬장을 채울 것입니다. 초과 물품들은 반드시 우리 창고에 채워져야 합니다. Mariposa는 서류보관함을 3층에 정리할 것입니다. 모든 파일을 고객들 이름 알파벳순으로 확실하게 정리해주세요. 또한 급여부서에서 서류를 정리하기 위해 도와달라는 요청이 있습니다. 이 일을 마치는 데에는 하루에 2시간이 걸려야 합니다.

만약 질문이 있다면 저의 사무실로 연락 주세요.

Floyd Mitchum

어휘 efficiently 능률적으로 inform 알리다 rotating 선회하는, 교대하는 distribute 분배하다 take charge of ~을 떠맡다 store 저장하다 excess supply 초과 물품 payroll 급여

---

135 (A) commensurately
(B) expansively
(C) fairly
(D) compatibly

해설 <be동사 + ----- + 과거분사>의 빈칸은 부사자리이다. 주어진 빈칸이 포함된 문장에서, 일이 ~하게 분배되도록 주별로 서로 교대 근무를 한다는 내용이 언급되어 있다. 따라서 공평하게 분배되도록 하겠다는 내용이 적절하므로 정답은 (C) fairly(공평하게)이다.

136
(A) replenish
(B) deplete
(C) neglect
(D) comprise

해설 동사 어휘문제이다. 주어진 단락의 내용은 Ela가 담당할 업무가 언급되어 있다. 빈칸 역시 그녀가 주문한 물건들이 도착했을 때, 해야 할 일을 언급하는 동사가 와야 한다. 따라서 부엌의 찬장을 채우는 업무를 할 것이다는 내용이 적절하므로 정답은 (A) replenish (보충하다, 다시 채우다)이다.

137
(A) has organized
(B) will organize
(C) organized
(D) will be organized

해설 동사시제문제이다. 주어진 지문은 다음 주에 직원들이 해야 할 일을 공지하는 것이다. 앞 문장들에서 Ela가 담당하게 될 일을 미래시제로 나열하고 있다. 따라서 주어진 문장역시 Mariposa가 다음 주에 할 일을 언급하는 것이 적절하므로 정답은 미래시제인 (B) will organize이다.

138
(A) Please make sure to arrange all the files in alphabetical order by customer name.
(B) Please be aware that we installed new copiers at each end of the 3rd floor hall way.
(C) I am writing to announce that we successfully passed the state fire inspection.
(D) It's two days before our quarterly evaluation of staff performance.

해설 빈칸 앞 문장에서 Mariposa가 서류보관함을 정리할 것이라는 내용이, 빈칸 뒤의 문장에서 급여부서에서 서류 정리 요청이 있었다는 내용이 언급되어 있다. 따라서 빈칸 역시 정리에 대한 내용이 언급되어야 하므로 정답은 (A)이다.

(A) 모든 파일을 고객들 이름 알파벳순으로 확실하게 정리해주세요
(B) 새로운 복사기를 3층 복도 양끝에 설치했다는 것을 알아주세요.
(C) 나는 우리가 화재 점검을 성공적으로 통과했다는 것을 알리기 위해 글을 쓰고 있습니다.
(D) 분기별 직원 업무성과 평가 이틀 전입니다.

Questions 139-142 refer to the following review.

Dining Review Exclusive

The Sicilias ★★★☆

by Shelly Croughton

Edisonburg City (April 20) - Chef Alfonso Prodi, a famous culinary artist who is a native of Cannes, France, ------- a **139.** pleasant French restaurant called The Sicilias on the Edisonburg Coast yesterday. Residents of Edisonburg were excited to ------- **140.** the dishes at the only French restaurant in the city. -------. **141.** Fortunately, the superb food more than compensated for the long wait to get a table. I suggest that you stay for dessert. The really delicious chocolate cake prepared by Chef Alfonso Prodi is ------- the best in Edisonburg. The Sicilias is the newest **142.** addition to the city'great restaurant scene, and I really cannot wait to go back!

독점 식당 리뷰
The Sicilias ★★★☆
Shelly Croughton 씀

Edisonburg City (4월 20일) – 프랑스 Cannes출신의 유명한 요리 예술가인 Chef Alfonso Prodi는 어제 Edisonburg Coast 에 The Sicilias라는 프랑스 레스토랑을 열었습니다. Edisonbug의 거주자들은 도시에 하나뿐인 프랑스 레스토랑에서 시식하게 되어 들떠 있었습니다. 지난 밤 자리가 마련되기를 기다리는 손님들이 인도를 따라 길게 줄 서 있었습니다. 다행스럽게도 테이블에 앉기 위해 긴 기다림은 최고의 음식으로 보상되었습니다. 저는 디저트를 위해 머무는 것을 당신에게 제안합니다. Chef Alfoso Prodi가 준비한 정말 맛있는 초콜릿 케이크는 Edisonburg에서 단연코 가장 최고입니다.

어휘 culinary 요리 resident 거주자 be excited 들뜨다 sample 시식하다 superb 최고의 compensate 보상하다

139
(A) is opening
(B) opening
(C) opened
(D) will have opened

해설 동사 시제문제이다. 주어진 문장 마지막에 yesterday라는 시제 힌트를 통해 유명한 요리 예술가가 어제 레스토랑을 '열었다'는 것을 알 수 있다. 따라서 정답은 과거시제인 (C) opened이다.

140
(A) sample
(B) remain
(C) satisfy
(D) expedite

해설 동사 어휘문제이다. 빈칸의 동사는 거주자들이 들떠 있는 이유를 설명해야 하며, 목적어인 dishes(요리)와 의미적으로 잘 어울려야 한다. 따라서 거주자들이 요리 시식에 들떠 있다는 의미가 자연스럽다. 정답은 (A) sample(시식하다)이다.

184

141

(A) To reserve a table, please call 555-0812 and spell your name.
(B) Chef Alfonso Prodi is also serving as a professor at Edisonburg university.
(C) Ratatouilles and Beef Bourguignon are the signature dishes of Sicilias.
(D) Last night, guests waiting for a table formed long lines down the sidewalk.

해설 빈칸 뒷 문장에서 다행스럽게도 테이블을 잡기 위한 그 긴 기다림은 음식으로 보상되었다는 내용이 나와 있다. 따라서 빈칸은 오래 기다려야 했다는 내용이 언급되어야 하므로 정답은 (D)이다.

(A) 예약을 하시려면 555-0812로 전화주시고 이름을 말씀해주세요.
(B) 셰프 Alfonso Prodi는 또한 Edisonburg 대학의 교수로 재직 중입니다.
(C) Ratatouilles와 Beef Bourguignon은 Sicilias를 대표하는 요리입니다.
(D) 지난밤 자리가 마련되기를 기다리는 손님들이 인도를 따라 길게 줄서 있었습니다.

142

(A) by far
(B) far away
(C) nearby
(D) far too

해설 빈칸은 be동사와 최상급(the best) 사이에서 수식을 하는 부사자리이다. 최상급 앞에서 최상급을 강조할 수 있는 by far가 문법상 적절하다. 따라서 정답은 (A) by far(단연코)이다.

Questions 143-146 refer to the following letter.

Hottest Fit Fitness

San Francisco'Best Fitness Club

33 New Montgomery Street, San Francisco, CA 94105

Mike Winslow

9087 Appletown Avenue

San Francisco, CA 94105

Membership Number 32456

Dear Ms. Winslow,

We would like to inform you that your membership at Hottest

Fit Fitness is scheduled to be renewed on 1 April. ------- our
143.

records, you signed up for the Automatic Renewal Program.

Previously, you ------- us to charge your yearly membership
144.

fee to your credit card, which starts with the numbers 1108. If

you would rather use ------- credit card or pay using a different
145.

method, please inform us before March 25 so that we can

update our records. Also, you can update your billing information

in three ways. First, you can visit www.Hottestfittown.com,

our secure website, click on My Information Modification, and

choose the section about your credit card. Second, you can call

our customer service department at 9162-0228. -------. If you
146.

don't take any further action, we will continue billing the current

credit card that we have on file.

Sincerely yours,

Regina Miller

Director of Club Membership

Hottest Fit Fitness

San Francisco'Best Fitness Club

33 New Montgomery Street, San Francisco, CA 94105

Mike Winslow

9087 Appletown Avenue

San Francisco, CA 94105

회원번호 32456

Winslow 씨께

저희는 4월 1일에 귀하의 Hottest Fit Fitness 멤버십이 갱신될 예정이라는 것을 알려드리고 싶습니다. 우리 기록에 따르면 당신은 Automatic Reneal Program에 등록하셨습니다. 이전에 당신은 1108로 시작하는 신용카드로 멤버십 비용을 지불했냐고 물어보았습니다. 만약 당신이 다른 신용카드를 사용하거나 다른 방법으로 지불을 하고 싶으시면 우리에게 3월 25일까지 알려주세요. 그러면 우리는 기록을 업데이트할 수 있습니다. 또한 당신은 비용 정보에 3가지 방법으로 업데이트할 수 있습니다. 우선 우리의 안전한 사이트인 www.Hottestfittown.com에 방문할 수 있는데 내 정보 수정을 클릭하시고 당신의 신용카드에 대한 부분을 선택하시면 됩니다. 두 번째로 9162-0228에 전화하셔서 우리의 고객 담당부서와 통화하실 수 있습니다. 마지막으로 당신은 Hottest Fit Fitness 지점에 들러서 안내데스크에 있는 직원과 얘기할 수 있습니다. 만약 아무런 조치도 취하지 않으시면 우리는 계속해서 우리 파일에 있는 현재의 신용카드로 비용을 청구할 것입니다.

진심을 담아

Regina Miller

클럽 멤버십 관리자

어휘 inform 알리다 be scheduled to ~할 예정이다 renew 갱신하다 charge 지불하다 would rather ~하겠다, 하고 싶다 method 방법 secure 안전한 section 부분 further 추가의 current 현재의 take action 조치를 취하다

143
(A) Accordingly
(B) In accordance
(C) According to
(D) Accordance

해설 빈칸이 our records라는 명사구 앞에 있으므로 전치사자리이다. 정답은 (C) According to(~에 따르면)이며 의미는 '우리 기록에 따르면'이다.

144
(A) asked
(B) suggested
(C) allocated
(D) compensated

해설 동사 어휘문제이다. 빈칸 앞에서 이미 등록을 했다는 내용이 나왔으므로, 빈칸의 동사는 '당신이 연간 멤버십 비용을 신용카드로 지불했는지를 물어보았습니다'라는 의미가 자연스럽다.

145
(A) other
(B) another
(C) the others
(D) each other

해설 빈칸은 명사 앞 수량형용사자리이다. 빈칸 뒤의 명사가 단수명사이므로 복수명사와 함께 쓰는 (A) other는 오답, 단독으로 쓰이는 (C) the others, (D) each other도 오답이다. 따라서 정답은 (B) another이다.

146
(A) Lastly, we have completed updating our website, so you can find more detailed information than before.
(B) Finally, you can drop by any Hottest Fit Fitness branch and talk to a representative at the reception desk.
(C) Thirdly, for every person you refer who then uses our service, you'll receive a 20% discount.
(D) Once more, your next payment is due on April 1, after which your name will be removed from our list.

해설 해설 앞 문장에서 비용 정보는 3가지 방법으로 업데이트하실 수 있다고 언급하면서 첫 번째와 두 번째 방법이 서술되어 있다. 따라서 빈칸은 남은 세 번째 방법을 언급하고 있어야 하므로 정답은 (B)이다.

(A) 최근에 우리의 홈페이지 업데이트를 완료했고 당신은 이전보다 더 자세한 정보를 찾을 수 있습니다.

(B) 마지막으로 당신은 Hottest Fit Fitness 지점에 들러서 안내데스크에 있는 직원과 얘기할 수 있습니다.

(C) 세 번째로 우리의 서비스를 이용하는 당신이 언급했던 모든 사람들을 위해 20프로 할인을 받을 것입니다.

(D) 하나 더 귀하의 이름이 우리 목록에서 지워지는 다음 지불기한은 4월 1일까지입니다.

PART 5

101

The company may ------- ticket sales to a maximum number per person and reserves the right to cancel any tickets purchased in excess of this number.
(A) connect
(B) restrict
(C) claim
(D) deny

회사는 1인당 최대 티켓 판매를 제한할 수 있고, 이 숫자를 초과하여 구매된 티켓을 취소할 권한을 가지고 있습니다.

해설 빈칸은 뒤의 명사 ticket sales(티켓 판매)를 목적어로 취하는 동사자리이다. 문맥상 적절한 동사는 (B) restrict(제한하다)이다.

어휘 reserve the right 권리를 갖다 purchase 구입하다 excess 지나침, 과잉 connect 연결하다 restrict 제한하다 claim 주장하다 deny 부인하다

102

Dining at Roma Station Park is always a ------- and genuinely authentic experience in Calgary.
(A) delightfulness
(B) delightfully
(C) delight
(D) delightful

Roma Station Park에서 식사하는 것은 항상 Calgary에서 즐겁고 진정으로 정통적인 경험입니다.

해설 빈칸은 등위접속사 and로 연결되는 형용사(delightful 매우 기쁜, 즐거운)자리이다. (A) delightfulness 명사 (B) delightfully 부사 (C) delight 동사

어휘 genuinely 진정으로 authentic 정통의 experience 경험 delightful 기쁜 delightfulness 유쾌함

103

Ms. Najad requested two color printers to be used only to ------- brochures for the upcoming product campaigns.
(A) printed
(B) prints
(C) printing
(D) print

Najad 씨는 곧 있을 상품 캠페인 책자를 인쇄하는 데에만 사용될 수 있는 컬러 프린트 두 대를 요청했다.

해설 빈칸은 to부정사 뒤에는 동사원형(print)이 온다.

어휘 request 요청하다 brochure 책자 upcoming 다가오는 product 상품 print 인쇄하다

104

Sales Director Manuel Park thinks that advertising ------- in print is no longer a strong method to attract potential customers.
(A) closely
(B) solely
(C) otherwise
(D) indeed

판매부장인 Manuel Park 씨는 오로지 인쇄매체의 광고가 잠재적인 고객들을 끌어들이기 위한 더 이상 강력한 방법이 아니라고 생각합니다.

해설 advertising in print는 '인쇄물에 의한 광고'이고 뒤에서 '이것이 더 이상 강력한 방법이 아니다'라고 하므로 문맥상 '오로지(solely) 인쇄물이 강력한 광고 수단이 아니다'는 의미가 자연스럽다.

어휘 advertising 광고 method 방법 attract 마음을 끌다 potential 잠재적인 customer 고객 closely 접근하여 solely 오로지, 단지 otherwise 그렇지 않으면 indeed 정말

105

Ramos Ramirez is going to distribute an ------- to each committee member before next Saturday's meeting.
(A) appointment
(B) agenda
(C) appearance
(D) expense

Ramos Ramirez 씨는 다음 토요일 미팅 전에 각각의 위원회 멤버들에게 안건을 배부할 것입니다.

해설 빈칸은 distribute에 대한 목적어자리로 선택지 중 의미가 적절한 단어는 (B) agenda(안건)이다.

어휘 distribute 배부하다 committee 위원회 appointment 약속 agenda 안건 appearance 외모 expense 비용

106

Part of Ms. Koop's job as production supervisor is to oversee daily operations, ------- providing support to her team members.
(A) so
(B) but
(C) as well as
(D) whereas

생산관리자로서 Koop 씨의 업무 일부는 팀원들에게 지원을 제공할 뿐만 아니라, 매일 운영을 감독하는 것입니다.

해설 빈칸은 의미가 적절한 접속사가 들어갈 자리이다. 앞부분에 '매일 운영을 감독'하고 뒤에는 '지원을 제공하는 것'이므로 의미를 덧붙이는 (C) as well as(~뿐만 아니라)가 정답이다.

어휘 production 생산 supervisor 관리자 oversee 감독하다 operation 작동, 운영 provide 제공하다 as well as ~에 더하여, 게다가 whereas 반면

107

------- Nike's sales have increased so dramatically is proof that its chief sales manager, Hochang Lee, has done a great job.
(A) With
(B) That
(C) If
(D) For

Nike's의 판매가 아주 극적으로 증가했다는 것은 판매 매니저 장Hochang Lee가 업무를 훌륭하게 해냈다는 증거입니다.

해설 빈칸은 의미가 적절한 접속사가 들어갈 자리이다. 빈칸 뒷부분부터 dramatically가 다시 주어의 역할을 할 수 있게 만들어야 하므로 명사절을 이끄는 접속사인 (B) That이 정답이다.

어휘 increase 증가하다 dramatically 극적으로 proof 증거

108

The human resources director is now evaluating trainees' performance ------- more thoroughly than the previous months.
(A) even
(B) too
(C) very
(D) so

인사부 이사는 현재 훈련생들의 성과를 이전 달보다 훨씬 더 철저하게 평가하고 있습니다.

해설 빈칸은 뒤의 비교급을 수식해 주는 단어가 들어갈 자리이다. 따라서 비교급 수식이 가능한 (A) even이 정답이 된다.
human resource 인사부 evaluate 평가하다 performance 성과 thoroughly 철저히 previous 이전의

109

As per the Canadian Railway guidelines, the railway does occasionally close at very ------- notice due to unforeseeable circumstances.
(A) brief
(B) short
(C) high
(D) low

Canadian Railway 지침서 대로, 철로는 예상치 못한 상황 때문에 아주 급한 공지로 때때로 폐쇄합니다.

해설 빈칸은 앞의 전치사 at과 notice 사이에 어울리는 형용사가 들어갈 자리이다. at short notice(급히, 갑자기)를 알아둔다면 해결이 용이한 문제이다.

어휘 railway 철로 occasionally 가끔 due to ~때문에 unforeseeable 예견할 수 없는 circumstance 환경

110

------- are the manuscripts needed to be reviewed and summarized.
(A) Encloses
(B) Enclosing
(C) Enclosed
(D) Enclose

검토되고 요약될 필요가 있는 원고가 동봉되어 있습니다.

해설 문장의 주어자리처럼 보이지만 주어로 들어갈 명사가 선택지에는 없다. 뒤에 be동사 are가 보이므로 문장이 도치되었다. enclose가 '동봉하다'라는 타동사인데 목적어가 없으므로 수동형인 (C) Enclosed가 정답이 된다.

어휘 enclose 동봉하다 manuscript 원고 need to ~ 필요로 하다 review 검토하다 summarize 요약하다

111

Selecting a house is a big decision and requires patience and a willingness to view ------- properties as possible.
(A) so much
(B) so many
(C) as many
(D) as much

집을 선택하는 것은 큰 결정이고 가능한 한 많은 부동산을 보기 위해 인내와 자발성을 요구합니다.

해설 빈칸은 as ~ as possible 구조이다. 빈칸 뒤의 명사가 properties로 복수이므로, (C) as many가 정답이다.

어휘 select 선택하다 decision 결정 require 요구하다 patience 인내 willingness 자발성 property 부동산, 재산

112

We will cease using the information you provided for the project ------- after your request has been received.
(A) vaguely
(B) measurably
(C) promptly
(D) originally

당신의 요청이 받아지고 난 직후에, 프로젝트를 위해 당신이 제공했던 정보를 사용하는 것을 중단할 것입니다.

해설 빈칸은 뒤의 after와 어울리는 부사가 들어갈 자리이다. after와 의미상 적절한 부사는 promptly로 promptly after는 '~ 직후에'라는 의미이다.

어휘 cease 중단하다 information 정보 provide 제공하다 request 요청 receive 받다 vaguely 모호하게 measurably 측정할 수 있게 originally 원래 promptly 지체 없이

113

If you have problems with starting your car, please refer to page 17 of the instruction manual ------- contacting a customer service representative.
(A) before
(B) even if
(C) during
(D) except

만약 당신이 자동차를 시동거는 것에 문제가 있다면, 고객서비스직원에게 연락하기 전에 설명서의 17페이지를 참조하십시오.

해설 빈칸은 의미가 적절한 전치사 또는 접속사가 들어갈 자리이다. 전체적인 문장의 해석으로 before(~전에)가 정답임을 알 수 있다.

어휘 refer 알아보도록 하다, 조회하다 instruction manual 설명서 contact 연락하다 representative 직원 even if ~에도 불구하고

114

The inspectors ------- that the school buses are compliant with all state regulations.
(A) replace
(B) influence
(C) associate
(D) certify

검사관은 학교버스가 모든 주 규정을 준수한다는 것을 증명합니다.

해설 빈칸은 that절을 받는 동사가 들어갈 자리이다. 선택지 중에 적절한 단어는 (D) certify(증명하다, 확인하다)이다.

어휘 inspector 검사관 compliant 준수 regulation 규정 replace 대신하다, 대체하다 influence 영향 associate 연상하다 certify 증명하다

115

One year after the merger, the executive team has been able to draw its initial conclusions and they are ------- positive.
(A) exceptional
(B) exceptionally
(C) exception
(D) except

합병 1년 후에, 중역진은 초기 결론을 이끌어낼 수 있었고 그들은 유난히 긍정적이었다.

해설 형용사 앞의 빈칸은 부사자리이므로 정답은 (B) exceptionally(뛰어나게, 예외적으로)이다.

어휘 merger 합병 executive 경영진 initial 초기의 conclusion 결론 exceptionally 뛰어나게, 예외적으로 exceptional 특출한 exception 예외

116

If you discover any physical ------- in our products, we will replace them free of charge or refund you the full amount.
(A) inconveniences
(B) mistakes
(C) misfortunes
(D) defects

만약 당신이 우리 제품에서 물리적인 결함을 발견한다면, 우리는 무료로 교체해 주거나 전액 환불을 해줄 것입니다.

해설 빈칸은 형용사 physical(물리적인)과 의미 연결이 어울리는 명사가 들어갈 자리이다. 그래서, defect(결함)가 연결되어, '물리적인 결함'의 의미로 적절해 보인다.

어휘 discover 발견하다 physical 물리적인 product 상품 replace 교체하다, 교환하다 free of charge 무료 refund 환불 inconvenience 불편 mistake 실수 misfortune 불운 defect 결점

117

With little difference between the services offered by logistics companies, contracts are awarded to ------- company offers the lowest price.
(A) whichever
(B) any
(C) these
(D) each

물류회사에 의해 제공된 서비스 사이에서의 작은 차이로, 최저가를 제공하는 어떤 회사든지 계약이 낙찰됩니다.

해설 빈칸은 뒤의 명사를 연결하면서 앞의 문장에 의미연결도 되어야 한다. 이 두 가지 요건을 충족시키는 단어는 선택지 중 (A) whichever(어느 쪽이든 ~한 것)이다. any, these, each는 문장을 연결할 수가 없다.

어휘 difference 차이 offer 제공하다 logistic 물류 contract 계약 be awarded to ~에게 수여되다. 주어지다

118

Health care providers are required to keep a patient's health information confidential ------- consent to release the information is provided by the patient.
(A) as
(B) unless
(C) nor
(D) either

만약 정보를 공개하기 위한 동의가 환자에 의해서 제공되지 않는다면, 의료서비스 제공업체는 환자의 건강정보를 기밀로 유지하도록 요청됩니다.

해설 빈칸은 의미가 적절한 접속사자리이다. 앞뒤 문장의 내용을 볼 때 '~하지 않는다면'의 의미로 (B) unless가 적절하다.

어휘 health 건강 require 요청하다 patient 환자 confidential 기밀의 consent 동의 unless ~하지 않는다면 nor ~도 아니다

119

KYL Accounting exclusively provides payroll services for restaurants, as ------- are their primary clients in the Hamilton area.
(A) their own
(B) these
(C) there
(D) them

KYL Accounting은 Hamilton 지역의 식당들이 주요한 고객이기 때문에, 식당만을 위한 급여관리서비스를 제공합니다.

해설 빈칸은 접속사 뒤에 주어가 와야 하는 자리이다. 주어로 가능한 these와 there 중에 there를 넣으면(there are ~있다) 해석이 어색해진다. 그래서, 앞 문장의 restaurants를 받는 (B) these가 정답이 된다.

어휘 exclusively 오로지, 독점적으로 provide 제공하다 payroll service 급여관리서비스 primary 주요한 client 고객

120

Within a short period of time, Lotus Metal Corporation has established a reputation as a ------- importer of quality stainless steel.
(A) fragile
(B) reliable
(C) memorable
(D) comfortable

짧은 시간 내로, Lotus Metal Corporation은 고품질 스테인리스의 믿을 만한 수입업체로서 명성을 쌓았다.

해설 빈칸은 뒤의 importer(수입업자)와 의미가 어울리는 형용사가 들어갈 자리이다. 선택지 중 회사와 의미 연결이 어울리는 단어는 (B) reliable(믿을 만한)이다.

어휘 establish 설립하다, 확립하다 reputation 명성, 평판 importer 수입업자 quality 고품질 fragile 부서지기 쉬운 reliable 믿을 수 있는 memorable 기억할 만한 comfortable 편안한

121

As a pharmacist, Dr. Duchamp's most ------- quality is the passion and commitment he shows to his patients.
(A) admiring
(B) admiration
(C) admirable
(D) admire

약사로서, Duchamp 박사의 가장 존경할 만한 자질은 그가 환자들에게 보여주는 열정과 헌신이다.

해설 빈칸은 명사 앞에 어울리는 품사가 들어갈 자리이다. 명사 앞의 빈칸은 형용사자리이다.

어휘 pharmacist 약사 passion 열정 commitment 헌신 patient 환자 admirable 존경스러운 admiration 존경

122

A real estate developer is in need of an ------- to design high-tech double-story houses at a low cost.
(A) architecturally
(B) architectural
(C) architect
(D) architecture

부동산 개발업체는 첨단 기술의 2층 집을 저가로 설계할 수 있는 건축가를 필요로 합니다.

해설 빈칸은 관사 뒤에 어울리는 명사가 들어갈 자리이다. 명사면서 의미가 적절한 것은 (C) architect(건축가)이다.

어휘 real estate 부동산 in need of ~을 필요로 하다 double-story 2층 architect 건축가 architecture 건축학

123

To use the machine safely, extension cords should be ------- only when necessary and only on a temporary basis.
(A) usage
(B) used
(C) using
(D) uses

기계를 안전하게 사용하기 위하여, 연장 코드는 반드시 필요할 때에만 일시적으로만 사용되어야 합니다.

해설 빈칸은 be동사 뒤에 적절한 형태의 단어가 들어갈 자리이다. be동사 뒤에 -ing나 -ed형태가 올 수 있는데, use는 '~을 사용하다'라는 타동사이며 목적어가 없으므로 수동형인 (B) used가 정답이다.

어휘 machine 기계 extension 연장 necessary 필요한 temporary 일시적인 basis 근거, 이유 usage 용법

124

Fedex ground shipping takes about 5 business days to deliver ------- express delivery takes only 2 days.
(A) despite
(B) whether
(C) until
(D) while

Fedex 일반배송은 배달하는 데 대략 5일이 걸리는 반면, 특급배송은 단지 2일이 걸린다.

해설 빈칸은 의미가 적절한 접속사가 들어갈 자리이다. 빈칸 앞뒤로 ground shipping(육상 운송)과 express delivery(빠른 배송)이 대치되는 개념으로 (D) while(반면)이 정답이 된다.

어휘 ground shipping 일반배송 deliver 배달 express delivery 특급배송 despite ~에도 불구하고 while 반면에

125

Available in a wide variety of sizes, our newly ------- line of luxury shoes are still made with the finest leather.
(A) updated
(B) updating
(C) update
(D) updates

매우 다양한 크기로 이용 가능한, 새롭게 업데이트 된 고급스러운 신발들은 여전히 가장 우수한 가죽으로 만들어졌다.

해설 빈칸은 명사를 수식해주는 형용사자리이다. 뒤의 line은 '제품군'의 의미로 '개선된'의 의미인 (A) updated가 정답이다.

어휘 available 이용 가능한 variety of 다양한 newly 새로 finest 가장 우수한 leather 가죽

126

Distributing a memo by email ------- paper versions may save several hours of labor, which over time could save the company a substantial amount of money.
(A) according to
(B) instead of
(C) throughout
(D) except

종이 대신 이메일에 의해 메모를 배포하는 것은 몇 시간의 노동을 절약할 수 있고, 또한 그것은 시간이 흘러 회사가 상당한 자금을 절약해줄 수 있다.

해설 빈칸 앞은 email 뒤는 paper versions이므로 '~ 대신에'라는 의미의 instead of가 정답이다.

어휘 distribute 배부하다 save 절약하다 labor 노동 substantial 상당한 instead of ~대신에 throughout 도처에

127

------- for changes to MYK membership must be made online using the electronic forms available.
(A) Requests
(B) Requested
(C) To request
(D) Requesting

MYK 멤버십 변경을 위한 요청은 이용 가능한 전자양식을 사용하여 온라인으로 이뤄져야만 합니다.

해설 빈칸은 문장의 주어자리이다. 주어로는 명사가 와야 하므로 (A) Requests(요청)가 정답이다.

어휘 electronic 전기 available 이용 가능한 request 요청

128

There were some attempts to grow bananas commercially in Honduras in the 1980s but these were only ------- successful.
(A) intriguingly
(B) regrettably
(C) marginally
(D) eloquently

1980년대 Honduras에서 상업적으로 바나나를 재배하려는 시도가 있었지만 오직 미미하게 성공적이었다.

해설 빈칸은 뒤의 successful(성공적인)과 의미연결이 적절한 부사가 들어갈 자리이다. 문맥상 (C) marginally(미미하게)가 자연스럽다.

어휘 attempt 시도 grow 기르다 commercially 상업적으로 intriguingly 흥미를 자아내어 regrettably 유감스럽게 eloquently 유창한 marginally 미미하게

129

With the aid of wireless remote devices, our service team guarantees that your vending machines always remain ------- stocked with the most popular selections.
(A) fully
(B) full
(C) fullest
(D) fuller

무선 원격장치의 도움으로 우리 서비스팀은 당신의 자판기가 항상 가장 유명한 상품으로 완전히 채워져 있다는 것을 보장합니다.

해설 빈칸 뒤의 stocked(과거분사)를 수식하는 품사는 부사(fully 완전히)이다.

어휘 aid of ~의 도움으로 guarantee 보장하다 vending machine 자판기 popular 인기 있는 remain (계속) 유지하다 fully 완전히

130

It is important to keep in mind that new operating systems are not always ------- with existing software needed for your printers.
(A) compatible
(B) alternative
(C) external
(D) formal

새로운 운영 시스템이 프린터에 필요한 기존의 소프트웨어로 항상 호환 가능한 것은 아님을 명심하는 것은 중요합니다.

해설 전치사 with와 어울리는 형용사 어휘를 골라보자. 선택지 중 with와 어울리는 형용사는 (A) compatible로, be compatible with는 '호환 가능하다'의 뜻이다.

어휘 keep in mind 명심하다 compatible 호환이 되는 alternative 대안 external 외부의 formal 격식을 차린, 정중한

ACTUAL TEST 06 ACTUAL TEST 07 ACTUAL TEST 08 ACTUAL TEST 09 ACTUAL TEST 10

PART 6

Questions 131-134 refer to the following article.

Around Town

-------. Marcus Verbeek, the event organizer, said that this year's
131.
performances were ------- the best event ever and wished to
132.
thank all the artists who joined in the celebration of the famous
island music. Many of the reggae bands that ------- this year
133.
were locals who have never been to Jamaica. Of course, the
big names in reggae, especially Stephen Marley, who came all
the way from Kingston, Jamaica, were the ones that attracted
the largest audiences. It is ------- that over 300 performers and
134.
more than 20,000 fans attended the concerts across the city.
The local tourism bureau estimates that this week-long event
brought more than $500,000 in tourism money to the local
economy.

Around Town

Reggage Fest는 시청 광장에서 10번째 연례 화려한 Sunday night 행사를 마무리했다. 행사 조직자인 Marcus Verbeek는 올해의 공연이 지금까지 공연 중에 최고였다고 말했고 유명한 아일랜드 음악의 축하행사에 함께 했던 모든 예술가들에게 감사하기를 희망했다. 올해 참여했던 많은 레게 밴드들은 Jamaica에 가보지 않은 사람들이었다. 물론, 레게의 유명인, Jamaica의 Kingston에서 먼 길을 달려온 Stephen Marley는 가장 많은 청중을 모은 사람이다. 시 전역에 300명 이상의 공연자와 20,000명 이상의 팬들이 참여했던 것으로 추정된다. 지역관광사무소는 이번 주 중 행사는 지역 경제에 500,000달러 이상을 벌어들였다고 예측한다.

어휘 organizer 조직자 yet 여태껏 celebration 축하행사 big name 유명인 attract 매료시키다 audience 청중 estimate 추정하다 over ~ 이상 more than ~ 이상 across the city 도시 전역에 bureau 사무실

131 (A) Coming Tuesday, Cansas City is holding a grand reggae festival at its city hall plaza.
(B) Reggae Fest wrapped up its 10th annual extravaganza Sunday night to a cheering crowd.
(C) Stephen Marley has been nominated for the reggae artist of the year award.
(D) This weekend, the Cansas Stadium will be closed to do a spring-cleaning for the coming reggae Fest.

해설 빈칸 다음 문장에서 행사 조직자가 올해의 공연히 여태 최고였다고 말했다는 내용이 나온다. 따라서 빈칸은 이 행사가 끝났다는 내용이 언급되는 것이 적절하므로 정답은 (B)이다.

(A) 다가오는 화요일, Cansas시는 시청 광장에게 레게축제를 개최한다.
(B) Reggage Fest는 시청 광장에서 10번째 연례 화려한 Sunday night를 마무리했다.
(C) Stephen Marley가 올해의 레게예술가 상에 후보 지명되었다.
(D) 이번 주말에, Cansas 경기장은 다가올 레게축제 봄 청소를 위해 폐쇄된다.

132
(A) chosen
(B) among
(C) polite
(D) prior

해설 빈칸 뒤에는 <the + 명사>가 왔기 때문에 선택지 중 전치사가 적합한 자리이다. 또한 be among the best event(최고 행사 중의 하나이다)를 알고 있는지 묻고 있다.

133
(A) will participate
(B) participate
(C) participated
(D) participating

해설 that절의 동사시제를 묻고 있다. 이미 행사가 끝났으므로 that절 역시 '올해 참가했던' 밴드라는 의미로 과거시제가 적절하다. 따라서 정답은 (C) participated이다.

134
(A) estimates
(B) estimating
(C) estimated
(D) estimator

해설 빈칸은 be동사 다음의 보어자리이다. 빈칸 뒤에는 진주어가 위치하고 목적어가 없으므로 수동태 형태가 정답이다. 의미적으로도 300명 이상의 공연자와 20,000명 이상의 팬이 참여했던 것으로 '추정된다'는 것이 자연스럽다.

Questions 135-138 refer to the following letter.

Michelle Zapatos

48 Main St

Boulder, Colorado

Dear Mr. Zapatos,

Thank you for 32 years of dedication to our company. We at Pueblo Imports want to celebrate your decades of excellence in employment by hosting a huge retirement party ------- you **135.** and all our departing workers. We hope that you will join us December 13th at the Miami Pueblo Country Club for a banquet dinner and speech from the President of Pueblo. You, ------- **136.** the other retiring employees, will be seated at the head table with the board of directors. Of course, your family is ------- **137.** to join this prestigious event as well. If you will be attending, please respond by filling in the attached card and leaving it with reception by November 15th at the latest. -------. **138.**

Sincerely,

Gabriel Daniels

Human Resources Manager

Enclosure

Michelle Zapatos
48 Main St
Boulder, Colorado

Zapatos 씨께

우리 회사에 대한 귀하의 헌신에 감사합니다. Pueblo Imports사는 귀하와 모든 떠나는 직원들을 기리기 위해 거대한 은퇴파티를 주최해서 수십 년간의 노고를 축하하고 싶습니다. Miami Pueblo Country Club에서 12월 13일 Pueblo사 사장님의 연설이 있으며 연회 식사를 위해 우리와 함께하시길 희망합니다. 귀하는 다른 은퇴하는 직원과 이사회와 함께 상석에 앉을 것입니다. 물론, 가족들도 권위 있는 이번 행사에 함께하신다면 환영합니다. 만약 당신이 참석하신다면, 늦어도 11월 15일까지 첨부된 카드를 작성하셔서 접수처에 제출하시어 응답을 주시길 바랍니다. 함께하실 손님의 수를 표시해 주시길 바랍니다.

진심을 담아

Gabriel Daniels
인사부장
동봉

어휘 dedication to ~에 대한 헌신 celebrate 축하하다 decades 수십 년 by hosting 주최함으로써 huge 거대한 retirement party 은퇴파티 honor 영예를 주다 along with ~와 함께 head table 상석 of course 물론 prestigious 저명한 reception 접수처, 환영회 at the latest 늦어도

135
(A) will honor
(B) to honor
(C) would honor
(D) to be honored

해설 한 문장에 동사는 반드시 하나만 있어야 한다. 이 문장에는 이미 동사(want)가 있으므로 더 이상의 동사는 필요 없다. 따라서 빈칸은 준동사(to부정사)자리이며, 빈칸 뒤에 목적어가 있으므로 능동태가 와야 한다.

136
(A) owing to
(B) even if
(C) along with
(D) in case of

해설 전치사 어휘문제이다. '다른 은퇴하는 직원들과 함께 귀하는 상석에 앉으십시오'라는 의미가 되어야 한다. 따라서 정답은 (C) along with(~과 함께)이다.

137
(A) customary
(B) welcome
(C) pending
(D) exclusive

해설 문맥상 적절한 형용사어휘를 찾는 문제이다. 가족들도 이 권위 있는 행사에 함께하는 것이 '환영된다'는 의미가 적합하므로 정답은 (B) welcome(환영하는)이다.

138
(A) Our janitor will then direct you to your reserved seat before the show begins.
(B) Your appointment as a new president will be announced at the end of the banquet.
(C) Don't forget to mark down the number of guests you will be bringing.
(D) This banquet attendance will be limited to permanent employees only.

해설 앞에서 가족들도 참석 가능하다는 내용이 언급되어 있고 빈칸의 바로 앞 문장에서 당신이 참석한다면 응답해달라는 내용이 나와 있다. 따라서 빈칸은 함께하실 손님의 수를 표시해달라는 의미가 적합하다. 따라서 정답은 (C)이다.

(A) 관리인은 쇼가 시작되기 전에 예약된 좌석까지 당신을 안내할 것입니다.
(B) 새 사장으로서 당신의 임명은 연회가 끝날 무렵에 발표될 것입니다.
(C) 함께하실 손님의 수를 표시해 주시길 바랍니다.
(D) 연회 참석은 정직원으로 제한됩니다.

Questions 139-142 refer to the following e-mail.

To: Auckland Office Managers <management@aros.com.nz>

From: Robert Fabian, IT Department <rfabian@aros.com.nz>

Re: Server Update

Date: 20 October

Attachment: admin password update procedure.txt

As the internal memo sent to all managers explained last week, we are ------- to upgrade our company servers. This will **139.** occur at midnight on August 24th and should be completed by Monday morning on August 26th.

All security protocols will be reset, which means you will need to enter a new password for your admin accounts. Please follow the procedure as ------- in the attachment included here. -------. **140.** **141.**

In additon, you must enter your new password within 24 hours of the servers going online. Do not use the ------- password as **142.** you had. Commit your new password to memory and do not write it anywhere.

수신: Auckland Office Managers ⟨management@aros.com.nz⟩

발신: Robert Fabian, IT Department ⟨rfabian@aros.com.nz⟩

제목: Server Update

날짜: 10월 20일

첨부: admin password update procedure.txt

지난주 모든 매니저들에게 발송된 내부 메모에서 설명했다시피, 우리는 회사 서버를 업그레이드하려고 합니다. 8월 24일 자정에 시작되고 8월 26일 월요일 아침까지 완료될 것입니다.

모든 보안 프로토콜은 초기상태가 되며 그렇게 함으로써 관리자 계정를 위해 새로운 비밀번호를 입력해야 합니다. 여기 포함된 첨부물에 설명된 대로 절차에 따르도록 합니다. 새로운 비밀번호가 입력될 때까지 네트워크에 접근할 수 없습니다.

게다가, 온라인에 서버가 열리면 24시간 내에 새로운 비밀번호를 입력해야 합니다. 이전에 사용했던 같은 비밀번호를 사용하지 마세요. 메모리에 새로운 비밀번호를 기억시키고 어디에도 적어놓지 마세요.

어휘 be about to V 막 ~하려고 하다 occur 일어나다, 발생하다 midnight 자정 reset 초기시키다 account 계정 procedure 절차 as explained 설명된 대로 in addition 게다가 go online 온라인에 접속하다 commit 기억시키다

139 (A) about
(B) reluctant
(C) concerned
(D) insecure

해설 빈칸 뒤 문장에서 서버 업그레이드가 8월 24일에 일어나고, 8월 26일에 완료된다는 내용이 나와 있으므로 '우리는 회사 서버를 업그레이드하려고 한다'는 의미가 적절하다. be about to V(막 ~하려고 하다)를 알면 금방 답을 찾을 수 있는 문제이다. 정답은 (A) about이다.

140
(A) explain
(B) explained
(C) explaining
(D) be explained

해설 as p.p(~된 대로)를 적용시키는 문제이다. 문맥상 여기 포함된 첨부물에 '설명된 대로' 절차를 따르도록 한다는 의미가 자연스럽다. 따라서 정답은 (B) explained이다.

141
(A) You have to attend the training seminar before accessing our new network system.
(B) Our company's network has the top security and is always protected from any DDOS attack.
(C) You will not be able to access the network until a new password has been entered.
(D) You can now log in to our website as regular maintenance has just been completed.

해설 빈칸 앞 문장에서 회사 서버 업그레이드와 새로운 비밀번호를 입력해야 함을, 빈칸 뒷 문장에서는 in addition을 이용해 24시간 이내에 새로운 비밀번호를 입력할 때 주의사항을 언급하고 있다. 따라서 빈칸 역시 주의해야 하는 내용이 언급되는 것이 자연스럽다.

(A) 당신은 새로운 네트워크 시스템에 접근하기 전에 훈련 세미나에 참석해야 합니다.
(B) 회사의 네트워크는 최고의 보안을 가지고 있으며 항상 DDOS 공격으로부터 보호됩니다.
(C) 당신은 새로운 비밀번호가 입력될 때까지는 네트워크에 접근할 수 없습니다.
(D) 당신은 정기 유지보수가 방금 완료되었기 때문에 웹사이트에 지금 로그인할 수 있습니다.

142
(A) both
(B) equal
(C) eager
(D) same

해설 빈칸은 명사를 수식하는 형용사자리이다. 앞에서 새로운 비밀번호를 입력해야 한다는 내용이 나와 있으므로 당신이 가지고 있던 '동일한' 비밀번호를 사용하지 마라가 의미상 적절하다. 따라서 정답은 (D) same이다. equal은 (수, 양, 가치 등이) 동일하다는 의미이므로 오답이다.

Questions 143-146 refer to the following letter.

Dear Mr. Moore,

We thank you for choosing Oceanblue Pools as your custom outdoor swimming pool contractor. Our professional pool installers ------- in the business for over 25 years and installed **143.** more than 1000 pools over that time. If the pool vinyl liner does become ripped or warped, make sure to contact our service department -------. We promise to come to your home and have **144.** the pool back in perfect ------- within 2 business days. We also **145.** provide a full range of pool maintenance services. -------. Please **146.** contact us if you have any additional questions regarding your pool.

Moore 씨께

맞춤 야외 수영장 계약자로서 Oceanblue Pools를 선택해주셔서 감사드립니다. 우리의 전문 수영장 실치자들은 25년 이상 일을 해왔고 1000개 이상의 수영장을 설치했습니다. 만약 수영장 비닐재가 찢어지거나 뒤틀린다면 서비스부서로 즉시 연락하십시오. 저희가 방문해서 이틀 안에 수영장을 완벽한 상태로 돌려놓겠습니다. 완전한 수영장 유지보수 서비스도 제공합니다. 혹한기를 대비하고 봄에 다시 개장할 수 있도록 수영장을 준비하는 것도 포함합니다. 수영장에 관한 추가 질문 있으면 연락 주십시오.

어휘 custom 맞춤의 pool vinyl liner 수영장 비닐재 rip 찢다 warp 휘다 condition 상태 a range of 다양한

143 (A) will be
(B) being
(C) have been
(D) has been

해설 빈칸은 동사 시제문제이다. 주어(installers)가 복수이고, 문장 뒤의 for over 25 years를 단서로 25년 이상 계속 일을 해왔기 때문에 현재완료시제가 적절하다. 따라서 정답은 (C) have been이다.

144 (A) later
(B) perfectly
(C) immediately
(D) extremely

해설 빈칸은 동사 contact를 수식하는 부사 어휘문제이다. 우리 서비스 부서에 즉시 연락하라는 의미가 적절하므로 정답은 (C) immediately(즉시)이다.

145
(A) schedule
(B) term
(C) appointment
(D) condition

해설 전치사구의 명사 어휘문제이다. '완벽한 상태'로 수영장을 돌려놓겠다는 의미가 적절하므로 정답은 (D) condition(상태, 조건)
이다.

146
(A) Our mowing and gardening service is highly recognized across this county.
(B) This includes preparing your pool for the cold season and to reopen it in the spring.
(C) Swimming is a good exercise especially for those who have heart problems.
(D) We only use environmentally friendly detergent for cleaning your house windows.

해설 (A) 우리 잔디와 정원 서비스는 전국에서 매우 인정받는다.
(B) 혹한기를 대비하고 봄에 다시 개장할 수 있도록 수영장을 준비하는 것도 포함한다.
(C) 수영은 심장 질환을 가진 사람을 위해 특히 좋은 운동이다.
(D) 우리는 집 창문을 청소하기 위해 친환경적인 세제만을 사용한다.

빈칸 앞에서, 수영장 설치와 유지보수를 언급하고 있으므로 혹한기 대비와 봄을 위해 준비하는 서비스도 포함된다는 내용이 자연스럽
다. 그러므로 정답은 (B)이다.

101

------- are already complete for the display booths at tomorrow's Wellness Food Fair.

(A) **Preparations**
(B) Preparation
(C) To prepare
(D) Preparing

내일 Wellness Food Fair에서의 전시 부스를 위한 준비는 이미 완료되었다.

해설 빈칸은 문장의 주어자리이다. 주어로는 명사가 와야 하고 동사가 are이므로 복수명사인 (A) Preparations가 정답이다.

어휘 complete 완료하다 display 전시 preparation 준비

102

Nowadays, many consumers find credit cards ------- and safe when they purchase items in stores.

(A) convene
(B) convenience
(C) convention
(D) **convenient**

요즘, 많은 소비자들은 상점에서 물건을 구매할 때, 신용카드를 더 편리하고 안전하다고 생각합니다.

해설 이 문장은 <find + 목적어(credit cards) + 목적보어>의 5형식구조이며 목적보어로는 형용사인 (D) convenient(편리한)가 적절하다.

어휘 nowadays 요즘 consumer 소비자 purchase 구입하다 convenient 편리한 convene 소집하다 convention 관습

103

Because the last board meeting focused on planning issues, it ran ------- late and left little time for important corporate issues.

(A) **quite**
(B) ever
(C) enough
(D) more

지난 이사회 미팅이 문제 계획에 집중했기 때문에, 꽤 늦게까지 진행되었고 중요한 회사문제를 위한 시간이 거의 없었다.

해설 빈칸은 뒤의 형용사 late(늦은)를 수식하는 부사자리이다. 선택지 중에서 late와 어울리는 부사는 quite(꽤)이다.

어휘 board meeting 이사회 미팅 issue 문제 corporate 기업의 quite 꽤 enough 충분한

104

The new machines are simply designed, so they are easy to operate and require ------- repairs.
(A) few
(B) little
(C) many
(D) any

새 기계가 단순하게 만들어졌고 그래서 작동하기 쉽고 수리를 거의 요구하지 않습니다.

해설 빈칸은 명사 repairs(수리)를 수식하는 형용사자리이다. 문맥상 '새로운 기계이니 수리가 필요치 않다'는 의미가 적합하므로 부정의 의미를 나타내는 (A) few가 정답이다. little은 셀 수 없는 명사(불가산명사)와 어울린다.

어휘 simply 간단히 operate 운영하다 require 요구하다 repair 수리

105

This series of ------- of the heroes of Korea were originally written approximately four hundred years ago.
(A) charts
(B) models
(C) careers
(D) biographies

한국 영웅에 관한 일련의 전기는 원래 대략 400년 전에 작성되었다.

해설 빈칸은 of the heroes(영웅들에 관한)와 의미연결이 적절한 명사자리이다. 또한 형용사 short(짧은)와의 연결도 고려해야 한다. 문맥상 적절한 명사는 biographies(자서전, 전기)이다.

어휘 hero 영웅 originally 원래 approximately 대략 chart 도표, 차트 career 직업 biographic 전기

106

Before you submit the monthly report, make sure that you go over it with great -------.
(A) care
(B) caring
(C) careful
(D) carefully

월간보고서를 제출하기 전에, 아주 주의 깊게 확실히 검토하세요.

해설 전치사 with 뒤에 어울리는 품사는 명사(care)이다. with care는 carefully의 의미이다.

어휘 submit 제출하다 make sure 확실히 하다 go over 검토하다 with care 주의 깊게

ACTUAL TEST 06 ACTUAL TEST 07 ACTUAL TEST 08 ACTUAL TEST 09 ACTUAL TEST 10

107

Our friendly, experienced staff will be happy to respond to any questions you may have ------- our vehicles, parts and services.
(A) regards
(B) regarding
(C) regard
(D) regarded

친절하고 숙련된 우리 직원들은 차량, 부품, 서비스에 관한 당신의 어떤 질문이라도 기꺼이 응답할 것입니다.

해설 빈칸은 뒤의 명사들을 연결해주는 전치사자리이다. 선택지 중에서 전치사는 (B) regarding(~에 관하여)이다.

어휘 friendly 친절한 respond to ~에 대응하다, 답하다 question 질문 vehicle 차량 regarding ~에 관하여 regard ~으로 여기다

108

Cecelia Ahern wrote ------- first book at just 21 and recently released her 11th novel: The Year I Met You.
(A) she
(B) hers
(C) herself
(D) her

Cecelia Ahern는 불과 21세에 첫 책을 집필했고 최근에 11번째 소설을 발표했다.

해설 빈칸은 명사 앞에 어울리는 형태의 대명사가 올 자리로, 소유격인 (D) her가 정답이 된다.

어휘 release 발표하다 novel 소설

109

Mr. Danilo Dalle needs to submit a ------- review of the book he read last week.
(A) future
(B) many
(C) short
(D) convenient

Danilo Dalle 씨는 지난주에 그가 읽었던 책의 짧은 서평을 제출할 필요가 있다.

해설 빈칸은 명사(review)를 적절하게 수식해주는 형용사자리이다. many 뒤에는 복수명사가 와야 한다. a many years (×) / a great [good] many years (o). 문맥상 short review(짧은 서평)가 어울린다.

어휘 submit 제출하다 review 검토하다 future 미래 convenient 편리한

110

It is our ------- that staff members should not take care of personal business while on duty.
(A) approval
(B) manual
(C) policy
(D) guide

직원들이 근무 중에 개인 업무를 처리해서는 안 된다는 것이 우리의 정책입니다.

해설 이 문장은 it(가주어)-that(진주어)구문으로 빈칸 뒤의 that절이 의미상의 주어가 된다. that절(근무 중에 개인 업무를 보면 안 된다)은 빈칸과 동격관계이다. 문맥상 that절과 동격관계가 될 수 있는 명사는 (C) policy(정책)이다.

어휘 take care of ~을 돌보다, 처리하다 approval 인정, 찬성 policy 정책

111

The hotel also boasts a fine-dining restaurant on its premises and ------- scenery on the grounds of the hotel.
(A) momentary
(B) picturesque
(C) multiple
(D) appeared

호텔은 또한 구내에 있는 훌륭한 레스토랑과 호텔 1층에 있는 그림 같은 경관을 자랑스럽게 여깁니다.

해설 명사 scenery(경치)와 어울리는 형용사를 골라보자. 선택지 중에서 (B) picturesque(그림 같은)가 가장 어울린다.

어휘 boast 자랑하다 premise 전제 scenery 경치 momentary 순간적인 picturesque 그림 같은 multiple 많은 appear ~인 것 같다

112

The downtown Hiltons hotel includes an ------- open-air courtyard that provides an informal seating area for guests.
(A) assessed
(B) entertained
(C) anticipated
(D) enclosed

시내의 Hiltons호텔은 손님들을 위해 격식 없이 편안한 좌석을 제공하는 담으로 둘러싸인 야외 안마당을 포함하고 있습니다.

해설 빈칸은 open-air courtyard(정원)와 어울리는 형용사가 들어갈 자리이다. 선택지 중 '담으로 둘러싸인'의 의미인 (D) enclosed가 어울린다.

어휘 include 포함하다 open-air 옥외의 courtyard 뜰, 마당 informal 편안한 assessed 평가된 entertain 접대하다 anticipated 기대하는, 대망의 enclosed 담으로 둘러싸인, 동봉된

ACTUAL TEST 06 ACTUAL TEST 07 ACTUAL TEST 08 ACTUAL TEST 09 ACTUAL TEST 10

113

With regional offices all ------- Australia, NASB provides support to help small businesses succeed.
(A) along
(B) across
(C) away
(D) broad

호주의 전역에 걸쳐 지사를 갖고 있는 NASB는 소기업이 성공하는 것을 지원합니다.

해설 빈칸은 지역을 나타내는 단어와 의미가 잘 어울리는 전치사자리이다. 전역을 나타내는 (B) across가 정답이다.

어휘 provide 제공하다 support 지원 broad 넓은

114

Replacement keys for your house can be ordered directly from the manufacturer ------- you have the house's proof of ownership.
(A) as though
(B) in fact
(C) more than
(D) provided that

당신 집의 대체 열쇠는 집의 소유 증거가 있다면 제조업체로부터 직접 주문될 수 있습니다.

해설 빈칸은 뒤의 문장을 연결하는 접속사자리이다. 앞뒤 문장의 해석으로 볼 때 (D) provided that(~가정할 때)이 정답이다.

어휘 replacement 교체, 대체 directly 곧장, 직접 manufacturer 제조자 proof 증거 as though 마치 ~인 것처럼 in fact 사실은 provided that 가정할 때

115

Not only is this a fantastic way to save energy, but you can also save almost $ 730 per year when you make the ------- improvements to your home.
(A) suggested
(B) suggest
(C) suggests
(D) suggesting

당신이 집에 제안된 개량공사를 할 때, 이것은 에너지를 절약하는 훌륭한 방법일 뿐만 아니라, 1년에 거의 730달러를 절약할 수 있다.

해설 빈칸은 뒤의 improvements(개량공사)와 연결이 적절한 형용사자리이다. '개량공사'는 제안을 받는 것이므로 (A) suggested가 정답이 된다.

어휘 not only ~뿐만 아니라 fantastic 환상적인 save 절약하다 improvement 향상, 개선 suggest 제안

210

116

The Regional Director of Operations will be responsible for leading a high performing team of sales representatives who consistently ------- company expectations.
(A) hail
(B) exceed
(C) believe
(D) command

운영지사장은 지속적으로 회사의 기대를 능가하는 영업사원 고성과팀을 이끄는 책임이 있다.

해설 빈칸은 목적어 company expectations(회사 기대)를 목적어로 취하는 동사자리이다. 선택지 중에서 (B) exceed(능가하다)가 연결이 자연스럽다.

어휘 regional 지역의 operation 운영 be responsible for ~에 책임이 있다 performing 실행할 수 있는 representative 대표 consistently 지속적으로 expectation 예상 hail 묘사하다 exceed 능가하다 command 명령하다

117

In addition to being a leading domestic producer, Muritos has been ------- successful in overseas markets.
(A) markedly
(B) permissibly
(C) intimately
(D) initially

Muritos는 선도적인 국내 생산자일 뿐 아니라 해외 시장에서도 눈에 띄게 성공적이었다.

해설 빈칸은 뒤의 successful(성공적인)과 의미연결이 적절한 부사가 들어갈 자리이다. 선택지 중 (A) markedly(현저하게)가 적절하다.

어휘 in addition to ~에 더하여 domestic 국내 successful 성공적인 overseas market 해외 시장 markedly 현저하게 permissibly 허용되어 intimately 친밀히 initially 처음에

118

Krachen College is pleased to offer two new professional development opportunities ------- educators in Moreton during the 2017 academic year.
(A) at
(B) for
(C) in
(D) as

Krachen대학교는 2017학년 동안 Moreton에서 교육자들을 위한 두 개의 새로운 직업 개발 기회를 제공하게 되어 기쁩니다.

해설 빈칸은 의미 연결이 적절한 전치사가 들어갈 자리이다. 문맥상 '교육자들(educators)을 위한 기회(opportunities)'가 적절하다.

어휘 be pleased to ~해서 기쁘다 professional 전문적인 opportunity 기회 educator 교육자 during ~ 동안

119

The results included in this report are ------- applicable to British pension plans.
(A) directs
(B) directing
(C) direct
(D) directly

이 보고서에 포함된 결과는 직접적으로 영국 퇴직연금 적립제도에 응용 가능합니다.

해설 형용사 앞의 빈칸은 부사(directly 직접)자리이다.

어휘 result 결과 include 포함하다 applicable 해당되는 directly 직접

120

Due to a high ------- of submissions, please understand that we will only contact you if your work fits our current needs.
(A) volume
(B) location
(C) point
(D) size

많은 양의 의뢰 때문에, 단지 당신의 작업이 우리의 현재 요구와 맞는다면 연락을 할 것이라는 점을 이해해주십시오.

해설 빈칸은 의미가 적절한 명사가 들어갈 자리이다. 빈칸 앞의 형용사 high와의 관계도 고려해 볼 때 정답은 (A) volume(양)임을 알 수 있다. high volume 많은 양

어휘 due to ~ 때문에 submission 의뢰, 제출 understand 이해하다 contact 연락하다 current 현재의 volume 양 location 장소 point 요점

121

An evaluation will be completed ------- after all requested information has been received by Creed Union.
(A) only
(B) when
(C) most
(D) now

평가는 모든 요청된 정보가 Creed Union에 의해서 접수된 이후에 완료될 것입니다.

해설 빈칸은 뒤의 접속사 after와 의미연결이 적절한 부사가 들어갈 자리이다. only after(단지 ~뒤에)라고 해야 연결이 매끄럽게 된다.

어휘 evaluation 평가 request 요청 information 정보

122

FORTUNE's new main office building, with floor space ------- 28,000 square meters, houses modern production facilities, warehouses and offices.
(A) processing
(B) completing
(C) earning
(D) totaling

총 28,000세곱미터에 달하는 면적을 가진 FORTUNE의 새로운 본사 건물은 현대적인 제조 시설, 창고와 사무실을 수용합니다.

해설 빈칸은 뒤의 28,000제곱미터를 목적어로 취하면서 floor space를 수식하는 단어가 올 자리이다. 선택지 중에서 total이 타동사로 '합계가 되다'의 의미이다. 이 문장은 floor space (which is) totalling 28,000 square meters의 형태이다.

어휘 modern 현대의 production 생산 facility 건물 warehouse 창고 office 사무실 processing 과정 completing 완전한 earning 소득 total 총, 전체의

123

We are going to replace the silver knobs with ------- ones to match the bookshelves, and we ordered a wall mount to hang the TV.
(A) darkness
(B) darkest
(C) darker
(D) darkly

책꽂이에 어울리게 하기 위해서 은색 손잡이를 조금 어두운 것으로 대체할 것이고, TV를 걸기 위해 벽걸이를 주문했습니다.

해설 빈칸은 대명사 ones를 수식하는 형용사자리이다. 선택지 중에서 형용사는 dark의 비교급인 (C) darker이다.

어휘 replace 대체, 교체하다 silver 은 knob 손잡이 book shelves 책 선반

124

------- of Mr. Ahn's mail should be forwarded to his assistant while he is out of town for a business trip next week.
(A) Everyone
(B) Each
(C) All
(D) Such

Ahn 씨의 모든 편지는 다음 주 출장 때문에 도시 밖에 있는 동안, 그의 조수에게 전달이 되어야 합니다.

해설 all of와 each of가 가능한 형태이긴 하지만, 뒤에 불가산명사 mail과 연결될 수 있는 건 all of이다. each of는 복수명사만 받을 수 있다. all of 뒤에는 복수명사 또는 불가산명사(셀 수 없는 명사)가 올 수 있다.

어휘 forward to ~로 전송하다 assistant 조수 business trip 출장 out of town 도심지를 벗어난

ACTUAL TEST 06 ACTUAL TEST 07 ACTUAL TEST 08 ACTUAL TEST 09 ACTUAL TEST 10

125

------- the country's largest shopping complex was finished, Lexis Construction had already planned to build a larger one.
(A) Unless
(B) By the time
(C) Due to
(D) Whenever

국가의 가장 큰 쇼핑 복합단지가 완공될 때, Lexis Construction은 이미 더 큰 쇼핑 복합단지를 건설하려고 계획했었다.

해설 빈칸 다음에 주어와 동사로 연결되면 빈칸은 접속사자리이다. 접속사는 절과 절을 연결시켜주는 역할을 한다. 우리가 흔히 알고 있는 접속사와 다른 형태의 By the time(~했을 때, ~했을 쯤) 역시 접속사이다. 빈칸이 있는 문장의 시제가 과거이고, 뒤 문장의 시제가 과거완료이므로, 이에 적절한 선택지는 by the time(~할 무렵에)이다. 다른 선택지들은 의미상 적절하지 않다. due to는 전치사구이다.

어휘 unless ~하지 않는 한 by the time ~할 무렵에 due to ~ 때문에 whenever ~할 때는 언제든지

126

A majority of the organization's members are physicians with an expertise in a ------- area of the neurological sciences.
(A) provided
(B) confident
(C) granted
(D) particular

대다수 조직의 멤버들은 신경과학의 특정한 분야에서의 전문지식을 가진 외과의사들이다.

해설 빈칸은 뒤의 area(분야)와 의미연결이 적절한 형용사가 들어갈 자리이다. 문맥상 특정한(particular) 분야(are)가 가장 적절하다. confident 자신감 있는

어휘 majority of 다수의 organization 조직 physician 외과의사 expertise 전문 지식 particular 특정한 neurological science 신경과학 grant 승인, 허락하다

127

We actively seek to support innovative technologies ------- decrease dependence on fossil fuels.
(A) if
(B) that
(C) when
(D) will

우리는 화석 연료에 대한 의존을 줄일 수 있는 혁신적인 기술을 지원할 것을 적극적으로 추구한다.

해설 빈칸은 technologies(기술들)과 동사(decrease)를 연결해주는 관계대명사자리이다. 앞의 명사(technologies)가 선행사가 되고, 뒤에 동사가 있으므로 주격 관계대명사 (B) that이 정답이다.

어휘 actively 적극적으로 innovative 혁신적인 technology 기술 decrease 감소하다 dependence 의존 fossil fuel 화석 연료

128 Australian Toy Corporate Is slowly inching its way ------- more entertaining games that boys and girls of all ages can play together.
(A) beside
(B) toward
(C) along with
(D) onto

Australian Toy Corporate는 모든 연령대의 남자아이와 여자아이가 함께 즐길 수 있는 더 재미있는 게임 쪽으로 천천히 방향을 움직이고 있다.

해설 빈칸은 앞의 명사 way(방향)와 연결이 적절한 전치사자리이다. 선택지 중 방향과 어울리는 전치사는 toward(~ 쪽으로, ~로 향해서)이다.

어휘 slowly 서서히, 천천히 towrd ~쪽으로, 향해서 beside ~ 옆에 along with ~에 따라 onto ~쪽으로

129 Failure to comply with the rules ------- in this manual will cause the warranty to be declared null and void.
(A) outlined
(B) outlining
(C) outlines
(D) outline

이 매뉴얼에 설명된 규정을 따르지 않으면 보증서는 아무 가치가 없고 무효가 될 것입니다.

해설 빈칸은 명사 rules 뒤에서 수식하기에 적절한 단어가 들어갈 자리이다. outline(간략히 설명하다)은 타동사인데, 뒤에 목적어가 없으므로 수동형인 outlined가 정답이다. 이 문장은 the rules (which are) outlined in this manual의 구조이다.

어휘 failure 실패 comply with 준수하다, 지키다 cause 야기하다 warranty 보증서 declare 선언, 공표하다 null 아무 가치 없는 void 무효 outline 간략히 설명하다

130 Meriton, which was formerly known as Riverside, is a desirable community to live in because of its ------- to downtown Brisbane and natural environments.
(A) direction
(B) diligence
(C) proximity
(D) site

예전에 Riverside로 잘 알려졌던 Meriton은 자연친화적인 환경과 Brisbane 시내와 가깝기 때문에 사는 데 호감이 가는 지역입니다.

해설 빈칸은 to이하(to downtown Brisbane and natural environments)와 의미연결이 적절한 명사가 들어갈 자리이다. 선택지 중에서 전치사 to와 어울리는 단어는 (C) proximity(가까움, 근접함)이다.

어휘 formerly 이전에 desirable 바람직한, 호감이 가는 diligence 근면, 성실

Questions 131-134 refer to the following letter.

Dear Mr. Gallon,

Don't miss any issue of The Weekly Financial Adviser! Please note that your subscription ------- on May 31. If you renew your
131.
subscription before that date, you will receive a copy of Modern Finance, the latest book from financial expert Tony Parsons.
-------. As you already know, The Weekly Financial Adviser
132.
provides readers with a ------- analysis of the most significant
133.
advancements in business and finance. We hope that you are satisfied with our timely reports, the ------- tips from Harbie
134.
Dellington and the humorous columns of Anayeli Tapia.

Sincerely,

Jane Ryan

Circulation Manager

Enclosure

Gallon 씨에게,

The Weekly Financial Adviser의 어느 한 부도 놓치지 마세요! 당신의 구독이 5월 31일에 만료된다는 점을 유념하세요. 만약 당신의 구독을 그 날짜 전에 갱신한다면, 재정전문가인 Tony Parsons 씨의 최신 책인 Modern Finance 한 권을 받게 될 것입니다. 당신이 작성하여 우리에게 우편으로 반송해야 하는 갱신 신청서가 동봉되었습니다. 당신도 이미 아시다시피, The Weekly Financial Adviser는 독자들에게 사업과 재무분야에서 가장 중대한 진보의 철저한 분석을 제공합니다. 우리는 당신이 시기적절한 보고서와 Harbie Dellington 씨의 투자 팁, 그리고 Anayeli Tapia씨의 유쾌한 칼럼에 만족하시기를 바랍니다.

안녕히 계십시오.

Jane Ryan
유통 관리자
동봉

어휘 please note that ~라는 점을 유념하세요 subscription 구독 renew 갱신하다 the latest 최신의 financial expert 재정전문가 thorough 철저한 analysis 분석 significant 중요한, 상당한 advancement 진보, 발전 be satisfied with ~에 만족하다 as well as ~뿐만 아니라 investment 투자 humorous 유쾌한

131 (A) is expired
(B) have been expired
(C) expires
(D) to expire

해설 that절의 동사자리이다. 동사가 아닌 (D)는 오답이고, expire는 자동사이므로 수동태가 불가능하다. 따라서 정답은 (C) expires 이다.

132
(A) We arranged a lecture by Parsons which is scheduled for June 1.
(B) There are a few more magazines you can select including Modern Finance.
(C) Enclosed is the renewal application you need to complete and mail back to us.
(D) We also receive letters from readers to be published in a newly added opinion section.

해설 빈칸 앞 문장이 갱신한다면 얻게 되는 이점이 언급되어 있으므로 빈칸은 갱신 방법이 언급되어야 한다.

(A) 우리는 6월 1일로 예정된 Parsons 씨의 강연을 마련했습니다.
(B) Modern Finance를 포함하여 당신이 선택할 수 있는 몇 가지 더 많은 잡지가 있습니다.
(C) 당신이 작성하여 우리에게 우편으로 반송해야 하는 갱신 신청서가 동봉되었습니다.
(D) 우리는 또한 새로이 추가된 독자의 의견란에 인쇄될 독자들의 편지도 받습니다.

133
(A) thorough
(B) absorbent
(C) skilled
(D) temporary

해설 명사 앞을 수식하는 형용사자리이다. 잡지의 장점을 제시하고 있는 내용이므로 철저한 분석을 제공한다는 의미가 적합하다. 따라서 정답은 (A) thorough(철저한)이다.

134
(A) investing
(B) invested
(C) investment
(D) invest

해설 빈칸 다음에 오는 tips와 어울리는 표현을 고르는 문제이다. 명사를 수식하는 형용사 '(A) investing 투자하는, (B) invested 투자된'은 해석상 적합하지 않다. 명사인 '(C) investment 투자'가 정답이다.

Dear Mr. Yamamoto,
 	
The Sukusima School and Office Supply thanks you for bringing
this to our ------- . We ------- that we made a mistake. We
     135.   **136.**
mistakenly delivered to you a different product due to the hectic
schedule of our newly hired inventory clerk, who was just hired
a couple of weeks ago.
 	
We deeply apologize for the inconvenience. For our part, we
are ------- to replace the equipment sent to you mistakenly free
   137.
of charge. The correct set of audio-visual equipment will be
delivered to you at your office tomorrow.
 	
------- . We will try not to make the same mistake in the future.
 138.
 	
Thank you!
 	
Respectfully yours,
 	
Keiko Yamada
General Manager
	Yamamoto 씨에게,
	
	우리 Sukusima School and Office Sup-
	ply가 이것에 주의를 기울이게 해주셔서 감
	사드립니다. 저희가 실수를 했다는 짐을 인
	정합니다. 몇 주 전에 고용된 신입 재고관
	리원의 너무 바쁜 일정 탓에 실수로 당신
	이 주문한 것이 아닌 다른 제품을 배달했
	습니다.
	
	이 불편에 대해 깊이 사과드립니다. 우리로
	서는, 무료로 실수로 배달된 장비를 교체할
	준비가 되어 있습니다. 오디오-시각 장비의
	정확한 세트가 내일 당신의 사무실로 배달
	될 것입니다.
	
	당신의 건설적인 지적에 매우 감사드립니
	다. 앞으로는 같은 실수를 하지 않도록 노
	력하겠습니다.
	
	감사합니다!
	
	존경을 담아
	
	Keiko Yamada
	총괄 관리자

어휘 bring to one's attention ~의 주의를 기울이게 하다 acknowledge 인정하다 hectic 정신없이 바쁜 inventory 재고 apologize for ~에 대해 사과하다 replace 교체하다 mistakenly 실수로 free of charge 무료로

135
(A) attendee
(B) attentive
(C) attention
(D) attended

해설 bring to one's attention(~의 주의를 기울이게 하다)이라는 관용표현을 묻는 문제이므로, 정답은 (C) attention이다.

136
(A) acknowledge
(B) impress
(C) carry out
(D) reserve

해설 빈칸 다음 문장에서 실수에 대해 설명하고 사과를 하고 있으므로 that절의 내용은 '실수를 했다'를 인정한다는 말이 가장 적절하다. 따라서 (A) acknowledge(인정하다)가 정답이다.

137
(A) ready
(B) hesitant
(C) qualified
(D) deliberate

해설 무료로 장비를 대체할 준비가 되었다(ready)는 말이 가장 적절하다.

138
(A) However, either way, you have to pay an additional $10.
(B) He is the only person who knows the situation.
(C) Your constructive comments are greatly appreciated
(D) We are looking forward to hearing your opinion about this new technology.

해설 앞 문단에서 자신들의 실수를 인정하고 제품을 무료로 교환해준다고 했고, 빈칸 뒤에 이어지는 문장에서 같은 실수를 반복하지 않겠다는 내용이 나와 있으므로 문제점을 지적해준 부분에 감사함을 언급하는 문장이 정답이다.

(A) 그러나, 어느 것이든, 당신은 추가로 10달러를 지불하셔야 합니다.
(B) 그가 상황을 아는 유일한 사람입니다.
(C) 당신의 건설적인 지적에 매우 감사합니다.
(D) 우리는 이 새로운 기술에 관한 당신의 의견을 듣는 데 관심이 있습니다.

Questions 139-142 refer to the following letter.

Dear Mr. Andrew Nagorski,

I ------- to you to bring to your attention the outstanding service
139.
I received from one of your employees at the Sacranton branch
of your pet cleaning company.

-------. I warned the shampooer, a Mrs. Clare, that Haru (my
140.
pet's name) can be very difficult around new people. She just
smiled and approached my dog ------- hesitation. After playing
141.
with him for a few minutes, he was completely relaxed and even
let her clean his ears without a fight.

I've never seen someone with more genuine affection for the
animals and I will definitely recommend ------- to all my dog
142.
owner friends.

Sincerely,

Robert Natale

Andrew Nagorski 씨에게

저는 당신의 애완동물 목욕회사의
Sacranton 지점에서 직원 중 한 명으로부
터 받은 우수한 서비스를 알려드리기 위해
이 글을 쓰고 있습니다.

지난주에, 저는 애완견의 목욕과 미용을 위
해 데려갔습니다. 미용사인 Clare 씨에게,
Haru(제 애완견의 이름)는 새로운 사람이
주위에 있으면 매우 어려워한다고 경고했
습니다. 그녀는 그저 웃으면서 제 애완견에
게 망설임 없이 다가갔습니다. 몇 분간 놀아
주자 개는 완전히 긴장을 풀었고 심지어 싸
우지도 않았고, 귀 청소도 하게 해줬습니다.

저는 애완견에게 이보다 진심어린 애정을
쏟는 사람은 한 번도 본 적이 없으며 그녀
를 애완견을 키우는 다른 친구들에게 분명
히 추천할 것입니다.

진심을 담아

Robert Natale

어휘 outstanding 뛰어난, 우수한 warn 경고하다 approach 접근하다, 다가가다 hesitation 망설임 completely 완전히 genuine 진
심 어린 affection 애정 definitely 분명히, 틀림없이 recommend 추천하다, 권장하다

139 (A) will write
(B) am writing
(C) to write
(D) wrote

해설 과거에 받았던 서비스에 대해서 현재 편지를 쓰고 있는 상황이므로 현재진행시제가 가장 자연스럽다. 따라서 정답은 (B) am
writing이다.

140
(A) Last week, I brought my pet dog over for a shampoo and cut.
(B) That day, your employee was very impolite and didn't pay any attention to my pet.
(C) Some time ago, my pet was trained to be a guide dog.
(D) The day before yesterday, I kept my pet outside for a long period.

해설 빈칸의 바로 앞 문장에서 자신이 받은 뛰어난 서비스에 대해서 알려주고 싶다는 내용이 나오고, 뒷 문장에서 과거에 있었던 경험을 말하고 있다. 그러므로, 빈칸은 과거의 내용을 구체적으로 말하기 전의 도입문장이 필요하다.

(A) 지난주에, 저는 애완견의 목욕과 미용을 위해 데려갔습니다.
(B) 그날, 당신의 직원은 매우 불친절했고 애완견에게 어떤 관심도 갖지 않았습니다.
(C) 언젠가, 저의 애완견은 안내견이 되기 위한 훈련을 받았습니다.
(D) 그저께, 저는 애완견을 오랜 시간 동안 밖에 내버려 두었습니다.

141
(A) except
(B) without
(C) unless
(D) instead

해설 빈칸은 명사 앞의 전치사자리이다. (C)는 접속사, (D)는 부사이므로 오답이고, 문맥상 '주저함 없이' 다가갔다는 내용이 가장 적절하다. 따라서 정답은 (B) without(~ 없이)이다.

142
(A) him
(B) her
(C) you
(D) them

해설 빈칸은 recommend의 대상이 되는 목적어자리이다. 칭찬받는 대상은 미용사인 Clare 씨이므로 (B) her가 정답이다.

Questions 143-146 refer to the following memo.

To: All staff of Telegraph Publishing

From: David Faber

Date: May 2

I am glad to give you some news about the exciting developments at Telegraph Publishing. For 25 years, our firm has ------- excellent publications in the English language in
143.
several countries in Asia.

To make Baliplus News more successful, Colin Falconer has been hired as Director for Circulation. We are delighted that he came to work with us, and Mr. Falconer has already outlined ambitious plans ------- the number of readers for this
144.
publication.

Also, our recent project, Babak Namazian, will begin production next month with Amos Badeah as the chief editor. Mr. Badeah was chosen from ------- hundreds of applicants for the position
145.
because he has expertise stemming from his 12 years with another publication. Mr. Badeah and the new art director, Donald Walf, will lead Babak Namazian.

-------.
146.

수신: Telegraph Publishing 전 스태프
발신: David Faber
날짜: 5월 2일

저는 여러분께 Telegraph Publishing사의 몇 가지 흥미로운 발전에 관한 소식을 전하게 되어 기쁩니다. 25년 동안 우리 회사는 훌륭한 영문 출판물을 아시아의 여러 국가에서 유통해왔습니다.

Baliplus News를 더욱 성공적으로 만들기 위해, Colin Falconer 씨가 배포부서의 이사로 고용되었습니다. 그가 우리와 함께 일하게 되어 기쁩니다. 그리고 Falconer 씨는 벌써 이 출판물의 구독자 수를 증가시킬 야심찬 계획들을 설명했습니다.

또한, 우리의 최근 프로젝트인 Babak Namazian는 Amos Badeah 씨를 편집장으로 하여 다음 달에 출판이 시작될 것입니다. Badeah 씨는 그 직책을 위한 수백 명의 지원자 중에서 12년간의 다른 출판물로부터 생겨난 전문지식 덕분에 뽑히게 되었습니다.

Badeah 씨와 그의 새로운 예술 감독인 Donald Walf 씨가 Babak Namazian을 이끌 것입니다.

우리는 이 새로운 직원들이 우리 회사에 가치 있는 자산이 될 것이고 잡지를 성공적으로 만든다는 것을 확신합니다.

143
   (A) distributed
   (B) disturbed
   (C) disordered
   (D) discarded

   해설 동사 어휘문제이다. 빈칸 뒤의 목적어가 훌륭한 영문 출판물이기 때문에 훌륭한 출판물을 배포하다는 의미가 적합하므로 정답은 (A) distributed(배포하다)이다.

144
(A) increase
(B) was increasing
(C) to increase
(D) increases

해설 완벽한 문장이 나왔고, 명사 plan 뒤를 수식하는 자리이기 때문에 to부정사가 적합하다.

145
(A) despite
(B) among
(C) about
(D) between

해설 전치사 어휘문제이다. 편집장 Mr. Badeah가 '수백 명의 지원자들 중에서 선택되었다'는 의미가 되어야 하므로 정답은 (B) among(셋 이상 ~ 사이에)이다.

146
(A) The recruitment is processed now and the successful applicant will be announced by the end of this month.
(B) Walf was an account manager for 7 years before being appointed for this position.
(C) Babak Namazian will be the last publication of our company because we decided to discontinue the other magazines.
(D) We are certain that these new employees will be valuable assets to our company and make the magazine successful.

해설 앞 문장에서 잡지를 더 성공적으로 만들기 위해서, 여러 사람이 고용되었다는 이야기를 하고 있다. 따라서 문장은 그들이 가치 있는 자산이 될 것이고, 잡지를 성공적으로 만들 것이라고 확신한다고 말하는 (D)가 적합하다.

(A) 채용은 현재 진행 중이며 합격자는 이달 말까지 발표될 것입니다.
(B) Walf 씨는 이 직책에 임명되기 전에 7년간 회계부장이었습니다.
(C) 우리 회사가 나머지 잡지들은 폐간하기로 결정했기 때문에 Babak Namazian은 우리 회사의 마지막 출간물이 될 것입니다.
(D) 우리는 이 새로운 직원들이 회사에 가치 있는 자산이 될 것이고 잡지를 성공적으로 만든다는 것을 확신합니다.

101

The warranty does not ------- any damage caused by accident, misuse, fire, flood, or improper installation.
(A) covered
(B) cover
(C) covering
(D) covers

보증서는 사고나 오용, 화재, 홍수 또는 부적절한 설치에 의한 어떠한 손상도 보상하지 않습니다.

해설 조동사 does 뒤의 빈칸은 동사원형(cover)이 온다.

어휘 warranty 보증서 cause 야기하다 accident 사고 misuse 오용 flood 홍수 improper 부적절한 installation 설치

102

Please be informed that utility bill payments ------- in person at the Cashier's Office will be processed immediately.
(A) making
(B) make
(C) made
(D) makes

출납 사무실에서 직접 이루어지는 공과금 지불은 즉시 처리된다는 것을 알려드립니다.

해설 빈칸은 앞의 payments(지불)를 수식하는 적절한 동사형태를 고르는 문제이다. make는 타동사인데 뒤에 목적어가 없으므로 made가 적절하다. utility bill payments (which are) made in person at the Cashier's Office의 구조이다.

어휘 inform 알리다 utility bill 공과금 in person 직접 immediately 즉시

103

The Seal Inc. agreed to make an ------- in US-based Ecoline Ltd, a provider of software for the hospitality sector.
(A) effectiveness
(B) investment
(C) alternative
(D) indication

Seal 사는 서비스분야에 소프트웨어를 제공하는 업체인 미국에 본사를 둔 Ecoline 사에 투자하는 것에 동의했습니다.

해설 빈칸은 동사 make와 어울리는 목적어(명사)가 들어갈 자리이다. make an investment는 '투자하다'의 의미를 가지며, 한 단어처럼 묶어서 외워두자.

어휘 agree to ~에 대해 동의하다, 합의하다 provider 제공업체 effectiveness 유효성 investment 투자 alternative 대안 indication 암시

104

States have the right ------- or ban the purchase and sale of alcohol on Sundays.
(A) restricted
(B) to restrict
(C) restricts
(D) restricting

여러 주들은 일요일마다 주류의 판매와 구매를 제한하고 금지할 권리를 가집니다.

해설 or 뒤의 동사원형을 통해 단서를 얻을 수 있고 right(권리)는 to부정사를 받는 명사라는 것을 알고 있다면 쉽게 풀 수 있는 문제이다.

어휘 right 권한 ban 금지하다 purchase 구입하다 sale 팔다 restrict 제한하다

105

To feed a growing population, agricultural land is ------- to expand globally in the next decade to match the increase in food demand.
(A) presented
(B) preferred
(C) projected
(D) proceeded

증가하는 인구에 음식을 공급하기 위해서, 농경지는 식품 수요의 증가에 부응하여 향후 10년간 세계적으로 확장할 걸로 예상된다.

해설 빈칸은 be to 사이에 의미가 적절한 단어가 들어갈 자리이다. 전체적인 의미로 볼 때 projected(예상된)가 정답이다.

어휘 feed 먹이를 주다, 밥을 먹이다 population 인구 agricultural land 농경지 expand 확장하다 globally 세계적으로 decade 10년 increase 증가하다 demand 수요 present 증정하다 prefer 선호하다 proceed 진행하다

106

------- the parking lot in front is being repaired, employees are advised to park their vehicles behind the main building.
(A) So
(B) In addition to
(C) While
(D) During

앞쪽의 주차장이 수리되는 동안, 직원들은 차량을 메인 빌딩 뒤에 주차하도록 조언받습니다.

해설 빈칸은 의미가 적절한 접속사가 들어갈 자리이다. 선택지 중에서 접속사는 (C) While뿐이다.

어휘 repair 수리하다 employee 직원 be advised to 조언을 받다 vehicle 차량 in addition to 게다가

107

------- Furious Autos salesman could offer a company credit application to customers purchasing one or more vehicles.
(A) Whichever
(B) Future
(C) Every
(D) When

모든 Furious Autos의 판매직원은 하나 또는 그 이상의 차량을 구매하는 고객들에게 회사 신용거래 신청서를 제공할 수 있습니다.

해설 빈칸은 주어인 salesman과 의미가 어울리는 단어가 들어갈 자리로 '모든'이란 의미의 every가 적절하다.

어휘 offer 제의하다 application 신청서 purchase 구입하다 vehicle 차량 future 미래 whichever 어느 쪽이든, 누구든

108

Many private art galleries and museums recently opened in the Burbank district, which was ------- an industrial area.
(A) immediately
(B) formerly
(C) fully
(D) closely

많은 개인 아트갤러리와 박물관은 예전에 산업지역이었던 Burbank 지역에 최근 개장했다.

해설 문맥상 어울리는 부사어휘를 고르는 문제이다. 선택지 중에서 '예전에'라는 의미의 formerly가 가장 자연스럽다.

어휘 private 사유의 museum 박물관 recently 최근에 district 지구, 지역 industrial area 산업지역 immediately 즉시 formerly 이전에 closely 바싹, 접근하여

109

Consumers are advised to do some preliminary research ------- making a purchase an air conditioner.
(A) from
(B) before
(C) for
(D) with

소비자들은 에어컨을 구매하기 전에 예비조사를 하도록 조언을 받습니다.

해설 문맥상 의미가 적절한 전치사를 고르는 문제이다. 앞부분은 '사전조사를 하도록 권유되다'이고 뒷부분은 '에어컨을 구매하다'이다. '에어컨을 구매하기 전에 사전조사를 하도록 권유되다'는 의미가 자연스럽다. (B) before가 정답이다.

어휘 be advise to ~하도록 조언 받다 consumer 소비자 preliminary 예비의 research 조사 purchase 구매

110

The Expo on November 11th offers auto designers from various countries an opportunity to meet ------- and view many concept cars in Chicago.
(A) as if
(B) inclusive
(C) one another
(D) otherwise

11월 11일의 엑스포는 다른 나라에서 온 자동차 디자이너들에게 서로를 만날 수 있고 Chicago에 있는 많은 콘셉트의 자동차를 볼 수 있는 기회를 제공합니다.

해설 빈칸은 동사 meet의 목적어자리이다. 선택지 중 목적어로 어울리는 단어는 (C) one another(서로서로)이다.

어휘 Expo 엑스포 offer 제공하다 various 다양한 opportunity 기회 as if 마치 ~인 것처럼 inclusive ~이 포함된 one another 서로서로 otherwise 그렇지 않으면

111

In the event that both candidates are ------- qualified for a job, other factors to determine merit should be considered, such as community service and any notable awards.
(A) equally
(B) lately
(C) punctually
(D) often

두 지원자가 동일하게 직책에 자격을 갖춘 경우, 장점을 결정할 수 있는 지역 봉사활동이나 눈에 띄는 수상과 같은 다른 요소들이 고려되어야 합니다.

해설 be동사와 과거분사 사이의 빈칸은 부사자리이며 문맥상 의미가 적절한 어휘를 선택해보자. equally(동등하게), lately(최근에), punctually(정각에), often(종종) 중에서 qualified(자격 있는)와 의미연결이 자연스러운 부사는 (A) equally(동등하게, 똑같이)이다.

어휘 candidate 지원자, 입후보자 qualified 자격 있는 determine 알아내다 merit 가치 consider 고려하다 notable 눈에 띄는

112

------- Elliot Electronics' stock price has increased recently, the company's board of directors is worried about the slowdown in the high-end electronics industry.
(A) Despite
(B) Whenever
(C) So that
(D) Although

Elliot Electronics의 주가가 최근에 증가했을지라도, 회사의 이사진들은 고품질 전자산업의 침체에 대해 걱정합니다.

해설 빈칸은 두 문장을 적절하게 연결해주는 접속사자리이다. 전체적인 문맥상 앞 문장과 뒤 문장은 서로 상반되는 의미이므로 양보절을 이끄는 although(비록 ~일지라도)가 정답이다. Despite는 전치사이다.

어휘 stock 주가 increase 증가하다 recently 최근에 worry 걱정하다 slowdown 침체, 둔화 industry 산업

 ACTUAL TEST 06 ACTUAL TEST 07 ACTUAL TEST 08 ACTUAL TEST 09 ACTUAL TEST 10

113

Mr. Watson reviewed the sales report from our Langley agency ------- and found five areas that need further marketing research.
(A) interestingly
(B) usefully
(C) significantly
(D) thoroughly

Watson 씨는 저희 Langley대리점의 판매 보고서를 철저하게 검토했고, 마케팅조사 가 좀 더 필요한 5개 부분을 발견했습니다.

해설 동사 review(검토하다)와 의미연결이 적절해 보이는 부사는 (D) thoroughly(철저하게)이다.

어휘 review 검토하다 further ~와 관련하여, 더 나아가 interestingly 흥미 있게 usefully 유용하게 significantly 상당히 thoroughly 대단히

114

Mr. Davison is a reliable lawyer who will help our company when we consider ------- our corporate headquarters to a new facility.
(A) has relocated
(B) to relocate
(C) relocating
(D) relocation

Davison 씨는 회사 본사를 새로운 건물로 이전하는 것을 고려할 때, 우리 회사를 도 와줄 믿을 만한 변호사입니다.

해설 빈칸은 동사 consider와 연결이 자연스러운 단어가 들어갈 자리이다. consider는 동명사를 목적어로 취하므로 정답은 (C) relocating이다.

어휘 reliable 믿을 수 있는 lawyer 변호사 consider 고려하다 corporate 기업의 headquarter 본사 facility 시설 relocate 이전하다

115

A number of quality ------- are made before new products are released to our customers.
(A) checked
(B) checking
(C) checkable
(D) checks

새로운 상품이 고객들에게 출시되기 전에 많은 품질 확인이 진행되었다.

해설 빈칸은 문장의 주어가 되는 명사자리이다. a number of(많은 ~) 뒤에는 복수명사가 오므로 정답은 (D) checks이다. 참고로 <a number of + 복수명사 + 복수동사> / <the number of + 복수명사 + 단수동사> 형태도 기억해두자.

어휘 release to 발표하다, 출시하다 quality 품질 product 상품

228

116 Free dellvery is available to customers who ------- a two-year maintenance contract for the product purchased.
(A) agree
(B) drive
(C) offer
(D) sign

무료배달은 구매된 제품에 대해 2년의 유지보수 계약서에 서명한 고객들에게 이용 가능합니다.

해설 빈칸에는 a two-year maintenance contract(2년의 유지보수 계약서)를 목적어로 취하는 적절한 의미의 동사가 들어가야 한다. 문맥상 '계약서에 서명하다(sign)'가 자연스럽다. agree(동의하다)는 자동사이므로 맨 먼저 탈락된다.

어휘 available 이용 가능한 customer 고객 maintenance 유지보수 contract 계약서 agree 동의하다

117 We are interested in learning ------- you still have an interest or might be available to work full-time this year.
(A) either
(B) nearby
(C) whether
(D) regarding

우리는 당신이 올해 정규직으로 일하는 데 여전히 관심이 있는지 또는 일할 시간이 있는지 아닌지 아는 것에 관심이 있습니다.

해설 빈칸은 동명사 learning 뒤에서 절을 받는 접속사자리이다. 정답은 명사절을 이끄는 접속사 (C) whether(~인지 아닌지)이다.

어휘 whether ~인지 아닌지 nearby 인근의 regarding ~에 관하여

118 ------- of the two accounting directors will be available on Thursday.
(A) Each other
(B) However
(C) Neither
(D) Anywhere

두 회계 이사들 중 어느 누구도 목요일에는 시간이 없을 것입니다.

해설 빈칸 뒤의 of와 잘 연결되는 단어는 선택지 중 neither이다. <neither of the + 명사>는 '둘 다 ~ 아니다'의 의미이다.

어휘 each other 서로 however 그러나 neither 둘 다 아닌 anywhere 어디에도

119

The vendors also must demonstrate that they have ------- to all equipment needed and that it is available within twenty-four hours.
(A) accessible
(B) access
(C) accesses
(D) accessed

상인들은 반드시 그들이 필요한 모든 장비를 이용할 수 있고 그것들은 24시간 이내에 사용 가능하다는 것을 증명해야 합니다.

해설 빈칸은 have를 목적어로 취하는 명사자리이며 셀 수 없는 명사(불가산명사)인 (B) access가 정답이다. <have + pp> 형태로 간주하여 accessed도 생각할 수도 있겠지만 access는 타동사로 바로 뒤에 목적어가 와야 한다.

어휘 vendor 상인 demonstrate 입증하다, 증명하다 equipment 장비 access 접근, 이용 accessible 접근 가능한

120

The most popular digital cameras on sale today contain ------- functions such as video capture and automatic focus.
(A) many
(B) every
(C) each
(D) a lot

오늘 할인 중인 가장 유명한 디지털 카메라는 비디오 캡처와 자동초점과 같은 많은 기능이 들어 있습니다.

해설 functions(기능)와 어울리는 수량형용사를 고르는 문제이다. 복수명사와 어울리는 (A) many(많은)가 정답이다.

어휘 contain ~이 들어 있다 function 기능

121

Before installing a new toner cartridge for the laser printer, it is extremely important that it ------- thoroughly first.
(A) shaking
(B) be shaken
(C) to shake
(D) shaken

레이저 프린터용 새 토너카트리지를 설치하기 전에, 처음에 토너 카트리지를 충분히 흔들어야 한다는 것이 매우 중요합니다.

해설 주어 뒤의 적절한 동사형태를 고르는 문제이다. important(중요한)는 의무·필수형용사로 it is important that S (should) V의 구조를 갖는다. 토너 카트리지가 흔들어져야 하기 때문에 수동형인 (B) be shaken이 정답이다.

어휘 extremely 매우 important 중요하다 thoroughly 철저히 shake 흔들다

122

------- one of the four packages we sent last night by courier has arrived at the destination yet.
(A) Never
(B) Not
(C) None
(D) No

배달원을 통해 지난밤 우리가 보냈던 4개의 소포들 중에 어떤 것도 아직 목적지에 도착하지 않았다.

해설 빈칸은 one of 앞에 어울리는 단어가 들어갈 자리이다. 부정부사인 never는 one과 어울리지 않는다. none이 대명사이기 때문에 그 뒤에 대명사 one을 다시 쓸 수 없다. no one은 사람을 나타내는 표현이므로 이 또한 어색하다. 그래서 정답은 not one of(어떠한 것도 ~않다)이다.

어휘 arrive 도착하다 destination 도착지

123

In spite of the scarcity of dependable skilled technicians, the office will open in June and the project will proceed as -------.
(A) planning
(B) is planned
(C) planned
(D) plan

믿을 만한 능숙한 기술자들이 부족함에도 불구하고 사무실은 6월에 개업하며 프로젝트는 계획된 대로 진행될 것입니다.

해설 빈칸은 앞의 as와 적절하게 연결되는 어휘형태를 묻고 있다. as + p.p.(~된 대로)의 의미를 알아두면 쉽게 해결 가능한 문제이다. as planned 계획된 대로

어휘 in spite of ~에도 불구하고 scarcity 부족 dependable 믿을 만한 proceed 진행하다

124

The new software program can ------- organizations to share information more quickly and efficiently.
(A) acquire
(B) enable
(C) overcome
(D) except

새로운 소프트웨어 프로그램은 기관이 더 빠르고 효율적으로 정보를 공유하는 것을 가능하게 합니다.

해설 빈칸은 organizations를 목적어로 취하고 to부정사를 받는 동사자리이다. 형태상 enable이 가장 적절하다.

어휘 organization 기관 efficiently 효율적으로 acquire 습득하다 enable 가능하게 하다 overcome 극복하다 except 제외하고는

ACTUAL TEST 06 ACTUAL TEST 07 ACTUAL TEST 08 ACTUAL TEST 09 ACTUAL TEST 10

231

125

The CEO's speech is scheduled ------- 11:30 A.M, following morning press conferences as part of Media Day activities.
(A) for
(B) upon
(C) in
(D) between

최고경영자 연설이 언론의 날 행사의 일환으로 아침 기자회견 이후인 11시 30분으로 예정되어 있다.

해설 빈칸은 is scheduled와 연결되는 전치사자리이다. be scheduled for는 '예정되어 있다'의 의미로 반드시 외워둬야 할 표현이다.

어휘 press conference 기자회견 be scheduled for 예정되다

126

Use of the new accounting system is strongly recommend as it works much ------- than present one although it might look very complicated.
(A) efficiently
(B) more efficient
(C) most efficiently
(D) more efficiently

새로운 회계시스템의 사용이 아주 복잡해 보이겠지만 현재의 시스템보다 훨씬 더 효율적으로 작동하기 때문에 강력하게 추천됩니다.

해설 빈칸은 뒤의 than과 어울리는 비교급자리이다. 동사 work(일하다)는 자동사이므로 빈칸에는 부사 비교급 형태인 (D) more efficiently가 정답이다.

어휘 strongly 강력하게 recommend 추천하다 present 현재의 complicated 복잡한 efficiently 효율적으로

127

The necessary documents should arrive by June 30 ------- prospective applicants to be considered for admission to our law school.
(A) in order for
(B) yet
(C) so that
(D) when

유망한 지원자가 우리의 로스쿨에 입학이 고려되기 위해서 필요한 서류들이 6월 30일까지 도착해야 합니다.

해설 to부정사에 대한 의미상의 주어가 applicants이므로 (A) in order for가 적절한 형태이다.

어휘 document 문서 necessary 필수의 arrive 도착하다 prospective 유망한 applicant 지원자 consider 고려하다 admission 입학

128
Clients of County Corporation have increased ------- since the public relations director started actively promoting the campaign.
(A) considering
(B) considered
(C) considerable
(D) considerably

County Corporation의 고객들이 홍보담당 이사가 적극적으로 캠페인을 홍보하기 시작한 이래로 상당히 증가했다.

해설 빈칸 앞의 increase는 '증가하다'의 자동사이므로 빈칸에는 부사가 들어가야 한다. 그래서 정답은 (D) considerably(상당히)이다.

어휘 client 고객 increase 증가하다 considerably 상당히 promote 촉진하다 considerable 상당한 actively 적극적으로

129
Queensland Elementary School offers a variety of after-school programs ------- on the arts and physical development.
(A) will focus
(B) focus
(C) have focused
(D) focusing

Queensland 초등학교는 예술과 신체발달에 집중하는 다양한 방과 후 프로그램을 제공합니다.

해설 빈칸 앞에 있는 명사 programs를 수식하는 어휘형태를 묻고 있다. 선택지 중 이에 적합한 형태는 focusing이다. 이 문장은 programs (which are) focusing on the arts and의 구조이다.

어휘 offer 제공하다 a variety of 여러 가지의 physical 신체의 development 개발 focus on 초점을 맞추다. 집중하다

130
Translink International Co. has used a global consulting group in an attempt to re-establish its ------- in Korea.
(A) provision
(B) summary
(C) presence
(D) description

Translink International사는 한국에서 입지를 다시 다지기 위한 시도로 글로벌 자문그룹을 이용해왔다.

해설 빈칸은 re-establish(재건하다)의 목적어(명사)자리이다. 문맥상 (C) presence(입지)가 가장 적합하다.

어휘 in an attempt to ~하기 위하여 re-establish ~을 재건하다 provision 공급 summary 요약 presence 입지 description 묘사, 서술

PART 6

Questions 131-134 refer to the following information.

Congratulations ------- your purchase of an Ichikami Food **131.** Processor. Our products are made tough and are dishwasher safe. Our famous lifetime warranty is our guarantee to ------- **132.** any unit which does not meet the high standards we hold. -------. Please make sure not ------- the food processor's **133.** **134.** outer shell in water. Only the removable plastic parts with the 'dishwasher safe' logo on them should be allowed to get wet.

Ichikami Food Processor의 구매를 축하 드립니다. 우리 상품들은 튼튼하게 만들어 져 있고 세척기로 세척해도 안전합니다. 우 리의 유명한 평생 보증기간은 높은 수준 을 충족시키지 못하는 장치는 어떤 것이든 지 교환해주겠다는 약속입니다. 하지만 보 증은 기계 내부의 전자장치의 손상은 포함 되지 않습니다. 만능 조리기구의 외부 케 이스를 물에 담그지 마세요. '식기 세척기 에 사용 가능'한 로고가 붙어 있는 떼어낼 수 있는 플라스틱 부품들만 물에 적실 수 있습니다.

어휘 purchase 구매 tough 튼튼한 dishwasher safe 식기 세척기에 사용 가능한 warranty 보증 guarantee 약속, 보장 replace 교 체하다 meet 충족시키다 cover 포함하다, 다루다 immerse 적시다, 담그다 food processor 만능 조리 도구 outer shell 외부 케이스 removable 제거 가능한, 떼어낼 수 있는

131 (A) of
(B) on
(C) in
(D) to

해설 전치사 어휘문제이다. 당신의 구매에 대해서 축하한다는 의미이므로 정답은 (B) on(~에 대해서)이다.

132 **(A) replace**
(B) design
(C) produce
(D) convert

해설 빈칸은 동사 어휘문제이다. 세척기의 평생 보증기간은 어떤 장치라도 '교환해주겠다'는 것을 보장한다는 의미이므로 정답은 (A) replace(교체하다)이다.

133

(A) However, the warranty does not cover any damage to the electronics inside the machine.
(B) Therefore, you are not eligible to get a full refund for these reasons.
(C) Additionally, we will deliver your items to your new address as specified in your previous letter.
(D) Similarly, please contact the manufacturer directly for the parts needed to be replaced.

해설 앞 문장에서 어떤 장치라도 교환해주겠다는 내용이 언급되었고, 빈칸 다음 문장에서는 주의사항이 언급되어 있으므로, 빈칸은 교환이 불가능한 부분을 언급하는 내용이 와야 한다.

(A) 하지만, 보증은 기계 내부의 전자장치 손상은 포함되지 않습니다.
(B) 그래서, 그러한 이유들 때문에 당신은 전액 환불을 받을 자격이 없습니다.
(C) 게다가, 우리는 당신의 이전 편지에 언급된 대로 새로운 주소로 물건들을 배달할 것입니다.
(D) 이와 비슷하게, 교체되어야 할 필요가 있는 부품들에 대해서는 제조업체에게 직접 연락하길 바랍니다.

134

(A) to immerse
(B) immersed
(C) immerse
(D) immersion

해설 <make sure to + 동사원형>는 '반드시 ~하다'라는 빈출표현이다.

Questions 135-138 refer to the following memo.

From: Jim O'Rourke

To: Eastbourne's Lumber employees

Date: March 23

Subject: John Greenspan retirement

------- **135.** more than 40 years working at Eastbourne's Lumber, John Greenspan will be retiring at the end of this week. As such, we will be holding a dinner in his honor on Friday, March 28th at 6 O'clock at the Berry Mix restaurant. We hope that you will be able to attend this special event to show Greenspan how ------- **136.** we are of his decades of hard work. -------. **137.** I will ------- **138.** your desk to get the money. We recommend a minimum contribution of 20 dollars.

Thank you,

Jim O'Rourke

Human Resources Manager

발신: Jim O'Rourke
수신: Eastbourne's Lumber 직원들
날짜: 3월 23일
제목: John Greenspan 퇴직

Eastbourne's Lumber에서 40년 이상 근무한 후에 John Greenspan 씨는 이번 주말에 사퇴할 것입니다. 그러한 이유로, 우리는 3월 28일 6시에 Berry Mix 레스토랑에서 그를 위해 저녁식사를 하려고 합니다. 수십 년 간의 근면함에 대해 우리가 얼마나 감사해하는지를 Greenspan 씨에게 보여줄 수 있는 이 특별한 행사에 참석하시길 바랍니다. 우리는 이번 주에 여러분 모두에게서 돈을 모아서 저녁식사비를 지불할 것입니다. 돈을 걷기 위해서 데스크를 잠깐 들르려고 합니다. 최소 20달러의 기부금을 권장합니다. 감사합니다.

감사합니다.

Jim O'Rourke
인사부장

어휘 retire 사퇴하다 as such 그러한 이유로 in one's honor ~에게 경의를 표하여, ~를 기념하여 attend 참가하다 appreciative 감사해하는 decade 10년 hard work 근면 come by 들르다 minimum 최소한의 contribution 기여, 기부금

135 **(A) After**
(B) Within
(C) Over
(D) Since

해설 전치사 어휘문제이다. 40년 이상 근무한 후에, 사퇴할 것이라는 의미가 적절하므로 정답은 (A) After(이후에)이다. since는 과거 시점과 함께 쓰이며 그 이후에 계속 ~했다는 내용이 이어져야 한다.

136
(A) appreciate
(B) appreciated
(C) appreciative
(D) appreciation

해설 타동사 show 뒤의 목적어자리에 명사절이 들어간 문장이다. <how+형용사 [부사] +주어 +동사>구문에서 동사 뒤에 형용사가 빠져 있으므로 how 뒤의 빈칸은 형용사자리이다. be appreciative of(~감사하다)를 알고 있다면 정답을 쉽게 찾을 수 있다.

137
(A) We will pay for this dinner with collections from all of you this week.
(B) To commemorate our 20th anniversary, we prepared gold medals for employees with long service.
(C) This event was delayed due to unavoidable circumstances.
(D) Greenspan will be out of town that day to lead a seminar at the 2017 Missouri Lumber Conference.

해설 (A) 우리는 이번 주에 여러분 모두에게 돈을 모아서 저녁식사비를 지불할 것이다.
(B) 20주년을 기념하기 위해서, 우리는 장기근속 직원들을 위해 금메달을 준비했다.
(C) 이번 행사는 불가피한 상황 때문에 연기되었다.
(D) Greenspan는 2017년 Missouri Lumber Conference에서 세미나를 이끌기 위해 그날 출장을 갈 것이다.

빈칸 다음 문장에서 돈을 걷기 위해 데스크로 간다는 내용이 나와 있으므로, 빈칸은 돈을 모을 것이라는 내용이 언급되어야 한다.

138
(A) continue on
(B) found out
(C) look for
(D) come by

해설 돈을 걷기 위해 당신의 자리에 '들르겠다'는 의미가 적절하므로 정답은 (D) come by(들르다)이다.

Questions 139-142 refer to the following e-mail.

To: Company Employees

From: Nicholas Baldwin

Date: September 12

RE: Vacation Scheduling

Attachment: spreadsheet

This email is to ------- all employees that our winter holiday
    139.
vacation period has decreased from 10 days to 1 this year.

We will ------- longer close our offices from December 23rd
   140.
to January 2nd, but instead will offer Christmas day only.

Employees are still welcome to use their personal vacation time

over this period. -------. Therefore, we have implemented a
    141.
merit system to determine ------- gets the most popular days.
      142.
Employees recognized for the most dedication to their job will

have priority for Christmas Eve and New Year'day vacation.

Please fill in the spreadsheet with your desired vacation times.

Thank you,

Nicholas Baldwin, Human Resources Director

수신: 회사 직원

발신: Nicholas Baldwin

날짜: 9월 12일

제목: 휴가 일정

점부: 스프레드시트

이 이메일은 우리의 겨울 휴가 기간이 올해 10일에서 1일로 줄어들었다는 것을 모든 직원들이게 알려주기 위한 것입니다. 우리는 12월 23일에서부터 1월 2일까지 사무실을 닫지 않을 것입니다. 하지만 그 대신 크리스마스는 휴일로 제공할 것입니다. 직원들은 여전히 이 기간 동안에 개인적인 휴가를 사용해도 좋습니다. 하지만 어떤 날도 사무실을 떠나는 직원이 전체의 5%가 넘어서는 안 됩니다. 그래서 우리는 누가 가장 인기 있는 휴가일을 받을 건지 결정하기 위해서 실적제를 도입했습니다. 그들의 업무에 가장 많은 헌신을 한 것으로 인정받는 직원들이 크리스마스이브와 새해 첫날의 휴가에 대한 우선순위를 가질 것입니다. 당신이 원하는 휴가기간을 스프레스시트에 기입해 주길 바랍니다.

감사합니다.

Nicholas Baldwin, 인사팀 관리자

어휘 remind 상기시키다 decrease 줄어들다, 감소하다 no longer 더 이상 ~하지 않다 instead 그 대신 cannot afford ~할 여유가 없다 implement 도입하다 merit system 실적제 determine 결정하다 recognize 인정하다 dedication 헌신 priority 우선순위, 우선권 fill in ~에 기입하다 desired 바라는

139 (A) comment
    (B) imply
    (C) remind
    (D) speak

해설 이 이메일은 휴가기간이 줄었다는 것을 '상기시키기 위한 것'이라는 해석이 적절하므로 정답은 (C) remind(상기시키다)이다.

140
(A) not
(B) no
(C) none
(D) never

해설 no longer(더 이상 ~않다)구문을 확인하는 문제이다. 따라서 정답은 (B) no이다.

141
(A) However, we cannot afford more than 5% of the workforce to be away from the office on any day.
(B) During this company vacation period, two of our security guards will be on duty alternately.
(C) Supervisors of each team will have a priority to choose their vacation date.
(D) We aim to boost our sales during the Christmas and New year peak season by 50%.

해설 빈칸 앞의 문장은 직원들이 개인적인 휴가를 사용해도 좋다는 내용이고 빈칸 다음 문장은 누가 인기 있는 휴가일을 받을 것인지를 결정하기 위한 방법이 언급되어 있으므로, 빈칸은 휴가일을 결정하는 것이 제한된다는 내용이 언급되어야 한다.

(A) 하지만 어떤 날도 사무실을 떠나는 직원이 전체의 5%가 넘어서는 안 됩니다.
(B) 회사 휴가 기간 동안, 보안요원들 중 두 명이 교대로 근무할 것입니다.
(C) 각 팀의 감독관들은 그들의 휴가일을 선택할 수 있는 우선순위를 가질 것입니다.
(D) 우리는 크리스마스와 새해 첫날 성수기에 우리의 판매를 50% 늘릴 것을 목표로 합니다.

142
(A) who
(B) what
(C) where
(D) when

해설 타동사 determine의 목적어자리에 명사절 접속사를 넣는 문제이다. '누가' 가장 인기 있는 휴가를 받을지 결정하는 것이라는 의미이므로 정답은 (A) who이다.

Questions 143-146 refer to the following letter.

Dear Valued Holsten Mall Customer, Because of loyal Holsten Mall shoppers like you, we are happy to announce the continuation of the reward program. After we announced last year that membership into the program would be free, many people -------. By spending just 500 dollars **143.** in one visit to the mall, shoppers were given a gift certificate for 10 dollars which could be used at ------- retail outlet in the **144.** building (food court and movie theatre not included). Also, every month the top 100 spenders were entered into a draw for a ------- to win a $1000 shopping gift certificate. This **145.** year, we hope to get even more customers into our reward program and are offering all new members a $5 gift certificate to be put toward any purchase of an item of $50 or more value. -------. To learn more about what membership means for you, **146.** please visit www.Holstenmall.com.	소중한 Holsten Mall 고객님께 당신과 같은 Holsten Mall의 단골 고객들을 위해, 보상프로그램이 지속된다는 것을 알리게 되어 기쁩니다. 작년에 프로그램 가입이 공짜라는 것을 발표하고 난 후에, 많은 사람들이 가입했습니다. 몰에 한번 방문하여 단지 500달러만 지불하면 손님들은 건물의 어떠한 소매점에 서라도(푸드코트와 극장을 제외한) 사용할 수 있는 10달러짜리 상품권을 받게 됩니다. 또한 매달 최상위 100명의 소비자들이 1000달러짜리 상품권을 받을 기회를 얻을 수 있는 경품행사에 입력됩니다. 올해 우리는 훨씬 더 많은 손님들이 우리의 보상프로그램에 가입하길 바라고 모든 새로운 멤버들에게 50달러나 그 이상의 아이템의 구매에 제시될 수 있는 5달러짜리 상품권을 제공할 것입니다. 이것은 우리의 소중한 고객들에게 감사를 표하는 Holsten의 여러 방식들 중 하나입니다. 당신에게 멤버십이 어떤 의미가 있는지를 알기 위해서 www.Holstenmall.com을 방문해 보길 바랍니다.

어휘 continuation 지속 reward 보상 realize 알게 되다 incredible 엄청난 gift certificate 상품권 retail outlet 소매점 draw 경품 추첨

143
(A) will join
(B) joined
(C) joins
(D) joining

해설 동사 시제문제이다. 우리가 작년에 프로그램이 공짜라는 걸 발표한 이후에, 많은 사람들은 어떠했는지를 나타내는 동사를 찾는다. 종속절의 시제가 announced 과거이고, 빈칸 다음 문장에서 역시 과거시제로 과거에 있었던 사실을 서술하고 있으므로, 빈칸도 과거시제가 적합하다. 따라서 정답은 (B) joined이다.

144
(A) no
(B) many
(C) any
(D) few

해설 수량형용사의 위치를 묻는 문제이다. (B), (D)는 가산 복수명사 앞에 써야 하므로 오답, 의미상 '어떤' 아울렛에서도 사용할 수 있는 상품권을 받았다가 적합하므로 정답은 (C) any이다.

145
(A) chance
(B) result
(C) matter
(D) event

해설 1000달러 쇼핑 상품권을 받을 수 있는 '기회'를 위해 경품 행사에 참가할 수 있다는 의미가 적합하므로 (A) chance(기회)가 정답이다.

146
(A) This reward program is a temporary event and only available to existing customers.
(B) It's one of the many ways Holsten says thank you to our fabulous customers.
(C) Your order has been processed and will arrive in 2 days.
(D) On January 3rd, the last day of our business, we are planning to celebrate our store's history.

해설 (A) 이 보상프로그램은 일시적인 행사이고 오직 기존의 고객들에게만 이용 가능하다
(B) 이것은 우리의 소중한 고객들에게 감사를 표하는 Holsten의 여러 방식들 중 하나이다.
(C) 당신의 주문은 처리되었고 이틀 안에 배송될 것이다.
(D) 1월 3일, 우리의 영업의 마지막 날, 우리는 가게의 역사를 기념할 계획이다.

첫 단락에서 단골 고객들을 위해 보상프로그램의 지속을 알리게 되어 기쁘다는 내용이 있었고, 어떤 혜택을 제공해주는지 서술하고 있다. 그러므로 이러한 혜택이 고객에게 감사를 표하는 방식이라는 언급이 자연스럽다.

101

All manufactured goods from this production facility have been thoroughly ------- for quality control.
(A) considered
(B) reached
(C) inspected
(D) planned

이 생산시설로부터 만들어진 모든 제조품들은 품질관리를 위하여 철저하게 검사됩니다.

해설 빈칸은 주어인 goods(제품)와 의미가 잘 어울리는 동사가 들어갈 자리이다. 빈칸 뒤의 for quality control(품질관리를 위해서)를 통해 '검사하다'의 의미인 inspected가 가장 적절하다는 것을 알 수 있다.

어휘 manufactured 제작된 good 물건 production 제조, 생산 facility 시설 thoroughly 철저히 inspect 검사하다 consider 고려하다 reach ~에 이르다

102

Once you ------- your travel plans, we will send you an itinerary related to your plans by e-mail.
(A) confirmed
(B) would confirm
(C) confirm
(D) will confirm

일단 당신의 여행 계획을 확인하고 나면, 우리는 이메일로 당신의 계획과 관련된 여행일정표를 보낼 것입니다.

해설 접속사 Once가 있고, 뒤 문장의 시제가 미래이므로, 빈칸이 있는 문장의 시제 역시 미래가 어울린다. 선택지 중 (D) will confirm 이 정답이다.

어휘 confirm 확인하다 travel 여행 send 보내다 itinerary 여행일정표 related to ~에 관련된

103

Riverdale Restaurant changes menu ------- seasonally depending on the availability of the fresh produce and seafood.
(A) options
(B) occasions
(C) results
(D) payments

Riverdale 레스토랑은 신선한 농산물과 해산물의 유용성에 따라서 계절별로 메뉴선택 사항들을 변경합니다.

해설 빈칸은 동사 changes(변경하다)의 목적어(명사)자리이다. 선택지 중에서 (A) options(선택사항)가 의미연결이 적절하다. changes menu options 메뉴 선택 사항들을 변경하다

어휘 change 변경하다 seasonally 계절에 따라 availability 유용성, 효용 fresh 신선한 occasion 때, 경우 result 결과 payment 지불

104

While most of the car dealers met their quota this month, ------- exceeded it.
(A) few
(B) much
(C) either
(D) whose

이번 달에 대부분의 자동차 대리점이 그들의 할당량을 충족시키긴 했지만 초과하지는 못했다.

해설 빈칸은 동사 앞의 주어자리이다. 앞 문장의 car dealers(자동차 딜러들)을 받는 복수대명사인 (A) few가 정답이다.
어휘 meet 충족하다 quota 할당량 exceed 초과하다

105

At this time of the year, catering service companies are busy ------- year-end parties and annual banquets.
(A) preparing
(B) prepares
(C) preparation
(D) to prepare

올해 이 시점에, 음식공급회사는 연말 파티와 연례 연회를 준비하느라 바쁩니다.

해설 빈칸 앞의 are busy와 의미연결이 적절한 형태를 골라보자. 숙어표현인 be busy -ing(~하는데 바쁘다)를 알고 있다면 쉽게 정답을 고를 수 있다.
어휘 annual 연간의 banquet 연회 prepare 준비하다

106

Employees are notified that conference rooms 1 and 2 will be ------- next Tuesday while the air-conditioning system is being repaired.
(A) irreversible
(B) allowable
(C) improbable
(D) inaccessible

직원들에게 회의실 1번과 2번이 에어컨이 수리되는 동안 다음 화요일에 접근할 수 없다고 통고되었다.

해설 빈칸은 앞의 주어 conference rooms 1 and 2와 의미가 어울리는 형용사자리이다. 선택지 중 inaccessible(접근할 수 없는)이 의미 연결이 적절하다.
어휘 employee 직원 repair 수리하다 be notified 통지를 받다 irreversible 되돌릴 수 없는 allowable 허용되는 improbable 사실 같지 않은 inaccessible 접근할 수 없는

ACTUAL TEST 06 ACTUAL TEST 07 ACTUAL TEST 08 ACTUAL TEST 09 ACTUAL TEST 10

107

In December, Heritage museum will feature over 45 works by the ------- oil painter Alex Bryson.
(A) completed
(B) renowned
(C) founded
(D) estimated

12월에 Heritage 박물관은 유명한 유화작가인 Alex Bryson의 45개가 넘은 작품을 전시할 것입니다.

해설 빈칸은 oil painter(유화작가)와 의미연결이 자연스러운 형용사자리이다. 선택지 중에서 renowned(유명한)가 가장 적절하다. renowned oil painter 유명한 유화 작가 completed 작성한 founded 기초의 estimated 견적의, 추측의

어휘 feature 전시하다, 특징으로 하다, 특별히 포함하다, 특징

108

Located at the heart of the Docklands, this airport is very popular due to its ------- to the financial centre of the City.
(A) achievement
(B) proximity
(C) competence
(D) exception

Docklands의 중심부에 있는 때문에, 이 공항은 도시의 금융 중심부에 근접함 때문에 아주 인기가 있습니다.

해설 빈칸은 문장의 내용에 어긋나는 명사가 들어갈 자리이다. 그리고 빈칸뒤에 전치사 to도 단서가 되어 이에 어울리는 단어는 (B) proximity(근접함)이다.

어휘 heart 중심부 proximity 근접함 financial centre 금융 중심부

109

Please make sure that the lid is screwed on ------- so the sauce does not leak.
(A) tightly
(B) strictly
(C) largely
(D) thinly

뚜껑을 꽉 돌려서 소스가 세지 않게 확실히 해주세요.

해설 빈칸은 앞의 동사 is screwed on(돌려서 조이다)과 의미가 어울리는 부사자리이다. 선택지 중에서 (A) tightly(단단히, 꽉)가 의미연결이 자연스럽다.

어휘 make sure ~을 확실히 하다 lid 뚜껑 be screwed on 돌려서 조이다 tightly 단단히 strictly 엄격히 largely 크게 thinly 얇게

110

Employers need to provide portable fire extinguishers by law ------- employees can access them in case of emergency.
(A) in order to
(B) owing to
(C) if
(D) so that

직원들이 비상시에 소화기를 이용하도록 하기 위해 고용주들은 법에 의해서 이동 가능한 소화기를 제공할 필요가 있습니다.

해설 빈칸은 뒤의 문장을 연결해주는 접속사자리이다. 빈칸 뒤의 문장에서 조동사 can과 연결되는 접속사는 so that(~하기 위해)임을 알 수 있다.

어휘 employer 직원 provide 제공하다 portable 휴대용의 extinguisher 소화기 access 접근 emergency 비상 in order to 위하여 owing to ~ 때문에

111

Even though the new policies were initially controversial, ------- effectiveness in assisting Quantas Papers Service has not been.
(A) they
(B) them
(C) their
(D) theirs

비록 새로운 정책들이 초기에는 논란이 되었을지라도, Quantas Papers Service를 돕는 정책의 효율성은 그렇지 않았다.

해설 빈칸은 뒤의 명사 effectiveness(효율성) 앞에 어울리는 대명사자리이다. 명사 앞에는 소유격이 와야 하므로, 정답은 (C) their 이다.

어휘 even though 비록 ~일지라도 policy 정책 initially 처음에 controversial 논란이 많은 effectiveness 효율성

112

Below are a few ------- ideas for how you can build relationships with customers and create brand loyalty.
(A) specific
(B) specify
(C) specifics
(D) specifies

고객들과 관계를 어떻게 맺고 브랜드 충성심을 어떻게 기르는지에 대한 몇 가지 구체적인 아이디어가 아래에 있다.

해설 빈칸은 명사(ideas)를 수식해주는 형용사자리이므로 정답은 (A) specific(자세한, 구체적인)이다.

어휘 below 아래에 relationship 관계 customer 고객 create 창조하다, 기르다 loyalty 충성심

ACTUAL TEST 06 ACTUAL TEST 07 ACTUAL TEST 08 ACTUAL TEST 09 ACTUAL TEST 10

245

113

If possible, you should apply online and upload electronic copies of documents ------- submitting paper applications.
(A) because of
(B) which
(C) instead of
(D) through

가능하다면, 온라인으로 지원해야 하고 지원서를 제출하는 것 대신에 서류의 전자사본을 업로드해야 합니다.

해설 빈칸은 앞뒤 의미를 적절히 연결해주는 전치사자리이다. 빈칸 앞에서는 '온라인으로 신청하고 전자문서를 업로드하라'이고 뒤에서는 '종이 지원서를 제출하는 것이다. 중간에서 '~ 대신에'라는 의미연결이 적합해 보인다.

어휘 apply 지원하다 electronic 전자 document 문서 submit 보내다 because of ~때문에 instead of ~ 대신에 through ~을 통해

114

The South English cruise industry ------- significant growth in its capacity and in the number of passengers embarking from U.K. ports.
(A) experientially
(B) experiential
(C) experienced
(D) experience

South English 크루즈산업은 수용량과 U.K 공항으로부터 탑승하는 승객들의 수에서 상당한 증가를 경험했다.

해설 주어 다음에 빈칸은 동사자리이다. experienced와 experience 중에서 주어인 industry와 어울리는 (C) experienced가 정답이다.

어휘 industry 산업 significant 상당한 growth 성장 capacity 수용량 passenger 승객 embarking 탑승

115

Thanks to the new high-tech scanner ------- other devices, it has become quite convenient for consumers to take superior quality prints.
(A) and
(B) yet
(C) only
(D) either

새로운 고품질 스캐너와 다른 장치 덕분에, 소비자들이 뛰어난 품질의 프린터를 가져오는 것이 꽤 편리해졌다.

해설 빈칸은 앞의 scanner와 뒤의 devices를 대등하게 연결해주는 접속사자리이다. 선택지 중 and는 앞뒤 문장성분을 대등하게 연결해주는 접속사이다.

어휘 quite 꽤 convenient 편리한 consumer 소비자 superior 우수한 quality 품질

116

There are several ------- in the airport terminal that sell a wide variety of typical Korean souvenirs.
(A) stored
(B) storing
(C) store
(D) stores

공항 터미널에 매우 다양한 일반적인 한국 기념품을 파는 몇몇 가게가 있다.

해설 빈칸은 앞의 수량형용사인 several에 연결이 적절한 명사가 들어갈 자리이다. several 뒤에는 복수명사가 와야 하므로 정답은 (D) stores이다.

어휘 several 다양한 sell 팔다 wide variety of 매우 다양한 ~ typical 일반적인 souvenir 기념품

117

The current version of the Win-Latex pillow has been lightened, making it the lightest ------- on the market.
(A) any
(B) either
(C) that
(D) one

Win-Latex 베개의 현재 버전은 그것을 현재 시장에서 가장 가벼운 베개로 만들면서 경량화되었다.

해설 빈칸은 the lightest 뒤에 어울리는 형태의 단어가 들어갈 자리이다. 형용사 뒤에 사용 가능한 선택지는 명사인 (D) one밖에 없다.

어휘 current 현재의 pillow 베개 lighten 가볍게 하다

118

The Pearl Bay Times article reports that several hospitals in the region have begun preparing ------- the shortage by recruiting new nurses.
(A) for
(B) to
(C) of
(D) as

Pearl Bay Times 기사는 이 지역에 있는 몇몇 병원들이 새로운 간호사를 고용함으로써 부족함을 준비하기 시작했다는 것을 보고합니다.

해설 빈칸 앞의 preparing과 어울리는 전치사가 들어갈 자리이다. prepare for(~을 준비하다)를 알고 있다면 쉽게 해결 가능한 유형이다.

어휘 article 기사 hospital 병원 region 지역 begin 시작하다 prepare 준비하다 shortage 부족 recruiting 채용, 고용 nurse 간호사

119

Due to unexpected health problems of one member of the Quintet, the ensemble's European tour will be postponed ------- further notice.
(A) onto
(B) until
(C) all
(D) with

Quintet 멤버 중 한 명의 예상치 못한 건강 문제 때문에, 추후 공지까지 단체 European 투어는 지연될 것입니다.

해설 빈칸은 뒤의 further notice와 의미연결이 어울리는 전치사가 들어갈 자리이다. until further notice(추후 공지가 있을 때까지)를 기억해 두면 쉽게 해결 가능하다.

어휘 due to ~ 때문에 unexpected 예상치 않은 health 건강 postpone 연기하다, 지연하다 further 추가의, 추후

120

If you don't have a computer, the school buildings are equipped with computer kiosks that you may use to complete the ------- form, before you begin your study.
(A) reimbursement
(B) training
(C) inventory
(D) enrollment

만약 컴퓨터를 갖고 있지 않다면, 학교는 공부를 시작하기 전에, 수강등록 신청서를 작성하기 위하여 당신이 사용할 수도 있는 컴퓨터실이 갖춰져 있습니다.

해설 빈칸은 뒤의 form(서식)과 의미연결이 자연스러운 명사자리이다. 빈칸 뒤에 '당신이 학업을 시작하기 전에'라는 표현을 통해 '수강등록 신청서'를 나타내는 enrollment form이 정답임을 알 수 있다.

어휘 be equipped with ~을 갖춘 computer kiosk 컴퓨터실 reimbursement 배상 inventory 물품 목록 enrollment 등록

121

Whether you are ------- seeking a new position or are simply interested in learning about exciting new opportunities, the Manhattan Lycos Network is a valuable tool to move your career forward.
(A) activate
(B) active
(C) activity
(D) actively

당신이 활발하게 새로운 직책을 찾든지, 흥미로운 새로운 기회에 대해서 아는 것에 간단히 관심이 있든지 간에, Manhattan Lycos Network는 경력을 쌓아주는 가치 있는 도구입니다.

해설 be동사와 분사 사이의 빈칸은 부사(actively 활발하게)자리이다.

어휘 whether ~인지 아닌지 seeking 탐색 simply 간단히 opportunity 기회 valuable 가치 있는 tool 도구 career 경력 actively 활발하게

122

Every shipment must be ------- to the attention of Andrew Morrel, the inventory manager.
(A) directed
(B) positioned
(C) included
(D) conditioned

모든 배송은 재고 매니저인 Andrew Morrei 씨의 주의로 보내져야 합니다.

해설 빈칸은 뒤의 to the attention of(~의 주의로)라는 표현으로 이와 어울리는 동사는 direct(보내다)이다. be directed to the attention of ~의 주의로 보내지다

어휘 shipment 배송 attention 주의 inventory 물품 목록 direct 보내다 position 두다 include 포함하다

123

Requests to book conference rooms should be submitted in writing to Dr. Pavalov ------- three business days in advance.
(A) by means of
(B) at least
(C) so that
(D) instead of

회의실 예약 요청은 적어도 영업일 3일 이전에 Dr. Pavalov 씨에게 서면으로 제출되어야 합니다.

해설 빈칸은 뒤의 three business days(3 영업일)이라는 기간의 단어와 의미가 어울리는 표현이 들어갈 자리이다. 선택지 중 at least(적어도)가 가장 적절하다. by means of ~의 도움으로 so that ~하기 위해 instead of ~ 대신에

어휘 request 요청 submit 보내다 business day 영업일 in advance 미리 at least 적어도

124

The conference will be cancelled due to inclement weather, but the preparation for it should continue ------- there will be full attendance.
(A) so
(B) which
(C) that
(D) as if

회의는 악천후 때문에 취소될 것이지만 회의 준비는 전원이 참석하는 것처럼 계속되어야 합니다.

해설 문맥상 '악천후로 인해 회의가 취소되지만 회의 준비는 모두가 참석할 것처럼 해야 한다'가 적절한 의미이므로 (D) as if(마치 ~인 것처럼)가 정답이다.

어휘 conference 회의 due to ~때문에 inclement weather 악천후 continue 계속되다 attendance 참석 as if 마치 ~인 것처럼

125

For tourists who want to visit Germany and Spain, New Dutch Express Ways ------- passengers with a bus service to and from Berlin and Madrid.
(A) commutes
(B) offers
(C) transports
(D) provides

독일과 스페인을 방문하길 원하는 관광객들을 위하여, New Dutch Express Ways는 탑승객들에게 Berlin과 Madrid를 왕복할 수 있는 버스 서비스를 제공합니다.

해설 빈칸은 전치사 with와 어울리는 동사자리이다. provide는 <provide + 사람 + with + 사물>의 형태로 쓰인다.

어휘 tourist 여행객 passenger 승객 commute 통근하다 offer 제의하다 transport 수송 provide 제공하다

126

Established in 2001, Richmond has become a ------- manufacturer of tennis balls, basketballs and soccer balls in Austria.
(A) moving
(B) talking
(C) serving
(D) leading

2001년에 설립된 Richmond는 호주에서 테니스, 야구와 축구공을 만드는 선도 제조업체가 되었다.

해설 빈칸 뒤의 manufacturer(제조업체)와 의미가 잘 어울리는 형용사 어휘를 고르는 문제이다. 선택지 중에서 leading(선도하는)이 적합하다. leading manufacturer 선도(하는) 제조업체

어휘 manufacturer 제조업체 establish 설립하다 leading 선도하는

127

Last year, the company's total sales rose ------- even the most hopeful predictions of its new president.
(A) beyond
(B) except
(C) besides
(D) therefore

작년에 회사의 전체 매출은 새로운 사장의 가장 희망하는 예측을 넘어서 상승했다.

해설 빈칸은 뒤에 명사구(the most hopeful predictions)를 받는 전치사자리이다. predictions(예측, 기대)와 어울리는 전치사는 (A) beyond(넘어서)이다.

어휘 rise 오르다 prediction 예측 beyond 넘어서 except 제외하고는 besides 게다가, ~ 외에 therefore 그러므로

128

Emit Otter ------- the shoe designs by the time he meets with the president of Onits Footgear next week.
(A) completes
(B) completed
(C) is completing
(D) will have completed

Emit Otter가 다음주에 Onit Footgear의 사장과 만날 때쯤이면, 그는 신발 디자인을 끝냈을 것입니다.

해설 빈칸에는 문맥에 어울리는 적절한 시제가 들어가야 한다. 이 문장은 by the time(~할 무렵)이 이끄는 문장으로 by the time 절이 현재시제일 때, 다른 문장은 미래완료시제라는 것을 알고 있다면 간단히 해결된다. 그래서 정답은 (D) will have completed이다.

어휘 by the time ~할 쯤 president 사장 complete 완료하다

129

Towers Innovations is seeking employees who have a cooperative spirit, strive to meet expectations, and have a ------- for serving clients.
(A) benefit
(B) passion
(C) career
(D) confirmation

Towers Innovations는 협동정신을 갖고, 기대를 충족시키는 것에 노력하고 고객 접대에 열정을 가진 직원들을 찾고 있다.

해설 빈칸은 의미가 적절한 명사가 들어갈 자리이다. 문맥상 '고객 접대에 대한 열정'의 의미이므로 passion이 정답임을 알 수 있다.

어휘 seeking 탐색 cooperative 협력적인 spirit 정신 strive to ~에 고군분투하다 expectation 예상, 기대 passion 열정 career 경력 confirmation 확인

130

All participants can stay at Central Hotel or Residence Suites, ------- is more comfortable.
(A) neither
(B) whichever
(C) everyone
(D) other

모든 참석자들은 Central Hotel이나 Residence Suites 중 더 편한 곳이면 어디든지 숙박할 수 있습니다.

해설 빈칸은 의미 연결을 적절히 하는 연결어가 들어갈 자리이다. 선택을 나타내는 (B) whichever(어느 것이든)가 적절하다.

어휘 applicant 지원자 stay 머무르다 comfortable 편안한 neither 어느 것도 ~아니다 other (그 밖의) 다른

Questions 131-134 refer to the following letter.

Dear Ms. Theresa,

My stay at your hotel was truly amazing, as it ------- me comfort
131.
and relaxation due to the many services you offer.

Hayatt Zilala is truly one of the best hotels in the U.S. as far as
offering world-class amenities to the guests is concerned. -------
132.
During my 3-night stay at your hotel, I was really aware of the
expenses I ------- by using the hotel's services. I was genuinely
133.
shocked when I went to pay my bill. I checked in on July 21
and checked out on July 24. For 3 nights' accommodation,
I was charged not $ 675 but $ 750. This is much higher than
expected, and I ------- there is a mistake with the bill. I hope you
134.
respond promptly to this letter and provide a refund for me.

Thank you very much.

Respectfully yours,

Jared Jones

Theresa 씨께

호텔에서의 숙박은 정말로 놀라웠습니다. 당신이 제공한 많은 서비스들 덕분에 저는 안락함과 휴식을 가질 수 있었기 때문입니다.

Hayatt Zilala는 손님들에게 세계적인 수준의 시설을 제공하는 미국에서 최고의 호텔 중 하나입니다. 하지만, 거기 있었을 때 신경 쓰이게 했던 게 한 가지 있었습니다. 호텔에서 3일간 숙박하는 동안에 호텔서비스를 이용함으로써 발생한 비용을 확실히 알게 되었습니다. 청구서를 지불하러 갔을 때, 정말로 충격을 받았습니다. 저는 7월 21일에 체크인을 했고, 7월 24일에 체크아웃을 했습니다. 3일의 숙박 동안, 저에게 675달러가 아닌 750달러가 청구되었습니다. 이것은 예상보다 훨씬 더 높은 금액입니다. 저는 청구서에 실수가 있었을 것이라고 생각합니다. 당신이 이 편지에 즉시 응답하고, 환불을 해주기를 원합니다.

감사합니다.

존경을 담아

Jared Jones

어휘 comfort 편안, 위안 relaxation 완화, 휴양 amenity 설비 incur 입다, 초래하다 genuinely 진짜, 정말로 accommodation 숙박 expect 예상하다 assume 여기다 respond 응답하다 promptly 신속히 refund 환불하다

131
(A) brought
(B) kept
(C) deposited
(D) consisted

해설 빈칸은 동사 어휘문제이다. 빈칸 뒤에 목적어, 목적보어인 형용사가 있기 때문에 5형식동사가 와야 한다. 의미상 그 호텔은 나에게 편함과 휴식을 '가져다 줬다'가 자연스럽다. 따라서 정답은 (A) brought(가지고 오다, 야기하다)이다.

132
(A) Additionally, I met several business colleagues there.
(B) However, there is just one thing that bothered me when I was there.
(C) Therefore, I would like to take the opportunity to visit your hotel again.
(D) Nonetheless, this was the best trip I've ever gone on.

해설 빈칸 앞에서는 이 호텔에서 경험한 좋은 점이 언급되어 있다. 하지만 빈칸 뒤의 내용은 비싼 비용에 대해 불만을 제기하고 있음으로 빈칸에는 문제점 제기의 도입문장이 필요하다. 따라서 정답은 (B)이다.

(A) 게다가, 저는 거기서 몇몇 사업 동료들을 만났습니다.
(B) 하지만, 거기 있었을 때 신경 쓰이게 했던 게 한 가지 있었습니다.
(C) 그러므로, 저는 당신의 호텔을 다시 방문할 기회를 가지고 싶습니다.
(D) 그럼에도 불구하고, 이것은 제가 경험했던 최고의 여행이었습니다.

133
(A) incurred
(B) incurring
(C) was incurred
(D) have been incurred

해설 명사(expenses)를 수식하는 목적격 관계대명사절의 동사 시제문제이다. 3일간 숙박하면서 '내가 초래했던 비용'이므로 정답은 (A) incurred이다.

134
(A) consider
(B) describe
(C) expect
(D) assume

해설 동사 어휘문제이다. 예상보다 많은 비용이 나왔고, 이것은 실수가 있을 것이라고 '예상한다'는 의미가 자연스럽다. 따라서 정답은 (D) assume(가정하다, 추측하다)이다.

ACTUAL TEST 06 ACTUAL TEST 07 ACTUAL TEST 08 ACTUAL TEST 09 ACTUAL TEST 10

Questions 135-138 refer to the following notice.

Attention to All Residents in the Edison Building Please be informed that annual maintenance work on the building's heating system will be ------- on Friday, April 12 from **135.** 9:00 A.M. until 4:00 P.M. This routine maintenance will prevent problems from occurring during the winter. To make work -------, **136.** some equipment will be placed in the upper hallways and main lobby. We are sorry for the noise and disturbance this work will cause. If any serious problems are found during the maintenance work, proper ------- will be taken and we will do **137.** our best to finish the additional work as quickly as possible. -------. You can also call 339-1672. **138.** We appreciate your patience and understanding. Rose Arkansas Building Manager	Edison Building 전 거주자께 알립니다 4월 12일 금요일 오전 9시부터 오후 4시까지 빌딩의 난방장치에 대한 연례 유지보수가 실시될 것이라는 것을 유념하길 바랍니다. 이 정기 보수작업은 겨울 동안에 문제가 발생하는 것을 막아줄 것입니다. 작업을 더 쉽게 하기 위해서, 몇몇 장비들이 위쪽 복도들과 메인 로비에 놓일 것입니다. 우리는 소음과 이 작업이 야기하는 방해에 대해서 사과드립니다. 만약 보수작업 동안에 심각한 문제가 발견된다면, 적절한 조치가 이루어질 것이고, 가능한 한 빨리 추가 작업을 끝내기 위해서 최선을 다할 것입니다. 이 작업에 대한 업데이트를 위해서는 엘리베이터 옆에 있는 관리 사무실에 들르십시오. 당신은 또한 339-1672로 전화할 수 있습니다. 여러분의 인내와 이해에 감사드립니다. Rose Arkansas 빌딩 관리인

어휘 resident 거주자 maintenance 유지보수 conduct 실시하다 routine 일상적인 prevent 막다, 예방하다 occur 일어나다, 발생하다 equipment 장비 upper 위쪽의 hallway 복도 disturbance 방해, 폐해 cause 야기하다 serious 심각한 proper 적절한 measure 조치 additional 추가적인 patience 인내심 understanding 이해

135
(A) recognized
(B) waived
(C) conducted
(D) demonstrated

해설 동사 어휘문제이다. 주어가 연례 보수작업이므로 의미상 (C) conducted(실시하다)가 정답이다.

136
(A) easier
(B) more easier
(C) easily
(D) more easily

해설 5형식동사 make의 목적보어자리이다. 부사인 (C), (D)는 오답이고, 비교급 more와 easier가 함께 쓰인 (B)는 문법상 불가능한 형태이므로 (A) easier가 정답이다.

137 (A) subscriptions
(B) trouble
(C) transactions
(D) measures

해설 형용사 proper를 수식하는 명사자리이다. 문제가 발생되면 취해져야 할 주어자리이므로 적절한 조치라는 의미로 (D) measures 가 정답이다.

138 (A) This work has been successfully completed and you can access anywhere in this building.
(B) Please move all your stuff to the employee lounge located on 3rd floor.
(C) For updates about this project, drop by the janitor's office next to the elevator.
(D) Please come up with ideas for making this transition more convenient for everyone.

해설 빈칸의 다음 문장에서 '너는 또한 전화할 수도 있다.'라고 연락방법을 한 가지 더 언급하고 있음으로 빈칸 역시 연락할 수 있는 방법이 제시되어야 한다.

(A) 이 작업은 성공적으로 완료되었고, 당신은 이 빌딩의 어느 곳이든 접근할 수 있습니다.

(B) 당신의 모든 짐들을 3층에 있는 직원 휴게실로 옮기길 바랍니다.

(C) 이 작업의 업데이트를 위해서는 엘리베이터 옆에 있는 관리사무실에 들르십시오.

(D) 모두를 위해 이행작업을 더 편리하게 하기 위한 아이디어를 생각해내길 바랍니다.

Questions 139-142 refer to the following letter.

From: International Radio Network Date: January 12 Subject: Membership Mr. Hernandez, Thank you for considering ------- our growing radio network. **139.** -------. Our goal is to join together as many different voices **140.** as possible from different cultures and languages for the purpose of expanding an understanding and tolerance of each other. All stations in the network have access to the best professionally produced programming of their sister stations. These programs can be custom tailored to your listeners'-------. **141.** Your membership fee will go into our legal fund which helps to keep all our stations on the air when they are threatened by government cutbacks. We have included a document that details some of the other benefits you ------- when you join the **142.** network. Thank you, International Radio Network	발신: International Radio Network 날짜: 1월 12일 제목: 멤버십 Hernandez 씨 우리의 성장하는 라디오 네트워크에 가입을 고려해주셔서 감사합니다. 우리는 중동지역의 파트너 방송국들을 모음으로써, 세계적인 청취율을 확장하려고 합니다. 우리의 목표는 서로서로의 이해와 관용을 확장시키기 위한 목적을 위해 다른 문화와 언어로부터 가능한 한 다양한 목소리들을 함께 결합하는 것입니다. 네트워크에 있는 모든 방송국들은 그들의 자매 방송국의 가장 전문적으로 생산된 프로그래밍에 접근합니다. 이 프로그램들은 청취자들의 기호에 맞춤제작 되었습니다. 당신의 회비는 정부의 예산 삭감으로 인해 위태로운 상태에 처한 모든 방송국들의 운영을 돕기 위한 합법적인 자금으로 쓰일 것입니다. 당신이 우리 네트워크에 가입했을 때 경험하게 될 다른 혜택들을 설명하는 서류를 포함시켰습니다. 감사합니다. International Radio Network

어휘 consider 고려하다 join 결합하다 growing 성장하는 goal 목표 culture 문화 purpose 목적 expand 확장하다 tolerance 용인, 관용 access 접근 professionally 전문적으로 produce 생산하다 custom 관습, 습관 tailor 맞추다 taste 맛, 기호 legal 법률과 관련된 fund 기금, 자금 threaten 협박하다, 위협하다 government 정부 cutback 삭감 include 포함하다 benefit 혜택 experience 경험하다

139 (A) to join
(B) joining
(C) joins
(D) joined

해설 동사 consider의 목적어자리이다. consider는 동명사 목적어를 취하는 동사이므로 정답은 (B) joining이다.

140
(A) We are seeking some qualified applicants to take the chief producer position at our new location.
(B) We are focusing on covering the irregularity of the Korean government these days.
(C) We are preparing to deliver our next issue to you and you will get it soon.
(D) We are looking to expand our global reach by gathering partner stations.

해설 빈칸 앞에서는 네트워크에 가입을 고려해줘서 감사하다는 내용, 빈칸 뒤에서는 우리가 다른 문화와 언어로부터 다양한 목소리를 결합하는 것을 목표로 한다는 내용이 언급되어 있다. 따라서 빈칸은 우리 네트워크가 다양한 회원국을 모으고 있다는 내용이 언급되는 것이 자연스럽다.

(A) 우리는 새 지점에서 책임 프로듀서 직책을 맡을 자격을 갖춘 지원자들을 찾고 있습니다.
(B) 우리는 요즘 한국 정부의 불규칙성을 다루는 데 집중하고 있습니다.
(C) 우리는 다음 호를 배달할 준비를 하고 있고, 당신은 곧 그것을 받을 것입니다.
(D) 우리는 파트너 방송국들을 모음으로써 세계적인 청취율을 확장하는 것을 생각하고 있습니다.

141
(A) tastes
(B) absences
(C) alteration
(D) sense

해설 명사 어휘문제이다. 이 프로그램들이 청취자들의 '기호'에 맞추어 맞춤제작 된다는 의미가 자연스럽다. 따라서 정답은 (A) tastes(맛, 기호)이다.

142
(A) experienced
(B) experience
(C) to experience
(D) will experience

해설 동사 시제문제이다. 첫 단락에서 네트워크 가입을 고려해줘서 감사하다는 내용이 언급되었고 아직 가입을 하지 않은 상태임을 알 수 있다. 따라서 혜택은 앞으로 당신이 가입하게 되었을 때 경험하게 될 미래의 일이므로 미래시제가 적합하다.

ACTUAL TEST 06 ACTUAL TEST 07 ACTUAL TEST 08 ACTUAL TEST 09 ACTUAL TEST 10

Questions 143-146 refer to the following e-mail.

To: Addington Stickler <astickler@ceprocookware.com>

From: Tira West <twest@ceprocookware.com>

Date: June 10

Subject: Brochure

Attachment: Revised draft

Dear Mr. Stickler,

Our marketing personnel are getting ready for the World Food and Cooking Exposition ------- in Vancouver from June 20 to
143.
June 23. As you already know, we will be displaying our -------
144.
line of stainless steel cooking and dining utensils ------- your
145.
team designed. Attached to this e-mail is a recently revised draft copy of the cookware brochure that we plan to give out at our display booth. We have put in more images and reflected the changes in the brochure that you have asked for. -------.
146.
Therefore, please go through it and let me know if there is anything you want to change before Wednesday afternoon.

Thanks,

Tira West

수신: Addington Stickler 〈astickler@ce-procookware.com〉

발신: Tira West 〈twest@ceprocookware.com〉

날짜: 6월 10일

제목: 홍보책자

첨부: 수정된 초안

Stickler 씨,

저희 마케팅 직원들은 6월 20일부터 6월 23일까지 Vancouver에서 열리는 World Food and Cooking Exposition을 준비하고 있습니다. 귀하가 이미 알고 있듯이 저희는 당신 팀이 디자인했던 최신 라인의 스테인리스 스틸 조리기구, 식기류를 전시할 것입니다. 전시 부스에서 나눠줄 계획인 최근에 수정된 조리도구 홍보책자의 초안이 이 메일에 첨부되었습니다. 저희는 더 많은 이미지를 넣었고, 당신들이 요청했던 변경을 책자에 반영했습니다. 저희는 최종 버전을 이번 주말까지 인쇄부서에 보내길 원합니다. 그러므로 그것을 살펴보고 수요일 오후 전까지 변경하고 싶은 것이 있는지 알려주길 바랍니다.

감사합니다.

Tira West

어휘 personnel 직원들, 인사과 get ready for ~을 위해 준비하다 latest 최신의, 최근의 utensil 기구, 도구 attach 붙이다. 첨부하다 revise 변경하다, 수정하다 draft 원고, 초안 cookware 취사도구 give out 나눠주다 reflect 비추다, 반사하다 go through 살펴보다, 검토하다

143
(A) holding
(B) is holding
(C) will be held
(D) to be held

해설 빈칸 앞은 완전한 문장이므로 빈칸은 수식하는 자리이다. 동사인 (B)와 (C)는 오답이다. 뒤에 목적어가 없기 때문에 수동태 형태인 (D) to be held가 정답이다.

144
(A) latest
(B) late
(C) last
(D) lately

해설 빈칸 명사를 수식하는 형용사자리이므로 부사인 (D)는 오답이다. 전시장에서 전시될 조리도구이기 때문에 '최신 조리도구'라는 의미로 (A) latest(최신의)가 정답이다.

145
(A) it
(B) who
(C) that
(D) what

해설 한 문장에 동사가 2개이므로 빈칸은 접속사자리이다. 앞에 사물명사인 utensils를 수식하고, 뒤에는 불완전한 문장이 왔기 때문에 (C) that이 정답이다.

146
(A) The printing division has informed us that they've finished printing our brochure.
(B) We tried the utensils you recommended, but they were not durable enough.
(C) We want to send the final version to our printing division by the end of this week.
(D) Without your help, we would have not taken those photographs.

해설 앞 문장에서 홍보책자가 수정되었다고 언급했고, 빈칸 뒤에서 그밖에 수정할 사항이 있으면 알려달라고 했기 때문에, 아직 인쇄가 완료된 것은 아니다. 그러므로 이번 주에 인쇄될 예정이라고 언급한 (C)가 가장 적절하다.

(A) 인쇄부서는 우리의 홍보 책자 인쇄를 끝냈다고 알렸습니다.
(B) 우리는 당신이 제안했던 조리도구를 사용해봤습니다. 하지만 그것들은 충분히 내구성을 갖추지 않았습니다.
(C) 우리는 최종 버전을 이번 주말까지 인쇄부서에 보내길 원합니다.
(D) 당신의 도움이 없었다면 그런 사진을 찍는 것은 어려웠을 것입니다.

정답표

Actual Test 01

101	(B)	108	(A)	115	(C)	122	(D)	129	(C)	136	(A)	143	(B)
102	(A)	109	(D)	116	(D)	123	(B)	130	(C)	137	(B)	144	(D)
103	(A)	110	(C)	117	(A)	124	(A)	131	(D)	138	(C)	145	(A)
104	(B)	111	(D)	118	(A)	125	(C)	132	(A)	139	(A)	146	(B)
105	(D)	112	(A)	119	(B)	126	(D)	133	(D)	140	(B)		
106	(B)	113	(C)	120	(D)	127	(D)	134	(A)	141	(B)		
107	(B)	114	(A)	121	(A)	128	(D)	135	(C)	142	(A)		

Actual Test 02

101	(B)	108	(A)	115	(D)	122	(C)	129	(A)	136	(C)	143	(D)
102	(A)	109	(A)	116	(C)	123	(B)	130	(A)	137	(A)	144	(C)
103	(D)	110	(B)	117	(C)	124	(A)	131	(A)	138	(B)	145	(D)
104	(D)	111	(C)	118	(D)	125	(B)	132	(D)	139	(D)	146	(C)
105	(D)	112	(D)	119	(D)	126	(A)	133	(C)	140	(C)		
106	(C)	113	(A)	120	(C)	127	(B)	134	(A)	141	(B)		
107	(A)	114	(B)	121	(C)	128	(A)	135	(C)	142	(D)		

Actual Test 03

101	(B)	108	(C)	115	(A)	122	(D)	129	(B)	136	(D)	143	(A)
102	(C)	109	(A)	116	(B)	123	(D)	130	(A)	137	(D)	144	(D)
103	(C)	110	(B)	117	(A)	124	(B)	131	(B)	138	(A)	145	(C)
104	(B)	111	(C)	118	(B)	125	(C)	132	(D)	139	(C)	146	(D)
105	(A)	112	(D)	119	(D)	126	(C)	133	(B)	140	(C)		
106	(D)	113	(A)	120	(A)	127	(C)	134	(B)	141	(C)		
107	(A)	114	(B)	121	(C)	128	(C)	135	(C)	142	(A)		

Actual Test 04

101	(C)	108	(A)	115	(B)	122	(C)	129	(A)	136	(A)	143	(D)
102	(A)	109	(D)	116	(D)	123	(C)	130	(D)	137	(B)	144	(A)
103	(D)	110	(B)	117	(C)	124	(D)	131	(A)	138	(B)	145	(C)
104	(A)	111	(B)	118	(D)	125	(B)	132	(C)	139	(D)	146	(A)
105	(D)	112	(C)	119	(D)	126	(C)	133	(C)	140	(A)		
106	(B)	113	(C)	120	(C)	127	(B)	134	(A)	141	(B)		
107	(D)	114	(D)	121	(A)	128	(D)	135	(C)	142	(A)		

Actual Test 05

101	(C)	108	(D)	115	(D)	122	(C)	129	(A)	136	(A)	143	(C)
102	(A)	109	(A)	116	(D)	123	(D)	130	(A)	137	(C)	144	(A)
103	(C)	110	(C)	117	(A)	124	(C)	131	(D)	138	(B)	145	(C)
104	(A)	111	(A)	118	(C)	125	(A)	132	(B)	139	(B)	146	(C)
105	(A)	112	(B)	119	(C)	126	(B)	133	(C)	140	(D)		
106	(A)	113	(A)	120	(D)	127	(D)	134	(B)	141	(A)		
107	(B)	114	(B)	121	(A)	128	(B)	135	(C)	142	(B)		

Actual Test 06

101	(C)	108	(C)	115	(A)	122	(B)	129	(D)	136	(A)	143	(C)
102	(A)	109	(B)	116	(D)	123	(A)	130	(A)	137	(B)	144	(A)
103	(A)	110	(B)	117	(C)	124	(A)	131	(C)	138	(A)	145	(B)
104	(C)	111	(C)	118	(A)	125	(A)	132	(D)	139	(C)	146	(B)
105	(C)	112	(C)	119	(B)	126	(A)	133	(A)	140	(A)		
106	(C)	113	(A)	120	(A)	127	(D)	134	(A)	141	(D)		
107	(B)	114	(A)	121	(C)	128	(D)	135	(C)	142	(A)		

Actual Test 07

101	(B)	108	(A)	115	(B)	122	(C)	129	(A)	136	(C)	143	(C)
102	(D)	109	(B)	116	(D)	123	(B)	130	(A)	137	(B)	144	(C)
103	(D)	110	(C)	117	(A)	124	(D)	131	(B)	138	(C)	145	(D)
104	(B)	111	(C)	118	(B)	125	(A)	132	(B)	139	(A)	146	(B)
105	(B)	112	(C)	119	(B)	126	(B)	133	(C)	140	(B)		
106	(C)	113	(A)	120	(B)	127	(A)	134	(C)	141	(C)		
107	(B)	114	(D)	121	(C)	128	(C)	135	(B)	142	(D)		

Actual Test 08

101	(A)	108	(D)	115	(A)	122	(D)	129	(A)	136	(A)	143	(A)
102	(D)	109	(C)	116	(B)	123	(C)	130	(C)	137	(A)	144	(C)
103	(A)	110	(C)	117	(A)	124	(C)	131	(C)	138	(C)	145	(B)
104	(A)	111	(B)	118	(B)	125	(B)	132	(C)	139	(B)	146	(D)
105	(D)	112	(D)	119	(D)	126	(D)	133	(A)	140	(A)		
106	(A)	113	(B)	120	(A)	127	(B)	134	(C)	141	(B)		
107	(B)	114	(D)	121	(A)	128	(B)	135	(C)	142	(B)		

Actual Test 09

101	(B)	108	(B)	115	(D)	122	(B)	129	(D)	136	(C)	143	(B)
102	(C)	109	(B)	116	(D)	123	(C)	130	(C)	137	(A)	144	(C)
103	(B)	110	(C)	117	(C)	124	(B)	131	(B)	138	(D)	145	(A)
104	(B)	111	(A)	118	(C)	125	(A)	132	(A)	139	(C)	146	(B)
105	(C)	112	(D)	119	(B)	126	(D)	133	(A)	140	(B)		
106	(C)	113	(D)	120	(A)	127	(A)	134	(A)	141	(A)		
107	(C)	114	(C)	121	(B)	128	(D)	135	(A)	142	(A)		

Actual Test 10

101	(C)	108	(B)	115	(A)	122	(A)	129	(B)	136	(A)	143	(D)
102	(D)	109	(A)	116	(D)	123	(B)	130	(B)	137	(D)	144	(A)
103	(A)	110	(D)	117	(D)	124	(D)	131	(A)	138	(C)	145	(C)
104	(A)	111	(C)	118	(A)	125	(D)	132	(B)	139	(B)	146	(C)
105	(A)	112	(A)	119	(B)	126	(D)	133	(A)	140	(D)		
106	(D)	113	(C)	120	(D)	127	(A)	134	(D)	141	(A)		
107	(B)	114	(C)	121	(D)	128	(D)	135	(C)	142	(D)		

ANSWER SHEET

Reading Comprehension Part V, Part VI

No.	A	B	C	D	No.	A	B	C	D	No.	A	B	C	D	No.	A	B	C	D	No.	A	B	C	D
101	Ⓐ	Ⓑ	Ⓒ	Ⓓ	111	Ⓐ	Ⓑ	Ⓒ	Ⓓ	121	Ⓐ	Ⓑ	Ⓒ	Ⓓ	131	Ⓐ	Ⓑ	Ⓒ	Ⓓ	141	Ⓐ	Ⓑ	Ⓒ	Ⓓ
102	Ⓐ	Ⓑ	Ⓒ	Ⓓ	112	Ⓐ	Ⓑ	Ⓒ	Ⓓ	122	Ⓐ	Ⓑ	Ⓒ	Ⓓ	132	Ⓐ	Ⓑ	Ⓒ	Ⓓ	142	Ⓐ	Ⓑ	Ⓒ	Ⓓ
103	Ⓐ	Ⓑ	Ⓒ	Ⓓ	113	Ⓐ	Ⓑ	Ⓒ	Ⓓ	123	Ⓐ	Ⓑ	Ⓒ	Ⓓ	133	Ⓐ	Ⓑ	Ⓒ	Ⓓ	143	Ⓐ	Ⓑ	Ⓒ	Ⓓ
104	Ⓐ	Ⓑ	Ⓒ	Ⓓ	114	Ⓐ	Ⓑ	Ⓒ	Ⓓ	124	Ⓐ	Ⓑ	Ⓒ	Ⓓ	134	Ⓐ	Ⓑ	Ⓒ	Ⓓ	144	Ⓐ	Ⓑ	Ⓒ	Ⓓ
105	Ⓐ	Ⓑ	Ⓒ	Ⓓ	115	Ⓐ	Ⓑ	Ⓒ	Ⓓ	125	Ⓐ	Ⓑ	Ⓒ	Ⓓ	135	Ⓐ	Ⓑ	Ⓒ	Ⓓ	145	Ⓐ	Ⓑ	Ⓒ	Ⓓ
106	Ⓐ	Ⓑ	Ⓒ	Ⓓ	116	Ⓐ	Ⓑ	Ⓒ	Ⓓ	126	Ⓐ	Ⓑ	Ⓒ	Ⓓ	135	Ⓐ	Ⓑ	Ⓒ	Ⓓ	146	Ⓐ	Ⓑ	Ⓒ	Ⓓ
107	Ⓐ	Ⓑ	Ⓒ	Ⓓ	117	Ⓐ	Ⓑ	Ⓒ	Ⓓ	127	Ⓐ	Ⓑ	Ⓒ	Ⓓ	137	Ⓐ	Ⓑ	Ⓒ	Ⓓ					
108	Ⓐ	Ⓑ	Ⓒ	Ⓓ	118	Ⓐ	Ⓑ	Ⓒ	Ⓓ	128	Ⓐ	Ⓑ	Ⓒ	Ⓓ	138	Ⓐ	Ⓑ	Ⓒ	Ⓓ					
109	Ⓐ	Ⓑ	Ⓒ	Ⓓ	119	Ⓐ	Ⓑ	Ⓒ	Ⓓ	129	Ⓐ	Ⓑ	Ⓒ	Ⓓ	139	Ⓐ	Ⓑ	Ⓒ	Ⓓ					
110	Ⓐ	Ⓑ	Ⓒ	Ⓓ	120	Ⓐ	Ⓑ	Ⓒ	Ⓓ	130	Ⓐ	Ⓑ	Ⓒ	Ⓓ	140	Ⓐ	Ⓑ	Ⓒ	Ⓓ					

ANSWER SHEET

Reading Comprehension Part V, Part VI

No.	A	B	C	D	No.	A	B	C	D	No.	A	B	C	D	No.	A	B	C	D	No.	A	B	C	D
101	Ⓐ	Ⓑ	Ⓒ	Ⓓ	111	Ⓐ	Ⓑ	Ⓒ	Ⓓ	121	Ⓐ	Ⓑ	Ⓒ	Ⓓ	131	Ⓐ	Ⓑ	Ⓒ	Ⓓ	141	Ⓐ	Ⓑ	Ⓒ	Ⓓ
102	Ⓐ	Ⓑ	Ⓒ	Ⓓ	112	Ⓐ	Ⓑ	Ⓒ	Ⓓ	122	Ⓐ	Ⓑ	Ⓒ	Ⓓ	132	Ⓐ	Ⓑ	Ⓒ	Ⓓ	142	Ⓐ	Ⓑ	Ⓒ	Ⓓ
103	Ⓐ	Ⓑ	Ⓒ	Ⓓ	113	Ⓐ	Ⓑ	Ⓒ	Ⓓ	123	Ⓐ	Ⓑ	Ⓒ	Ⓓ	133	Ⓐ	Ⓑ	Ⓒ	Ⓓ	143	Ⓐ	Ⓑ	Ⓒ	Ⓓ
104	Ⓐ	Ⓑ	Ⓒ	Ⓓ	114	Ⓐ	Ⓑ	Ⓒ	Ⓓ	124	Ⓐ	Ⓑ	Ⓒ	Ⓓ	134	Ⓐ	Ⓑ	Ⓒ	Ⓓ	144	Ⓐ	Ⓑ	Ⓒ	Ⓓ
105	Ⓐ	Ⓑ	Ⓒ	Ⓓ	115	Ⓐ	Ⓑ	Ⓒ	Ⓓ	125	Ⓐ	Ⓑ	Ⓒ	Ⓓ	135	Ⓐ	Ⓑ	Ⓒ	Ⓓ	145	Ⓐ	Ⓑ	Ⓒ	Ⓓ
106	Ⓐ	Ⓑ	Ⓒ	Ⓓ	116	Ⓐ	Ⓑ	Ⓒ	Ⓓ	126	Ⓐ	Ⓑ	Ⓒ	Ⓓ	135	Ⓐ	Ⓑ	Ⓒ	Ⓓ	146	Ⓐ	Ⓑ	Ⓒ	Ⓓ
107	Ⓐ	Ⓑ	Ⓒ	Ⓓ	117	Ⓐ	Ⓑ	Ⓒ	Ⓓ	127	Ⓐ	Ⓑ	Ⓒ	Ⓓ	137	Ⓐ	Ⓑ	Ⓒ	Ⓓ					
108	Ⓐ	Ⓑ	Ⓒ	Ⓓ	118	Ⓐ	Ⓑ	Ⓒ	Ⓓ	128	Ⓐ	Ⓑ	Ⓒ	Ⓓ	138	Ⓐ	Ⓑ	Ⓒ	Ⓓ					
109	Ⓐ	Ⓑ	Ⓒ	Ⓓ	119	Ⓐ	Ⓑ	Ⓒ	Ⓓ	129	Ⓐ	Ⓑ	Ⓒ	Ⓓ	139	Ⓐ	Ⓑ	Ⓒ	Ⓓ					
110	Ⓐ	Ⓑ	Ⓒ	Ⓓ	120	Ⓐ	Ⓑ	Ⓒ	Ⓓ	130	Ⓐ	Ⓑ	Ⓒ	Ⓓ	140	Ⓐ	Ⓑ	Ⓒ	Ⓓ					

ANSWER SHEET

Reading Comprehension Part V, Part VI

No.	A	B	C	D	No.	A	B	C	D	No.	A	B	C	D	No.	A	B	C	D	No.	A	B	C	D
101	Ⓐ	Ⓑ	Ⓒ	Ⓓ	111	Ⓐ	Ⓑ	Ⓒ	Ⓓ	121	Ⓐ	Ⓑ	Ⓒ	Ⓓ	131	Ⓐ	Ⓑ	Ⓒ	Ⓓ	141	Ⓐ	Ⓑ	Ⓒ	Ⓓ
102	Ⓐ	Ⓑ	Ⓒ	Ⓓ	112	Ⓐ	Ⓑ	Ⓒ	Ⓓ	122	Ⓐ	Ⓑ	Ⓒ	Ⓓ	132	Ⓐ	Ⓑ	Ⓒ	Ⓓ	142	Ⓐ	Ⓑ	Ⓒ	Ⓓ
103	Ⓐ	Ⓑ	Ⓒ	Ⓓ	113	Ⓐ	Ⓑ	Ⓒ	Ⓓ	123	Ⓐ	Ⓑ	Ⓒ	Ⓓ	133	Ⓐ	Ⓑ	Ⓒ	Ⓓ	143	Ⓐ	Ⓑ	Ⓒ	Ⓓ
104	Ⓐ	Ⓑ	Ⓒ	Ⓓ	114	Ⓐ	Ⓑ	Ⓒ	Ⓓ	124	Ⓐ	Ⓑ	Ⓒ	Ⓓ	134	Ⓐ	Ⓑ	Ⓒ	Ⓓ	144	Ⓐ	Ⓑ	Ⓒ	Ⓓ
105	Ⓐ	Ⓑ	Ⓒ	Ⓓ	115	Ⓐ	Ⓑ	Ⓒ	Ⓓ	125	Ⓐ	Ⓑ	Ⓒ	Ⓓ	135	Ⓐ	Ⓑ	Ⓒ	Ⓓ	145	Ⓐ	Ⓑ	Ⓒ	Ⓓ
106	Ⓐ	Ⓑ	Ⓒ	Ⓓ	116	Ⓐ	Ⓑ	Ⓒ	Ⓓ	126	Ⓐ	Ⓑ	Ⓒ	Ⓓ	135	Ⓐ	Ⓑ	Ⓒ	Ⓓ	146	Ⓐ	Ⓑ	Ⓒ	Ⓓ
107	Ⓐ	Ⓑ	Ⓒ	Ⓓ	117	Ⓐ	Ⓑ	Ⓒ	Ⓓ	127	Ⓐ	Ⓑ	Ⓒ	Ⓓ	137	Ⓐ	Ⓑ	Ⓒ	Ⓓ					
108	Ⓐ	Ⓑ	Ⓒ	Ⓓ	118	Ⓐ	Ⓑ	Ⓒ	Ⓓ	128	Ⓐ	Ⓑ	Ⓒ	Ⓓ	138	Ⓐ	Ⓑ	Ⓒ	Ⓓ					
109	Ⓐ	Ⓑ	Ⓒ	Ⓓ	119	Ⓐ	Ⓑ	Ⓒ	Ⓓ	129	Ⓐ	Ⓑ	Ⓒ	Ⓓ	139	Ⓐ	Ⓑ	Ⓒ	Ⓓ					
110	Ⓐ	Ⓑ	Ⓒ	Ⓓ	120	Ⓐ	Ⓑ	Ⓒ	Ⓓ	130	Ⓐ	Ⓑ	Ⓒ	Ⓓ	140	Ⓐ	Ⓑ	Ⓒ	Ⓓ					

ANSWER SHEET

Reading Comprehension Part V, Part VI

No.	A	B	C	D	No.	A	B	C	D	No.	A	B	C	D	No.	A	B	C	D	No.	A	B	C	D
101	Ⓐ	Ⓑ	Ⓒ	Ⓓ	111	Ⓐ	Ⓑ	Ⓒ	Ⓓ	121	Ⓐ	Ⓑ	Ⓒ	Ⓓ	131	Ⓐ	Ⓑ	Ⓒ	Ⓓ	141	Ⓐ	Ⓑ	Ⓒ	Ⓓ
102	Ⓐ	Ⓑ	Ⓒ	Ⓓ	112	Ⓐ	Ⓑ	Ⓒ	Ⓓ	122	Ⓐ	Ⓑ	Ⓒ	Ⓓ	132	Ⓐ	Ⓑ	Ⓒ	Ⓓ	142	Ⓐ	Ⓑ	Ⓒ	Ⓓ
103	Ⓐ	Ⓑ	Ⓒ	Ⓓ	113	Ⓐ	Ⓑ	Ⓒ	Ⓓ	123	Ⓐ	Ⓑ	Ⓒ	Ⓓ	133	Ⓐ	Ⓑ	Ⓒ	Ⓓ	143	Ⓐ	Ⓑ	Ⓒ	Ⓓ
104	Ⓐ	Ⓑ	Ⓒ	Ⓓ	114	Ⓐ	Ⓑ	Ⓒ	Ⓓ	124	Ⓐ	Ⓑ	Ⓒ	Ⓓ	134	Ⓐ	Ⓑ	Ⓒ	Ⓓ	144	Ⓐ	Ⓑ	Ⓒ	Ⓓ
105	Ⓐ	Ⓑ	Ⓒ	Ⓓ	115	Ⓐ	Ⓑ	Ⓒ	Ⓓ	125	Ⓐ	Ⓑ	Ⓒ	Ⓓ	135	Ⓐ	Ⓑ	Ⓒ	Ⓓ	145	Ⓐ	Ⓑ	Ⓒ	Ⓓ
106	Ⓐ	Ⓑ	Ⓒ	Ⓓ	116	Ⓐ	Ⓑ	Ⓒ	Ⓓ	126	Ⓐ	Ⓑ	Ⓒ	Ⓓ	135	Ⓐ	Ⓑ	Ⓒ	Ⓓ	146	Ⓐ	Ⓑ	Ⓒ	Ⓓ
107	Ⓐ	Ⓑ	Ⓒ	Ⓓ	117	Ⓐ	Ⓑ	Ⓒ	Ⓓ	127	Ⓐ	Ⓑ	Ⓒ	Ⓓ	137	Ⓐ	Ⓑ	Ⓒ	Ⓓ					
108	Ⓐ	Ⓑ	Ⓒ	Ⓓ	118	Ⓐ	Ⓑ	Ⓒ	Ⓓ	128	Ⓐ	Ⓑ	Ⓒ	Ⓓ	138	Ⓐ	Ⓑ	Ⓒ	Ⓓ					
109	Ⓐ	Ⓑ	Ⓒ	Ⓓ	119	Ⓐ	Ⓑ	Ⓒ	Ⓓ	129	Ⓐ	Ⓑ	Ⓒ	Ⓓ	139	Ⓐ	Ⓑ	Ⓒ	Ⓓ					
110	Ⓐ	Ⓑ	Ⓒ	Ⓓ	120	Ⓐ	Ⓑ	Ⓒ	Ⓓ	130	Ⓐ	Ⓑ	Ⓒ	Ⓓ	140	Ⓐ	Ⓑ	Ⓒ	Ⓓ					

ANSWER SHEET

Reading Comprehension Part V, Part VI

No.	A	B	C	D	No.	A	B	C	D	No.	A	B	C	D	No.	A	B	C	D	No.	A	B	C	D
101	Ⓐ	Ⓑ	Ⓒ	Ⓓ	111	Ⓐ	Ⓑ	Ⓒ	Ⓓ	121	Ⓐ	Ⓑ	Ⓒ	Ⓓ	131	Ⓐ	Ⓑ	Ⓒ	Ⓓ	141	Ⓐ	Ⓑ	Ⓒ	Ⓓ
102	Ⓐ	Ⓑ	Ⓒ	Ⓓ	112	Ⓐ	Ⓑ	Ⓒ	Ⓓ	122	Ⓐ	Ⓑ	Ⓒ	Ⓓ	132	Ⓐ	Ⓑ	Ⓒ	Ⓓ	142	Ⓐ	Ⓑ	Ⓒ	Ⓓ
103	Ⓐ	Ⓑ	Ⓒ	Ⓓ	113	Ⓐ	Ⓑ	Ⓒ	Ⓓ	123	Ⓐ	Ⓑ	Ⓒ	Ⓓ	133	Ⓐ	Ⓑ	Ⓒ	Ⓓ	143	Ⓐ	Ⓑ	Ⓒ	Ⓓ
104	Ⓐ	Ⓑ	Ⓒ	Ⓓ	114	Ⓐ	Ⓑ	Ⓒ	Ⓓ	124	Ⓐ	Ⓑ	Ⓒ	Ⓓ	134	Ⓐ	Ⓑ	Ⓒ	Ⓓ	144	Ⓐ	Ⓑ	Ⓒ	Ⓓ
105	Ⓐ	Ⓑ	Ⓒ	Ⓓ	115	Ⓐ	Ⓑ	Ⓒ	Ⓓ	125	Ⓐ	Ⓑ	Ⓒ	Ⓓ	135	Ⓐ	Ⓑ	Ⓒ	Ⓓ	145	Ⓐ	Ⓑ	Ⓒ	Ⓓ
106	Ⓐ	Ⓑ	Ⓒ	Ⓓ	116	Ⓐ	Ⓑ	Ⓒ	Ⓓ	126	Ⓐ	Ⓑ	Ⓒ	Ⓓ	135	Ⓐ	Ⓑ	Ⓒ	Ⓓ	146	Ⓐ	Ⓑ	Ⓒ	Ⓓ
107	Ⓐ	Ⓑ	Ⓒ	Ⓓ	117	Ⓐ	Ⓑ	Ⓒ	Ⓓ	127	Ⓐ	Ⓑ	Ⓒ	Ⓓ	137	Ⓐ	Ⓑ	Ⓒ	Ⓓ					
108	Ⓐ	Ⓑ	Ⓒ	Ⓓ	118	Ⓐ	Ⓑ	Ⓒ	Ⓓ	128	Ⓐ	Ⓑ	Ⓒ	Ⓓ	138	Ⓐ	Ⓑ	Ⓒ	Ⓓ					
109	Ⓐ	Ⓑ	Ⓒ	Ⓓ	119	Ⓐ	Ⓑ	Ⓒ	Ⓓ	129	Ⓐ	Ⓑ	Ⓒ	Ⓓ	139	Ⓐ	Ⓑ	Ⓒ	Ⓓ					
110	Ⓐ	Ⓑ	Ⓒ	Ⓓ	120	Ⓐ	Ⓑ	Ⓒ	Ⓓ	130	Ⓐ	Ⓑ	Ⓒ	Ⓓ	140	Ⓐ	Ⓑ	Ⓒ	Ⓓ					

ANSWER SHEET

Reading Comprehension Part V, Part VI

No.	A	B	C	D	No.	A	B	C	D	No.	A	B	C	D	No.	A	B	C	D	No.	A	B	C	D
101	Ⓐ	Ⓑ	Ⓒ	Ⓓ	111	Ⓐ	Ⓑ	Ⓒ	Ⓓ	121	Ⓐ	Ⓑ	Ⓒ	Ⓓ	131	Ⓐ	Ⓑ	Ⓒ	Ⓓ	141	Ⓐ	Ⓑ	Ⓒ	Ⓓ
102	Ⓐ	Ⓑ	Ⓒ	Ⓓ	112	Ⓐ	Ⓑ	Ⓒ	Ⓓ	122	Ⓐ	Ⓑ	Ⓒ	Ⓓ	132	Ⓐ	Ⓑ	Ⓒ	Ⓓ	142	Ⓐ	Ⓑ	Ⓒ	Ⓓ
103	Ⓐ	Ⓑ	Ⓒ	Ⓓ	113	Ⓐ	Ⓑ	Ⓒ	Ⓓ	123	Ⓐ	Ⓑ	Ⓒ	Ⓓ	133	Ⓐ	Ⓑ	Ⓒ	Ⓓ	143	Ⓐ	Ⓑ	Ⓒ	Ⓓ
104	Ⓐ	Ⓑ	Ⓒ	Ⓓ	114	Ⓐ	Ⓑ	Ⓒ	Ⓓ	124	Ⓐ	Ⓑ	Ⓒ	Ⓓ	134	Ⓐ	Ⓑ	Ⓒ	Ⓓ	144	Ⓐ	Ⓑ	Ⓒ	Ⓓ
105	Ⓐ	Ⓑ	Ⓒ	Ⓓ	115	Ⓐ	Ⓑ	Ⓒ	Ⓓ	125	Ⓐ	Ⓑ	Ⓒ	Ⓓ	135	Ⓐ	Ⓑ	Ⓒ	Ⓓ	145	Ⓐ	Ⓑ	Ⓒ	Ⓓ
106	Ⓐ	Ⓑ	Ⓒ	Ⓓ	116	Ⓐ	Ⓑ	Ⓒ	Ⓓ	126	Ⓐ	Ⓑ	Ⓒ	Ⓓ	135	Ⓐ	Ⓑ	Ⓒ	Ⓓ	146	Ⓐ	Ⓑ	Ⓒ	Ⓓ
107	Ⓐ	Ⓑ	Ⓒ	Ⓓ	117	Ⓐ	Ⓑ	Ⓒ	Ⓓ	127	Ⓐ	Ⓑ	Ⓒ	Ⓓ	137	Ⓐ	Ⓑ	Ⓒ	Ⓓ					
108	Ⓐ	Ⓑ	Ⓒ	Ⓓ	118	Ⓐ	Ⓑ	Ⓒ	Ⓓ	128	Ⓐ	Ⓑ	Ⓒ	Ⓓ	138	Ⓐ	Ⓑ	Ⓒ	Ⓓ					
109	Ⓐ	Ⓑ	Ⓒ	Ⓓ	119	Ⓐ	Ⓑ	Ⓒ	Ⓓ	129	Ⓐ	Ⓑ	Ⓒ	Ⓓ	139	Ⓐ	Ⓑ	Ⓒ	Ⓓ					
110	Ⓐ	Ⓑ	Ⓒ	Ⓓ	120	Ⓐ	Ⓑ	Ⓒ	Ⓓ	130	Ⓐ	Ⓑ	Ⓒ	Ⓓ	140	Ⓐ	Ⓑ	Ⓒ	Ⓓ					

ANSWER SHEET

Reading Comprehension Part V, Part VI

No.	A	B	C	D	No.	A	B	C	D	No.	A	B	C	D	No.	A	B	C	D	No.	A	B	C	D
101	Ⓐ	Ⓑ	Ⓒ	Ⓓ	111	Ⓐ	Ⓑ	Ⓒ	Ⓓ	121	Ⓐ	Ⓑ	Ⓒ	Ⓓ	131	Ⓐ	Ⓑ	Ⓒ	Ⓓ	141	Ⓐ	Ⓑ	Ⓒ	Ⓓ
102	Ⓐ	Ⓑ	Ⓒ	Ⓓ	112	Ⓐ	Ⓑ	Ⓒ	Ⓓ	122	Ⓐ	Ⓑ	Ⓒ	Ⓓ	132	Ⓐ	Ⓑ	Ⓒ	Ⓓ	142	Ⓐ	Ⓑ	Ⓒ	Ⓓ
103	Ⓐ	Ⓑ	Ⓒ	Ⓓ	113	Ⓐ	Ⓑ	Ⓒ	Ⓓ	123	Ⓐ	Ⓑ	Ⓒ	Ⓓ	133	Ⓐ	Ⓑ	Ⓒ	Ⓓ	143	Ⓐ	Ⓑ	Ⓒ	Ⓓ
104	Ⓐ	Ⓑ	Ⓒ	Ⓓ	114	Ⓐ	Ⓑ	Ⓒ	Ⓓ	124	Ⓐ	Ⓑ	Ⓒ	Ⓓ	134	Ⓐ	Ⓑ	Ⓒ	Ⓓ	144	Ⓐ	Ⓑ	Ⓒ	Ⓓ
105	Ⓐ	Ⓑ	Ⓒ	Ⓓ	115	Ⓐ	Ⓑ	Ⓒ	Ⓓ	125	Ⓐ	Ⓑ	Ⓒ	Ⓓ	135	Ⓐ	Ⓑ	Ⓒ	Ⓓ	145	Ⓐ	Ⓑ	Ⓒ	Ⓓ
106	Ⓐ	Ⓑ	Ⓒ	Ⓓ	116	Ⓐ	Ⓑ	Ⓒ	Ⓓ	126	Ⓐ	Ⓑ	Ⓒ	Ⓓ	135	Ⓐ	Ⓑ	Ⓒ	Ⓓ	146	Ⓐ	Ⓑ	Ⓒ	Ⓓ
107	Ⓐ	Ⓑ	Ⓒ	Ⓓ	117	Ⓐ	Ⓑ	Ⓒ	Ⓓ	127	Ⓐ	Ⓑ	Ⓒ	Ⓓ	137	Ⓐ	Ⓑ	Ⓒ	Ⓓ					
108	Ⓐ	Ⓑ	Ⓒ	Ⓓ	118	Ⓐ	Ⓑ	Ⓒ	Ⓓ	128	Ⓐ	Ⓑ	Ⓒ	Ⓓ	138	Ⓐ	Ⓑ	Ⓒ	Ⓓ					
109	Ⓐ	Ⓑ	Ⓒ	Ⓓ	119	Ⓐ	Ⓑ	Ⓒ	Ⓓ	129	Ⓐ	Ⓑ	Ⓒ	Ⓓ	139	Ⓐ	Ⓑ	Ⓒ	Ⓓ					
110	Ⓐ	Ⓑ	Ⓒ	Ⓓ	120	Ⓐ	Ⓑ	Ⓒ	Ⓓ	130	Ⓐ	Ⓑ	Ⓒ	Ⓓ	140	Ⓐ	Ⓑ	Ⓒ	Ⓓ					

ANSWER SHEET

Reading Comprehension Part V, Part VI

No.	A	B	C	D	No.	A	B	C	D	No.	A	B	C	D	No.	A	B	C	D	No.	A	B	C	D
101	Ⓐ	Ⓑ	Ⓒ	Ⓓ	111	Ⓐ	Ⓑ	Ⓒ	Ⓓ	121	Ⓐ	Ⓑ	Ⓒ	Ⓓ	131	Ⓐ	Ⓑ	Ⓒ	Ⓓ	141	Ⓐ	Ⓑ	Ⓒ	Ⓓ
102	Ⓐ	Ⓑ	Ⓒ	Ⓓ	112	Ⓐ	Ⓑ	Ⓒ	Ⓓ	122	Ⓐ	Ⓑ	Ⓒ	Ⓓ	132	Ⓐ	Ⓑ	Ⓒ	Ⓓ	142	Ⓐ	Ⓑ	Ⓒ	Ⓓ
103	Ⓐ	Ⓑ	Ⓒ	Ⓓ	113	Ⓐ	Ⓑ	Ⓒ	Ⓓ	123	Ⓐ	Ⓑ	Ⓒ	Ⓓ	133	Ⓐ	Ⓑ	Ⓒ	Ⓓ	143	Ⓐ	Ⓑ	Ⓒ	Ⓓ
104	Ⓐ	Ⓑ	Ⓒ	Ⓓ	114	Ⓐ	Ⓑ	Ⓒ	Ⓓ	124	Ⓐ	Ⓑ	Ⓒ	Ⓓ	134	Ⓐ	Ⓑ	Ⓒ	Ⓓ	144	Ⓐ	Ⓑ	Ⓒ	Ⓓ
105	Ⓐ	Ⓑ	Ⓒ	Ⓓ	115	Ⓐ	Ⓑ	Ⓒ	Ⓓ	125	Ⓐ	Ⓑ	Ⓒ	Ⓓ	135	Ⓐ	Ⓑ	Ⓒ	Ⓓ	145	Ⓐ	Ⓑ	Ⓒ	Ⓓ
106	Ⓐ	Ⓑ	Ⓒ	Ⓓ	116	Ⓐ	Ⓑ	Ⓒ	Ⓓ	126	Ⓐ	Ⓑ	Ⓒ	Ⓓ	135	Ⓐ	Ⓑ	Ⓒ	Ⓓ	146	Ⓐ	Ⓑ	Ⓒ	Ⓓ
107	Ⓐ	Ⓑ	Ⓒ	Ⓓ	117	Ⓐ	Ⓑ	Ⓒ	Ⓓ	127	Ⓐ	Ⓑ	Ⓒ	Ⓓ	137	Ⓐ	Ⓑ	Ⓒ	Ⓓ					
108	Ⓐ	Ⓑ	Ⓒ	Ⓓ	118	Ⓐ	Ⓑ	Ⓒ	Ⓓ	128	Ⓐ	Ⓑ	Ⓒ	Ⓓ	138	Ⓐ	Ⓑ	Ⓒ	Ⓓ					
109	Ⓐ	Ⓑ	Ⓒ	Ⓓ	119	Ⓐ	Ⓑ	Ⓒ	Ⓓ	129	Ⓐ	Ⓑ	Ⓒ	Ⓓ	139	Ⓐ	Ⓑ	Ⓒ	Ⓓ					
110	Ⓐ	Ⓑ	Ⓒ	Ⓓ	120	Ⓐ	Ⓑ	Ⓒ	Ⓓ	130	Ⓐ	Ⓑ	Ⓒ	Ⓓ	140	Ⓐ	Ⓑ	Ⓒ	Ⓓ					

ANSWER SHEET

Reading Comprehension Part V, Part VI

No.	A	B	C	D	No.	A	B	C	D	No.	A	B	C	D	No.	A	B	C	D	No.	A	B	C	D
101	Ⓐ	Ⓑ	Ⓒ	Ⓓ	111	Ⓐ	Ⓑ	Ⓒ	Ⓓ	121	Ⓐ	Ⓑ	Ⓒ	Ⓓ	131	Ⓐ	Ⓑ	Ⓒ	Ⓓ	141	Ⓐ	Ⓑ	Ⓒ	Ⓓ
102	Ⓐ	Ⓑ	Ⓒ	Ⓓ	112	Ⓐ	Ⓑ	Ⓒ	Ⓓ	122	Ⓐ	Ⓑ	Ⓒ	Ⓓ	132	Ⓐ	Ⓑ	Ⓒ	Ⓓ	142	Ⓐ	Ⓑ	Ⓒ	Ⓓ
103	Ⓐ	Ⓑ	Ⓒ	Ⓓ	113	Ⓐ	Ⓑ	Ⓒ	Ⓓ	123	Ⓐ	Ⓑ	Ⓒ	Ⓓ	133	Ⓐ	Ⓑ	Ⓒ	Ⓓ	143	Ⓐ	Ⓑ	Ⓒ	Ⓓ
104	Ⓐ	Ⓑ	Ⓒ	Ⓓ	114	Ⓐ	Ⓑ	Ⓒ	Ⓓ	124	Ⓐ	Ⓑ	Ⓒ	Ⓓ	134	Ⓐ	Ⓑ	Ⓒ	Ⓓ	144	Ⓐ	Ⓑ	Ⓒ	Ⓓ
105	Ⓐ	Ⓑ	Ⓒ	Ⓓ	115	Ⓐ	Ⓑ	Ⓒ	Ⓓ	125	Ⓐ	Ⓑ	Ⓒ	Ⓓ	135	Ⓐ	Ⓑ	Ⓒ	Ⓓ	145	Ⓐ	Ⓑ	Ⓒ	Ⓓ
106	Ⓐ	Ⓑ	Ⓒ	Ⓓ	116	Ⓐ	Ⓑ	Ⓒ	Ⓓ	126	Ⓐ	Ⓑ	Ⓒ	Ⓓ	135	Ⓐ	Ⓑ	Ⓒ	Ⓓ	146	Ⓐ	Ⓑ	Ⓒ	Ⓓ
107	Ⓐ	Ⓑ	Ⓒ	Ⓓ	117	Ⓐ	Ⓑ	Ⓒ	Ⓓ	127	Ⓐ	Ⓑ	Ⓒ	Ⓓ	137	Ⓐ	Ⓑ	Ⓒ	Ⓓ					
108	Ⓐ	Ⓑ	Ⓒ	Ⓓ	118	Ⓐ	Ⓑ	Ⓒ	Ⓓ	128	Ⓐ	Ⓑ	Ⓒ	Ⓓ	138	Ⓐ	Ⓑ	Ⓒ	Ⓓ					
109	Ⓐ	Ⓑ	Ⓒ	Ⓓ	119	Ⓐ	Ⓑ	Ⓒ	Ⓓ	129	Ⓐ	Ⓑ	Ⓒ	Ⓓ	139	Ⓐ	Ⓑ	Ⓒ	Ⓓ					
110	Ⓐ	Ⓑ	Ⓒ	Ⓓ	120	Ⓐ	Ⓑ	Ⓒ	Ⓓ	130	Ⓐ	Ⓑ	Ⓒ	Ⓓ	140	Ⓐ	Ⓑ	Ⓒ	Ⓓ